CANADIAN HERITAGE PRESERVATION

Eric P. Jokinen

LONE PINE

Copyright © 1987 by Lone Pine Publishing and Eric P. Jokinen

First Printing 1987 5 4 3 2 1

Printed in Canada

All rights reserved.

No part of this book may be reproduced in any form without permission in writing from the publishers, except by a reviewer who may quote brief passages in a magazine or newspaper.

The Publisher
Lone Pine Publishing
#414 10357 109 St.
Edmonton, Alberta T5J 1N3

Typesetting by Pièce de Résistance Typographers, Edmonton

Printed in Canada by Co-op Press
Edmonton, Alberta

Canadian Cataloguing
in Publication Data

Jokinen, Eric
  Canadian Heritage Preservation

Includes index.
ISBN 0-919433-36-7 (bound).
ISBN 0-919433-40-5 (pbk.)

1. Historic buildings—Canada—Conservation and restoration. I. Title.

NA109.C3J64 1985   720'.28'80971   C85-090117-0

This book is dedicated to Capt. Eric E. Jokinen,
and Mr. Welsford A. Marshall, P. Eng.

CONTENTS

Acknowledgements 6
Introduction 7
Chapter 1: The Issues 9
Chapter 2: Design Techniques 14
Chapter 3: Structural Techniques 19
Chapter 4: Residential Construction 51
Chapter 5: Project Studies 70
Chapter 6: Applications in Canada 126
Chapter 7: Innovative Solutions 147
Chapter 8: Summary 152

Appendix A 154
Glossary 155
Bibliography 156
Index 157

ACKNOWLEDGEMENTS

This book would not have been possible without the initiative provided by Richard Kilstrom, Heritage Officer for the City of Edmonton, Planning Department. Richard suggested I undertake a study of the methods available to conserve historic structures in urban settings. He arranged major funding for research from the City of Edmonton (Planning Department and Real Estate / Supply Services Department). Recognition is also due to Messrs. Arni Fullerton, Kulbir Singh, Duncan Fraser, Bob Warren, Dave Thurston and John Bachinsky for their efforts.

Substantial research funding was also provided by the Province of Alberta through Alberta Culture. In addition to administering the research grants, Fritz Pannekoek, Rino Basso and Peter Pratt of Alberta Culture's Historic Sites Service provided invaluable support and comments.

Recognition is also due my partners, Pat Quinn and Dirk Dressel, whose patience and financial support were indispensable. A.M. "Mickie" Holland and Janos Dvorszak acted as architectural consultants to the project and provided many useful comments.

Particularly worthy of recognition are those in my Edmonton office who assisted in all phases of this book. I give special thanks to Gord Anderson, Dwight Redden and Julien Fagnan for their research contributions, Kris Carlson who did an outstanding job in preparing the technical illustrations and Janice Rowley for word processing.

Among the specialty contractors who contributed technical advise, I gratefully acknowledge the contributions of Mr. Russ Renneberg (W & R Foundations Ltd.) for underpinning, Mr. Hans Webersdorfer for timber restoration and Mr. Gary Robertson for photogrammetric surveys.

Harry Ala-Kantti, Robert Gordon and D'Arcy Cote provided photos and information on the project studies in Ottawa.

Earl Fraser, Paul Tuckwell and Derek Buck assisted with Barrington Place in Halifax. Messrs. G. des Aulniers and A. Cote of Quebec City provided invaluable assistance with the Quebec Post Office project.

John Harrison and Howard Johnson of the WZMH Group provided background for the Boston study project. The WZMH Group also assisted with the 336 Bay Street project in Toronto. This information was supplemented by further data provided by Mr. A. Alberga of Imbrook Properties.

Ken London of ARCOP Associates and Richard Clark (Trizec Corp.) helped out with the Hollinsworth study. ARCOP Associates Montreal staff also provided ample information on the Maison ALCAN preservation project. ALCAN staffer Lorne Walls supplemented this data with additional information and photos.

Rob Way, Jose Calvo and Dr. Rusty Morgan were most helpful on the Carnegie Library project in Vancouver.

Blake Pratt and Mike Szyling of the University of Alberta and Gerry Tersmete of the Alberta Association of Architects must be recognized for their contribution to the project studies on their respective facilities. Steve Sorenson of P&M Construction provided photos costs for one of the University of Alberta projects.

Ysreal Seinik (New York) and W. Thoen (Boston) provided information on several of the innovative techniques mentioned.

Neil Robinson of the IBI Group, Calgary and Dudley Thompson of the Prairie Partnership, Winnipeg were most generous in supplying information on the Ranchmen's Club and the Manitoba Teacher's College respectively.

Background on the Queens Quay Terminal in Toronto was supplied by Mr. Jacob Astrug of the Zeidler Roberts Partnership, Walter Blackwell of M.S. Yolles and Partners, and Mr. Dairmid Murphy of Olympia and York.

Many other people in the conservation, design, construction and development industries were consulted and provided invaluable information and encouragement. Their contributions are very much appreciated.

Finally, the patience and perseverance of my editors, Grant Kennedy, Karin Blouw and Zanne Cameron eased the burden of producing my first published work. Their support and input is very much appreciated.

Eric P. Jokinen
Edmonton, Alberta
December 1986

INTRODUCTION

A great deal of technical literature exists on specific building elements and materials and much of it is applicable to heritage conservation. But when it comes to the more global aspects of historic building conservation there does not appear to be a single comprehensive reference. Thus this book gives an overview of the methods and materials available for preservation. This information is supplemented with examples of how these methods can be used in a Canadian context.

The term "Heritage Preservation" is meant to be synonymous with "Structural Engineering" in the context of this book. Mechanical and electrical systems in historic buildings are normally so outdated they must be completely replaced. Once the shell of a heritage project has been defined structurally, the installation of new mechanical and electrical systems can proceed. The core of this book is thus structural engineering.

But heritage conservation is hardly confined to engineering matters. The process involves varied categories of interested groups. First, we have the dedicated volunteer conservationists, preservation societies and historical boards. Next come the heritage officers of urban and rural planning departments, and provincial and federal cultural agencies. They are followed by the professionals and contractors who advise on various aspects of the project and ultimately carry out the preservation process. Last—but certainly not least—are the owners of historic properties. This last group includes private real estate developers, individual owners of historic homes, trustees of heritage parks and government employees responsible for the property management of historic sites.

There will be something of interest in this book for each of these groups. But the real purpose of the book is to compile, in one source, possible solutions to a wide variety of heritage conservation challenges. It will prove particularly useful to non-engineers who have a crazy idea but aren't quite sure how it can be done. One example is running a subway tunnel diagonally under an eight-storey building. (See Chapter 5.)

Because this book is intended to be used by a wide cross-section of people, detailed engineering terminology and analysis have been kept to a minimum. Any development of the kind envisioned here will ultimately require the involvement of a structural engineer well-versed in the more esoteric and detailed engineering aspects of the preservation process.

Much of *Canadian Heritage Preservation* revolves around the renovation of historic buildings to accommodate a new use. Some of my fellow engineers will decry the lack of historic civil engineering structures in this book. Unfortunately, civil engineering structures do not lend themselves to a change in use.

Many historic civil engineering structures have been lovingly restored. They now function mainly as museum pieces. The Rideau Canal is a prime example of this. But how many new uses can one find for a canal lock, hydro-electric dam or railway trestle? Wait! Yes, there is another use for a 70-year-old, 30-metre-high railway trestle. One can install an artificial waterfall on it!

Photo I.1: High Level Bridge, Edmonton

Photo I.1: High Level Bridge, Edmonton

The first and last chapters cover the human aspects of heritage conservation and their impact on the engineering process. The remaining chapters deal with the techniques available to implement the preservation process. Small-scale (residential) conservation projects are covered in Chapter 4. Large-scale heritage projects, and their design and construction, are well documented in Chapters 2 and 3. Individual projects are surveyed in Chapter 5. A series of hypothetical projects are presented in Chapter 6 and a number of unusual approaches to specific problems are covered in Chapter 7.

The technical chapters contain many examples which will appeal to those less technically inclined. Some examples taken from other countries have been used because the particular techniques displayed have not been tried in Canada. In all instances, however, the know-how and materials required to implement the techniques illustrated do exist in Canada.

The most difficult phase in writing *Canadian Heritage Preservation* was the selection of which projects to include. Many were considered during the course of research. A number of these were studied in some detail and regretfully put aside. The in-depth studies finally adopted range from coast to coast and illustrate almost all the construction techniques discussed elsewhere in the book.

Most books about a specific area of interest start with an historic overview of developments in the field. I have purposely avoided this because the entire book is about history. The difficulty in dealing with our built heritage in Canada is the varied span of history in the different parts of the country. In Quebec City, structures tend to be historically significant if they have reached their first centenary. In Western Canada, a building may have historic importance at the age of 30 years.

Heritage conservation projects often become the focus for highly emotional confrontation. The first chapter of the book discusses these issues.

When holding forth on any controversial topic, one must take sides. No attempt has been made to provide universal solutions to the controversial issues raised in this book, because no universal solutions exist. The opinions offered here are solely my own, born of an abiding interest in local history and heritage conservation.

Chapter 1

THE ISSUES

THE VALUE OF HERITAGE CONSERVATION

The issue is: "Why save that old building?" The simple answer is: "Because it is part of our cultural heritage." Other elements of our cultural heritage, particularly visual and literary works of art, are easily preserved in museums, private collections and libraries. Even "bad" art is often preserved if it illustrates the development of a particular style or artist.

Unfortunately, buildings do not lend themselves very well to storage. This only seems feasible for smaller pioneer structures which can be moved to historic sites such as Upper Canada Village and the Ukrainian Cultural Heritage Village. Certain buildings, such as churches and provincial legislatures, can be maintained in their original locations, fulfilling the same function for which they were built. Carefully maintained, these buildings also function as living artifacts. However this is neither feasible nor desireable for other buildings; particularly historic buildings in urban settings where land costs and taxation are prohibitively high.

Many fine examples of our architectural and engineering heritage are lost due to purely economic circumstances. Yet it would be unthinkable to destroy any other art-form by a recognized artist for monetary reasons. The same value must be applied to our architectural heritage as is applied to other art-forms that are equally irreplaceable. A unique characteristic of our architectural heritage lies in the fact that it can be recycled to lead a useful, and often economically viable life.

Another major factor causing the loss of historically significant buildings is public confrontation. In the case of a project which will receive public funding, particularly municipal grants, the entire population of the community often becomes involved in the controversy. Conservationists present unassailable arguments with dire warnings of the consequences that will result from ignoring our roots. Their opponents use equally unassailable arguments for the need to set priorities, invoking issues like housing for the poor and job creation. Unfortunately the anti-conservationists don't seem to believe in or understand the value of old buildings (this is somewhat akin to the concept that if one doesn't go to parks, one's town shouldn't spend money on them). These arguments are self-defeating. Heritage conservation projects are labour intensive; much more so than demolition and new construction, and hence are ideal sources of employment creation. There are also many examples of historic properties being converted to re-use as subsidized accommodation for the poor and elderly. These properties have the advantage of being in older neighbourhoods where the facilities are most needed.

A completely different situation develops when a heritage structure controlled by the private sector is threatened. The tax structure in Canadian municipalities makes it a very expensive proposition to maintain an historically important building in a depressed real-estate market. The owners, often residents in other cities or even in other countries, face a common choice: demolish the structure in order to gain some immediate relief from property taxes while earning revenue from the inevitable parking lot; or maintain the structure at considerable expense until market conditions allow redevelopment of the original building. Enter the conservation activists with simplistic answers and immovable positions, usually released to the press before the owner or politicians are aware of any brewing controversy. The stage is then set for confrontation with the owner placed, quite unwittingly, in opposition to conservation.

This issue must be resolved through co-operation between, for example, the private sector and government. The Queens Quay Terminal in Toronto is just such an example. Here, the local historical board had the major facade and clock tower designated as heritage resources. The federal government, as owner, solicited development proposals from private industry. The project has been redeveloped as a commercial venture. The inclusion of a major cultural amenity (a 450-seat dance theatre) by the federal government has helped to ensure the overall viability of the private developer's large investment.

The cost of redeveloping a sound structure will, in most instances, equal the cost of replacing it with a new building. This is the hard cost, but what of the intangibles? What price can we put on our heritage?

This question is difficult to answer. However, we do know that dedicated groups and individuals can alter the course of history, or the course of its destruction. That such actions succeed in preserving parts of our heritage implies that the community does value architectural artifacts. As with most irreplaceable art-forms, that value is "priceless."

WAYS AND MEANS

There are many ways to finance and build a conservation project in Canada. The most commonly used construction delivery methods are:

-Construction Management: the construction process is managed and directed by the owner or a professional construction manager.

-Fixed Price Tender: construction is carried out by a general contractor awarded a lump-sum contract based on a complete set of design documents.

-Fast Tracking: construction is started before the design is complete.

-Cost Plus: a contractor provides all services, labour and materials at his cost plus a specified fee or mark-up, normally without any guarantee as to the final

CONFRONTATION equals DEMOLITION

overall price.

-Do-It-Yourself: substantial labour input is provided by the owner.

The construction method selected will be largely dependent on the scale and complexity of the project. Some factors affecting the final selection are: the degree of construction knowledge of the owner; budgeting and cost control restraints; the local construction market; and time restraints.

The design process is the foundation of any conservation project. In this area there are few options. A team of professionals experienced in historic building design should be retained as a first step in the overall process. Normally an architect heads the design team. He or she appoints the remaining design team members and recommends the construction method most suitable to the project.

The importance of retaining design professionals experienced in heritage conservation cannot be overemphasized. Their experience can add to the success of the project in many ways, including: familiarity with sources of original drawings; understanding of deterioration and repair processes for traditional building materials; and awareness of the impact of new technology and materials on traditional materials. An architect familiar with the conservation process can also assist with the historic evaluation of a structure by identifying the vintage of various additions to the original. This requires a sound knowledge of traditional materials observed during the initial survey.

The feasibility of any preservation project begins and ends with economics. The most worthwhile and logical of plans are impossible without adequate funding. Financial assistance is usually not available as a direct grant for construction, but monies can be obtained in a number of indirect ways.

Federal and provincial job-creation subsidies are available to cover the labour costs of community backed projects. Funding is sometimes available from charitable foundations for projects with outstanding historical significance. Projects with wide public appeal often benefit from the donation of funds, labour, services and materials from the community at large.

Design professionals can provide assistance with preliminary budgeting. This budgeting is invaluable as a guide for determining the overall scale of the project. Once economic feasibility is established, budget updating is usually provided by a friendly contractor, a professional cost consultant or a construction manager together with the design team.

IS IT VALID TO CHANGE AN HISTORIC STRUCTURE?

After a community or property owner has decided that a heritage structure is to be preserved, debate ensues as to the future uses of the exterior and interior spaces. One of the surest ways to ensure preservation of a building is to find a viable use for that building. This often requires changes, both internally and externally. The thought of major additions, vertically or horizontally seems abhorrent to some, but these additions may be essential to the new use. Without a purpose the structure may become a neglected artifact, doomed ultimately to destruction.

The idea that historic buildings must not be altered seems inconsistent with the very history one is trying to preserve. Any building which has survived a half-century or more has seen many changes. Any contemporary alterations, provided they are in character, will some-day also be history.

Architectural and engineering research often reveals that supposedly complete and inviolate buildings were designed originally for vertical and horizontal additions. One may also find that the most pleasing aspects of a heritage property are actually part of a later addition.

In conclusion, any addition or alteration which is sympathetic to the original design is acceptable. Such changes may be essential to ensure that conservation does occur.

DO-IT-YOURSELF

Current teachings in home renovation courses recommend retaining a professional contractor for construction delivery. Given that preservation projects are more complicated than conventional home renovations, a professional contractor would appear to be indispensable for heritage conservation. This is not true in all cases.

Granted, large-scale projects requiring heavy lifting and specialized techniques like pre-stressing need professional construction supervision. However, for smaller projects undertaken by an individual, family or community organization, the do-it-yourself approach can contribute substantially to the success of the project.

First, there is a sense of commitment and pride in any project wrought by your own hands. This sense of pride does exist in skilled tradesmen, but the commitment to the project ends when they move on to the next job.

Next consider the value of "sweat equity." For each

dollar we pay a tradesman, we must first earn anywhere from $1.25 to $2.00 to cover our income-tax liabilities. Donations of money to registered heritage groups are tax-deductible, but there are the hidden costs of setting up and administering a foundation. These costs tend to dilute the value of the donation. The common argument against sweat equity is that you can make more at your chosen profession than you can contribute in bumbling attempts at carpentry. This may be so, but you can't practice law, medicine or whatever 24 hours a day. Physical labour in a different environment from your career can rejuvenate your spirit and an old building at the same time.

The alleged lack of construction skills among lay people is a challenge in any do-it-yourself conservation project. But knowledge of these skills is readily

Photo 1.3: Fibreglass or Terra-cotta?

available. Architects and engineers from the professional design team are thoroughly familiar with the skills required for a building project, even if they do not possess the skills themselves. There is also a wealth of do-it-yourself books on almost every conceivable topic.

Of course, manual skill cannot be learned from a book. But a do-it-yourself project has plenty of scope for trial and error. The inefficiencies of this method are more than offset by the cost-savings realized through "sweat equity."

One further advantage of construction by an owner is the ability to phase a project. Any undertaking handed over to a general contractor must be legally defined and carried to completion without delay. Such a contract can be altered or terminated only at considerable additional cost. A do-it-yourself project allows the proponents to proceed at their own pace, dependent on availablity of funds and enthusiasm for the project.

AUTHENTICITY

Authenticity in the preservation process often becomes a subsequent controversy to the initial "preservation or demolition" debate. We saw earlier that the question of additions and alterations to a heritage property can lead to a polarization of the various conservation interests. Similarly, debate inevitably rages around the methods and materials used to accomplish the ultimate goal of conservation.

Some may favour total fidelity to the original skills used to create the oldest portion of the structure. Others may take a more liberal approach, such as fibreglass reproductions of terra-cotta castings. The purist approach is fine for museum-type settings. This is particularly valuable where the old techniques can be practised as part of the activities of an institutional heritage setting. A fine example is the water-powered sawmill at Upper Canada Village.

In a more contemporary setting, individuals or businesses seldom have the resources to pursue these idealistic goals. Instead they must adapt modern materials and methods to the preservation process. These adaptations are in themselves innovative and stimulating.

The public facades of historic buildings are often the only portions of the structure worth saving. Possible options are: to dismantle and reassemble after the new frame is up; to support the facades in place during the construction process; to demolish all elements and reproduce with new materials later on; or to dismantle, store and re-use in a different location.

Every preservation project is unique. For this reason there can be no universal answer to the question of authenticity.

Different materials require varied treatments. Unique stone carvings must be preserved, repaired and re-used. Terra-cotta is in limited supply and can be easily reproduced in fibreglass. Old brick can also be readily reproduced in "antiqued" new bricks. The practice of numbering and dismantling large quantities of old brick is questionable! Half of them are often broken in the process. Innovative techniques like the large-scale panelization of masonry prove to be good compromises. These techniques are explored in more detail in the following chapters.

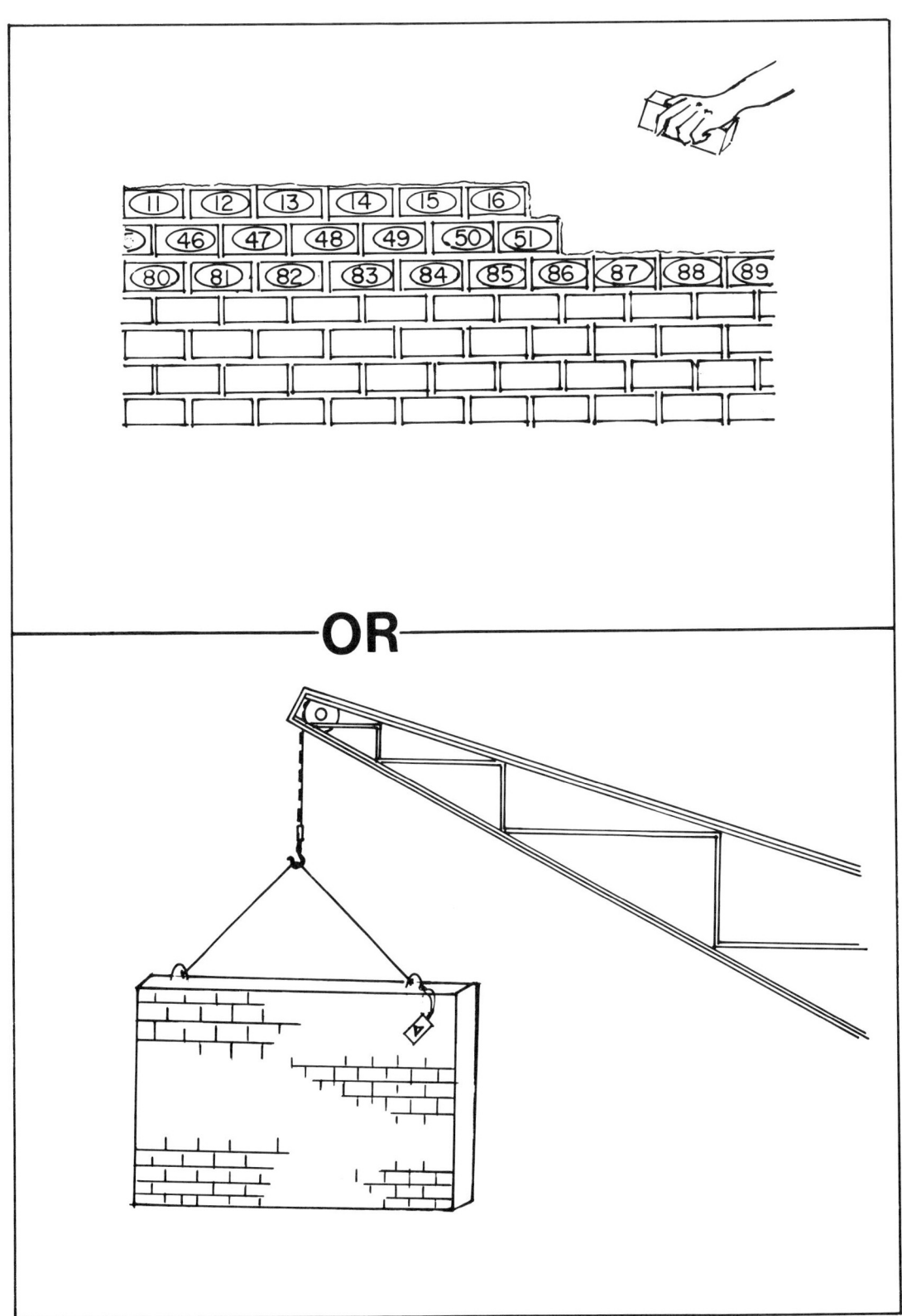

Figure 1.1 - Dismantle or panelize?

Chapter 2

DESIGN TECHNIQUES

EVALUATION OF EXISTING STRUCTURES

Structural evaluations of heritage buildings are normally initiated for two reasons. A survey may be undertaken as the result of a routine maintenance inspection uncovering visible signs of distress.

Otherwise, a formal evaluation is often the prelude to the rehabilitation of a structure for a new use. A change in use may require increased load capacity, or building codes may dictate upgrading to new standards. In the extreme, the building may have deteriorated or been damaged to the point where safety is threatened. In each case, the type of review varies dependent on the project's particular demands.

Current techniques used in analyzing the properties of materials and systems are very helpful in determining a structure's capabilities. The soundness of any evaluation, however rests ultimately in the experience and judgement of the investigating engineer. Anyone who undertakes to modify a heritage structure must first understand its architectural, historical, and structural integrity as fully as possible.

The Investigation

A preliminary assessment involves a thorough on-site visual examination to determine the type of construction and materials employed in the structure and to survey their condition. Signs of deterioration and distress are noted, and documented with photographs and sketches. Specimens for laboratory analysis are collected and simple field tests are conducted. These provide a basis for the initial assessment of the condition and capacity of the structural components. Loads due to the current use are established and related to the known or assumed original design loads. Past owners and occupants may be sought out to determine the load history of the structure. They can often assist by providing insight into the renovation history of the building while pinpointing maintenance problem areas in the past.

Off-site investigation includes theoretical analysis of the structural system aided by the information obtained from specimen tests and documents. A detailed set of construction documents often provides more information than can be obtained from the most elaborate on-site investigation. Time spent finding construction drawings or people involved in the construction industry when the project was built is often a good investment.

The results of these investigations can then be presented in a preliminary report. This report includes an assessment of necessary repairs or renovations and further investigation required. If the past performance of a building is known, and if construction and loading history are well documented and no signs of distress or deterioration are found, no further structural investigation may be necessary. On the other hand, the investigation may become a major project if the engineer must certify the adequacy of a building for which little of the original documentation exists.

Original Drawings

Anyone involved in the modification of an historic building is elated to find copies of the original construction drawings. The discovery usually comes after much detective work.

Unfortunately the elation is often short-lived. Usually a visit to the site with these documents reveals major changes made to the basic design prior to, or during the course of construction. Although potentially very valuable, such documents may resemble but not represent the as-built or present-day structure. Revisions were often required during construction due to unforeseen problems with the design. In some cases completely different building systems have been implemented for economic reasons. Many such changes to the original construction documents are never formally documented or have been lost.

Differences may also occur due to renovations made without documentation or, in some cases, without proper engineering input. A common example is the removal of part of an interior partition without considering its load-bearing function. Structural elements are also frequently removed or a system's stability compromised by storefront renovations. Structural materials such as steel and concrete are less prone to unauthorized modification due to the inherent difficulty in removing them. In contrast, wood is easily damaged by indiscriminate holes or notches. Complete framing systems may have been revised without authorization. In many instances, the damaged structure has deformed and transferred loads to unintended elements. The designer is then faced with the danger of inadvertently removing a non-structural element which, during the life of the building, has become an essential part of the structural frame.

Safe Load Evaluation

A detailed evaluation of a structure's load carrying capacity can be done by load test or computation. Load tests are used where no drawings or material records exist. They are limited, however, by practical size, and use in structures that give considerable warning prior to failure. The most commonly tested elements are floor systems. They are easily loaded and usually undergo extensive cracking and deflection before failure. Load testing of columns, walls and foundations is often not feasible. More complex systems, such as transfer girders, may be tested using a scale model or a similar but disposable structure. Load testing requirements that verify structural adequacy are normally covered in construction material standards such as the Canadian Standard Association's "Code for the Design of Concrete Structures for Buildings."

Load capacity verification by computation requires the following: a three dimensional description of the structure and its components; the strength properties of the materials; and the state of repair or distress.

The complexity and cost of recreating structural drawings through field measurement of the existing structure are determined by the extent to which architectural finishes and building services conceal the components. Access is required to determine not only the size, location and connection detail of these members but their condition as well.

The use of photogrammetry, a three dimensional photographic recording technique, can aid in drawing re-creation. It is especially useful in documenting facades and other decorative elements which are to be dismantled. Photogrammetry can also be used as a tool of analysis, assisting in determining the sequence of building movements and deformations. This technique is discussed in more detail in Chapter 3.

An examination to determine the state of repair or to record signs of distress should include drawings of all defects or deformations. An integral part of this work is the study of cracks: a technique requiring a thorough knowledge of structural systems and their behavior. One must first distinguish between active cracks and those which occurred in the original construction (for example shrinkage cracks in concrete). Active cracks should be monitored over a full year, if possible, to separate thermal movements from those caused by settlement or distress. Crack movement can be monitored by setting steel points on either side of the crack and measuring the distance between them using a dial micrometer such as the DEMEC mechanical strain gage. Crack history thus obtained can be used to assess the potential for further distress of the structure.

Foundations

Foundations are difficult to examine. The best test of a foundation system is its performance over a long period of time. The examination of other elements of the structure will indicate if there have been excessive settlements—a sure indicator of the quality of foundations. Excavations may be required in the basement levels to determine a typical footing type, size and condition. Soil bearing capacities can be evaluated by laboratory testing of samples taken from the test excavation, supplemented by hand samples or machine-augered investigations at other locations on the site.

Timber Construction

Wood members must be examined for: decay; checks and cracks; the tightness of bolted connections; corrosion of metal hardware; excessive wear; insect damage; and human damage such as holes and notches. In some cases visual grade marks on the member surface can be used to determine strength properties. If these are not available, wave propagation tests may be used to measure strength and elasticity. Probes and penetration tests will indicate the extent of decay.

Radiographic examinations (x-ray) will reveal grain direction, decay, splits, checks, knots, insect damage, member location and joint detail behind architectural finishes.

Masonry

Masonry distress may be indicated by spalling (flaking of the surface), decay of mortar or by the corrosion of lateral fixing hardware. Most methods of evaluating in-situ strength of masonry and mortar are destructive. Mortar strength can be estimated by a scratch test. Sounding with a hammer will indicate overall soundness and the degree of bond between the mortar and the masonry units. Hammer tests also assist in locating voids. Drilling can be used to determine the overall wall thickness and composition. Visual inspection of inaccessible spaces is possible through the use of fiber-optics inspection scopes. High-frequency ultrasonics will detect invisible cracks and voids and can serve as a measure of strength. X-rays and pacometers (magnetic detectors) will locate reinforcement. If a suitable location can be found, cores, panels, and cubes can be cut from the masonry and subjected to lab tests.

Concrete Structures

Distressed concrete members may exhibit cracking, spalling and deflection. Stains resulting from the rusting of reinforcement are also a primary indicator of potential problems. Reinforced concrete can be the most expensive building material to investigate. Strength can only be assessed through detailed information about the contained reinforcement (bar size, quantity, spacing and length, location, deformation, and strength). Numerous non-destructive procedures have been developed to aid in reinforced concrete evaluation, but all have limitations. The most common approach is a detailed visual examination aided by non-destructive tests. These are then supplemented by the results of destructive tests. Cores of concrete are removed and crushed to determine compressive strength, and concrete cover (surface concrete) may be removed in certain areas to reveal reinforcement details. This may then be followed by load tests on certain building elements if required.

Some non-destructive aids and their application to the investigation of reinforced concrete follow:
Rebound hammer - indication of strength
Windsor probe - indication of strength
Pacometers (magnetic detectors) - location and size or depth of reinforcement if within 180 mm. of the surface
Acoustic emissions - detect growing cracks under loaded condition
Acoustic impact (chain drag, hammer) - detect voids and debonding of concrete cover
Ultrasonics - determine thickness of concrete
X-Rays - indicate density and thickness, locate voids and reinforcement
Radar - detect voids

Destructive tests vary from pullout tests, which cause local surface damage but give a simple, quick and inexpensive indication of concrete strength, to the drilling of cores which are then examined and tested in a laboratory. Petrographic examination is the most sophisticated of the concrete evaluation methods currently available. This technique involves the examination of a sample under a microscope. The sample may also be x-rayed. This allows the petrographer to determine the composition of the original concrete mix, the quality of its various components and the degree of curing (hydration) of the cement in the mix.

Structural Steel

Structural steel members must be checked for corrosion, local buckling, tightness of bolted connections, cracks in connecting welds, and for human damage such as holes. Magnetic particle and x-ray inspection can be used to check the condition of the steel, welds and rivets. Bolt torque is checked manually. In many cases a suitable location can be found to take a small sample to determine yield strength and other properties of the steel. Accurate determination of the properties of cold rolled shapes, built-up sections, or pipe can be very time consuming.

Intuition

One evaluation technique that cannot be learned from a book is the use of intuition and curiosity. A qualified investigator is able to draw on past experience with other buildings to make judgement calls on the soundness of a given structure. An insatiable curiosity will lead the investigator to explore a seemingly irrelevant clue. This answer may shed light on a seemingly unrelated problem in another area. The most common example would be rust stains in an area where they normally would not occur. This implies the passage of water, perhaps through a void which was previously undetected.

The curiosity mentioned above is the most valuable research tool available to an architect or engineer investigating an older building. One of the first structures I investigated was a reinforced concrete building of 1910 vintage in Ottawa. Reinforced concrete was then in its infancy in Canada and concrete quality control was non-existent. The lack of bond between the river-bed gravel aggregate and the rest of the concrete was the major concern. Oldtimers in the construction industry were consulted and a retired contractor finally offered the most plausible explanation. He recalled that the sand and gravel used in concrete at the time were brought by barge up the Ottawa River. The river was used extensively for the transport of logs in booms. The tannic acid in the tree bark would leach out and coat the river bed gravel. This coating decreased the amount of bond possible between the aggregate and the cement paste.

Judgement calls in evaluating an older existing structure are almost inevitable. It is often impossible to obtain enough information about the structure or foundations to do even a rudimentary analysis, short of literally destroying the structure in a testing program. Hence the need to pass judgement based on what little information is available.

The structure's history is the best guide. If it has performed well and been reasonably maintained, there is no reason why it should not continue to do so. The building in Ottawa suffering from tannic acid coating was a case in point. Drawings for the reinforcing steel were available and a detailed analysis was possible. This analysis revealed that the frame had been designed for the self-weight of the structure only. No allowance had been made for live loads due to the occupancy of the building. Assuming the drawings were correct, a rational decision was called for. The design appeared to be seriously deficient. But the structure had performed very well over a span of 60 years and showed no signs of distress. The recommendation was that the structure continue to be used as originally intended, but that no major alterations be made to the structure.

Final Report

The report of the findings resulting from a detailed evaluation will include the location and description of the defects discovered, an assessment of the seriousness of each, and recommendations for rectifying them. The load capacity of the existing structure is assessed along with a description of the alterations required to increase it, where necessary. Alterations required to update the structure to the requirements of building officials and the functional and cost implications of all required work is reported as well.

RELAXATION OF CODE REQUIREMENTS

Most Canadian building codes offer some relief from mandatory requirements for existing buildings. The Alberta Building Code, a typical model code, offers the following as assistance to restoration or renovation work. Clauses quoted have been edited to clarify their intent.

Para.1.2.1.2 The rehabilitation or change of an existing building, that has been designated by an acceptable authority as having a significant level of safety is acceptable for its intended use.

Para.1.5.7.4 The authority having jurisdiction shall accept any existing construction or condition if the construction or condition does not constitute an unsafe condition.

The above clauses provide considerable latitude to a building inspector in assessing the safety of an existing building. Any prerogative or privilege must be accompanied by a corresponding responsibility. A recent court decision has held a municipal building official responsible for deficiencies in a building erected in his jurisdiction. A building inspector is expected to exercise reasonable caution because of the expectations of the community he or she serves. He is confronted with the difficult task of passing judgement on the the work of a number of highly specialized consultants while not necessarily possessing all of their knowledge himself. The following sections of the Alberta Code provide a mechanism for the building inspector to consider unorthodox solutions to specific problems.

Para.2.6.1.1 The provisions of the Code are not intended to limit the appropriate use of materials, appliances, equipment or methods of design, or construction not specifically authorized herein.

Para.2.6.1.2 Any person desirous of providing an equivalent to satisfy one or more of the requirements of the Code shall submit sufficient evidence to demonstrate that the proposed equivalent will provide the level of performance required by the Code.

Para.2.6.1.3 Materials, systems, equipment and procedures not specifically described herein, or which vary from the specific requirements in the Code, or for which no recognized test procedure has been established, may be used if it can be shown that they are suitable on the basis of past performance, or on the basis of acceptable tests or evaluation.

The Code is even more specific as it relates to alternate structural design methods and materials.

Para.2.6.2.1(1) Buildings and their structural components whose designs are not in conformance with the Code may be designed by one of the following methods:

a) Analysis based on generally established theory
b) Evaluation of a full-scale structure or a prototype by a loading test
c) Studies of model analogues, provided the design is carried out by a person especially qualified in the specific methods applied, and provided the design ensures a level of safety and performance at least equivalent to that provided for, or implicit in, the requirements of the Code.

Para.2.6.3.1 Any material may be used provided it is shown to be satisfactory for the purpose intended and to be at least the equivalent of the quality, strength, effectiveness, fire resistance, durability and safety required by this Code.

The Code even recognizes that codes and standards used by other jurisdictions can be useful in resolving unusual circumstances within a specific project.

Para.2.6.4.1 The results of tests based on test standards other than as described in this Code may be used provided such alternative test standards will provide comparable results.

The above sections of the Alberta Building Code allow municipal building plan checkers a reasonable degree of flexibility in applying code requirements to restoration or renovation projects.

It has been my experience that building inspectors are prepared to listen to and accept reasonable arguments for relaxations in most sections of the Code, with one notable exception. The section dealing with exit requirements is enforced rigorously, with no exemptions. It is difficult to argue against the enforcement of this particular requirement because of the risks to human life involved.

Before any detailed building plans for restoration work are started, it is strongly recommended that the consultant initiate preliminary discussions with a senior plan checker to determine what concessions or trade-offs may be applied to his or her particular restoration project.

It is worth noting that the provision of sprinklers (when not normally required) ultimately allows plan checkers the highest degree of flexibility when dealing with other code requirements.

It is extremely important for the consultant to maintain dialogue with a senior plan checker during the various drawing development stages. This on-going interactive process usually enables both parties to arrive at reasonable solutions to all the building code requirements.

The interpretation of requirements in most building codes can be appealed if a building owner feels he has been unfairly treated. This should be a last resort as such appeals will cause costly delays. Also, an atmosphere of confrontation will inevitably pervade any future dealings with the building official related to that project. It is usually far easier to negotiate and trade concessions directly with the authority having jurisdiction.

In my own experience, and the experience of others interviewed during the course of research for this book, a project has never been abandoned due to excessive code requirements. Restoration projects provide as much scope for creative technical minds as the most avant-garde new design.

Chapter 3

STRUCTURAL TECHNIQUES

The techniques discussed in this chapter are in common use in new building construction throughout North America. Their adaptation to conservation work should present no difficulties when done in consultation with contractors and design professionals familiar with the preservation process.

Each technique is discussed in a general way to familiarize the reader with what is available. Every topic could form the basis for a textbook, in fact, many excellent texts are available on most of these topics (see bibliography). What follows are the more familiar techniques. In Chapter 4 more imaginative solutions to specific problems are examined.

SELECTIVE DEMOLITION

Economic restraints often preclude the total retention of a heritage building when a property is redeveloped. In many cases a portion containing the most notable heritage attributes can be preserved and incorporated in the new project. This technique—removing the insignificant, damaged or unwanted parts while preserving without damage those parts to be integrated with the new construction—is called selective demolition. It is not unlike common demolition and is governed by the National Building Code, CSA Standard S350-M1980 and local construction safety regulations.

Selective demolition can be carried out in many different ways, each with different ramifications. The most spectacular method employs small explosive charges. These are meticulously placed and fired in a precise pattern to destroy key structural elements, causing the building to break up and collapse under its own weight. Although quick and safe when done by experienced people, the potential for damage due to blast-induced vibrations or unexpected "overkill" often rules out the use of explosives in selective demolition. There is also danger to adjacent properties. This technique has been used in most of Canada's major cities and is a major spectator event. The date of the blast is usually a highly guarded secret, but is normally set early on a Sunday morning. However, the boarding up of neighbouring buildings on a Saturday is a dead give-away, resulting in large crowds gathering for the event. The inherent danger results in very high insurance costs, not to mention the fees charged by the highly specialized explosives contractor.

The other extreme is the slow removal, piece by piece, of unwanted portions of the building. This method is labour intensive, but can be aided by mechanical means such as bars, saws, drills, pneumatic hammers, and a crane to assist in lifting and supporting pieces. Relatively uncommon tools are also available to assist hand demolition.

Concrete or similar materials can be broken by "silent explosives"; a process whereby an expansive powder, liquid carbon-dioxide cartridges or an hydraulic device is placed in a series of drilled holes. Outward pressure causes the member to break into smaller pieces. Similarly, radar or microwaves can vapourize internal water in concrete, causing it to crack. Practical application of this technique has been very limited to date.

A thermic lance (high temperature flame thrower) creates a concentration of heat that cuts through reinforced concrete efficiently. Its use is often restricted by the potential fire hazard. The hydrojet, a stream of water under high pressure, can also be used to aid demolition cutting but is limited at present to softer materials, like mortar.

The major safety concerns when using selective demolition are insuring the stability of the remaining portion of the building at each stage of removal, and preventing rubble from building up to the point of overstressing parts of the remaining structure.

A wrecking ball will speed demolition, but the im-

Photo 3.1: Selective Demolition

Photo 3.1: Selective Demolition

pact of the ball causes considerable vibration and the extent of the break-up and fall of material is difficult to control. Its use in selective demolition is limited to those portions of the structure previously separated by at least 6 metres from the "desirable" parts to be retained. An hydraulic excavator equipped with a shielded "pusher arm" or a grapple can be used to push a building apart. This application should be considered similar to the use of a wrecking ball and restricted to previously separated portions of the building.

When executing selective demolition of a building, one can not over-emphasize the importance of insuring the stability of both the portion to be retained and the part being demolished. It is also important to protect newly exposed surfaces from the weather to prevent drastic changes in moisture levels in the portions to be retained.

MINOR ADDITIONS

The addition of a new element will often facilitate the adaptation or upgrading of a heritage structure. The new element can be as simple as a new exit stair added to the back of of a building, or it can be more elaborate, such as the 9 metre by 5.3 metre elevator and service core added to the Hollinsworth Building in Calgary (see Project Study 5, Chapter 5).

Photo 3.2: Toronto Free Theatre

When incorporating a new element such as a stair in a structure, the strength and integrity of the structural frame must not be impaired by the new opening. Exterior additions must be visually compatible with the original building. The new glass-walled lobby of the Toronto Free Theatre provides an attractive contrast to the walls of the old brick buildings it connects.

Photo 3.3: York Theatre

ROCK EXCAVATION

On sites where construction involves rock excavation, the owner of an adjacent heritage property has two major concerns. Contrary to popular belief, continuity and homogeneity are not common properties of rock. Rock more often contains numerous discontinuities such as mud seams, cavities and fissures. Some bedrock is also susceptible to weathering and freezing when exposed. Even plastic flow of rock can occur in some circumstances. Most existing structural foundations bearing on bedrock exert high bearing stresses on the founding material. It is of paramount importance that a geotechnical engineer be consulted while determining construction procedures in such cases. Recommended procedures may include requirements for stabilizing rock formations, for underpinning of adjacent structures, or for special precautions necessary to prevent weather-induced deterioration of the rock.

The other major concern arises from blasting, a common tool of rock excavation. Damage due to airblasts or flying rock is a possibility, but can be prevented through skilled and careful blasting techniques. Damage caused by vibrations induced in the ground and propagated to the heritage building is more probable. Determining an acceptable charge of explosive material depends upon knowledge of the blast-caused ground motions and reliable damage criteria for the type of building involved.

When blasting, it is common practice to use a distributed series of explosive charges fired at intervals a few milliseconds apart. This technique, known as multiple delay blasting, provides improved fragmentation of material and greatly reduces the vibration level for a given weight of explosives. Given a certain type or class of historic building, an estimate of a safe weight of explosives in each individual delay can be obtained with the help of Figures 3.1 and 3.2. As the degree of propagation of blast vibrations varies greatly with different soil types, a test blast is normally conducted at the site. The resulting peak particle velocity measured at the subject building is then used to select the most appropriate values for the particular site.

The response of a structure to ground motion is perhaps best determined by a complete dynamic analysis. This is expensive, time consuming, and can be inaccurate considering the simplifying assumptions that must be made. The peak particle velocity caused by a blast wave referenced to damage critera indices for different building types can be a reliable means of determining safe blast charges. Peak particle velocity can be measured on location by an electromagnetic detector connected to a recording instrument. A less elaborate measure can be obtained using an "impact noise meter". Although portable seismographs and accelerographs do not measure particle velocity directly, the velocity can be interpolated from records they produce. This makes them a good complement to the other measurement devices mentioned.

Different portions of a building may be damaged by the same amount of explosives, depending on their distance to the blast. Within 6 metres, damage may be confined to random cracking or movement along old planes of weakness in a small portion of an adja-

BUILDING CLASS	PEAK PARTICLE VELOCITY (mm/sec)	SCALED DISTANCE (mm kg)
I	100	4500
II	50	9000
III	25	13500
IV	13	22500

Class I: Structures of substantial construction.
Class II: Relatively new residential structures in sound condition.
Class III: Relatively old residential structures in poor condition.
Class IV: Old residential structures in very poor condition.

Note: If structure is subjected to repeated blasting, or if blasting is done without instrumentation, lower the category by one.

Figure 3.1: Blast Design Criteria

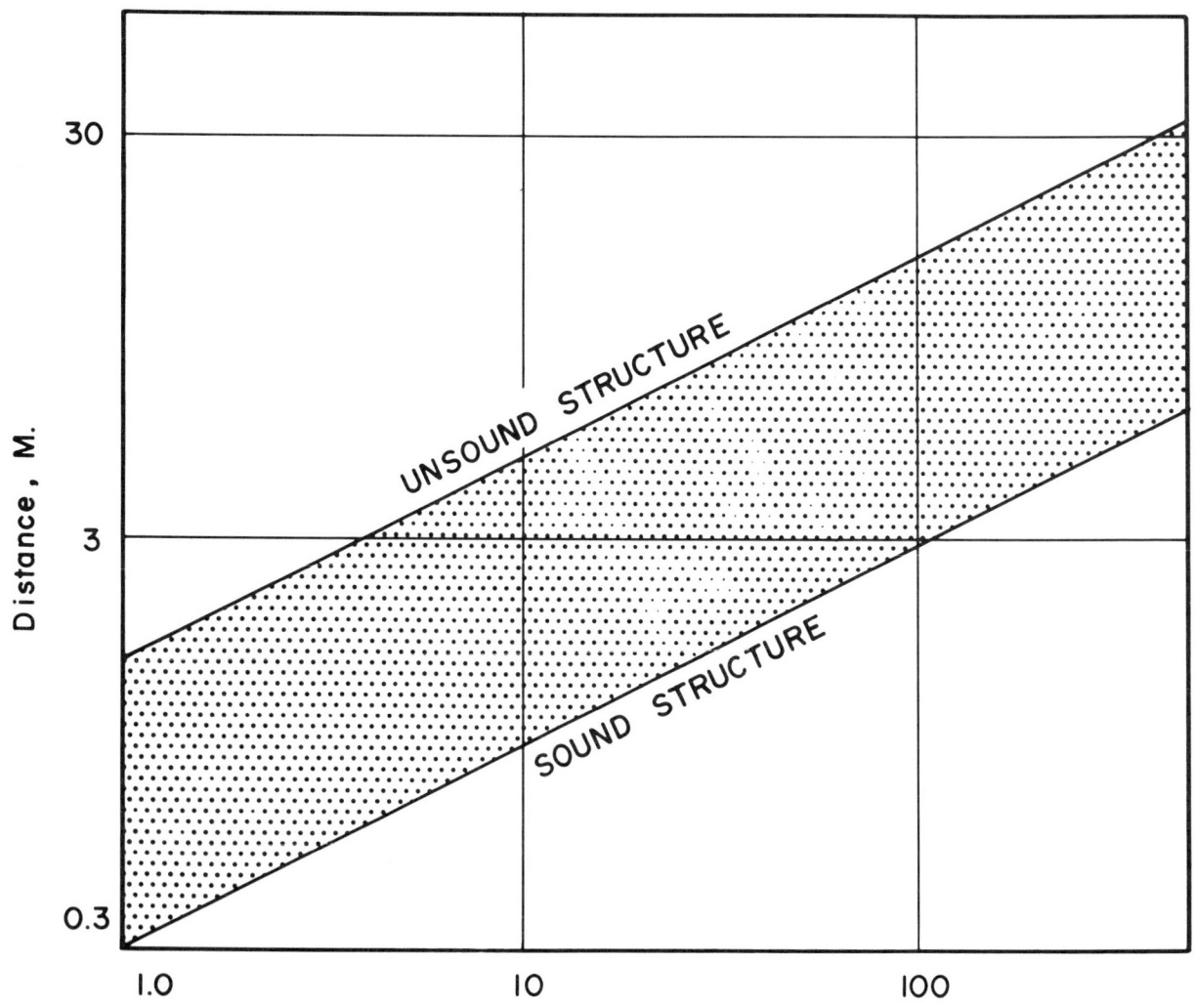

Relative Quantity of Explosives

Figure 3.2: Safe Charge Weight

cent basement wall. Beyond 30 metres however, the blast can affect the entire building, causing shaking similar to a small earthquake. Typical damages are shearing-type failures at wall or wall-floor intersections, horizontal movement along joints in masonry walls and cracking at corners of openings and points of restraint.

It is interesting to note that humans normally object to blast movements that are least damaging for structures. Final blast sizes are often selected for public tolerance levels rather than for structural damage criteria.

It is imperative that an "as-found" survey of the heritage structure be undertaken prior to any blasting. The ensuing documents must then be accepted by all parties. A monitoring program which measures and records the movements resulting from each blasting operation provides a means of verifying charge weights and provides warning of potential problems.

In some situations there are alternatives to blasting. The use of expanding powders or hydraulic tools to break up rock or concrete was discussed under the topic "Selective Demolition" and, in certain cases, are equally applicable to rock excavation. Similarly, cutting via high pressure water may be considered. Soft rock and shale can be cut with a rock saw. One version looks much like an oversized chain saw mounted on an hydraulic backhoe. The saw allows precision cutting and reduces the potential for damage due to overexcavation.

EXCAVATION SHORING

An excavation adjacent to a heritage structure affects the surrounding ground and thus has the potential to affect the structure as well. The National Building Code of Canada states :
"Every excavation shall be undertaken in such a manner as to prevent movement which would cause damage to adjacent properties, existing structures, utilities, roads and sidewalks at all stages of construction ....".

The movement associated with an excavation is commonly a lateral yielding of the soil and its support system toward the excavation. Corresponding vertical settlement occurs in the adjacent earth mass. The extent of soil movement is normally limited to a certain horizontal distance from the edge of the excavation. In granular soils (sand,gravel) this distance is one to one and one-half times the depth of the excavation. For soft to firm clays this distance can approach two, to two and one-half times the depth and even greater than three times when poor workmanship is involved. With poor construction methods, erratic movements can occur due to loss of ground or erosion of soil behind a shoring wall. Such bank failures usually occur without warning and can bring down an adjacent building. In urban areas considerable damage to utilities is caused by building excavation activities and the resulting press coverage is embarrassing to all involved in the project.

The stability of the excavation cut must also be considered. Failures are generally small and shallow in granular material but can be deep and massive in clays, often involving soil to a considerable distance behind the excavation limits. Changes in groundwater level due to dewatering activities for the excavation may precipitate stability failures or cause settlement of adjacent soil. Even the sloped sides of a simple excavation must be protected from the weather and maintained to insure their continued stability.

There are a variety of retaining-type shoring systems available to support the walls of an excavation if space does not allow a sloped cut. The implications to an adjacent building varies for different systems. Retaining-type shoring systems may be considered as having two components: a face in contact with the soil, and a lateral support system to hold the face in place.

The most common face structure is composed of soldier piles at a one to two and one-half metre spacing, with timber lagging between as shown in Figure 3.3. Typically a soldier pile is constructed by placing a steel wide-flange section into a machine-augered hole which is then backfilled with lean or weak mix concrete or other like material. In some instances, a steel pipe, a steel H-pile, or a precast concrete pile can be used in place of the wide-flange shape. It is also possible to use driven piles, but this procedure must be questioned when used adjacent to a heritage structure. The displacement of soil associated with pile driving can cause an uplift of adjacent property. The soil-transmitted vibrations from the pile-driving may also cause cracking of building finishes. Changes in the soil structure due to piling vibrations can cause settlement of foundations. In extreme cases, soft clays and silts have been known to liquefy with rather spectacular results.

After soldier pile installation, and as excavation proceeds, lagging is placed between the piles to support the soil face. Any voids behind the lagging are filled with sand or grout to ensure firm support for the adjacent soil. Wood is the most commonly used lagging material but steel or precast panels have been used successfully.

This system is often the most economical face struc-

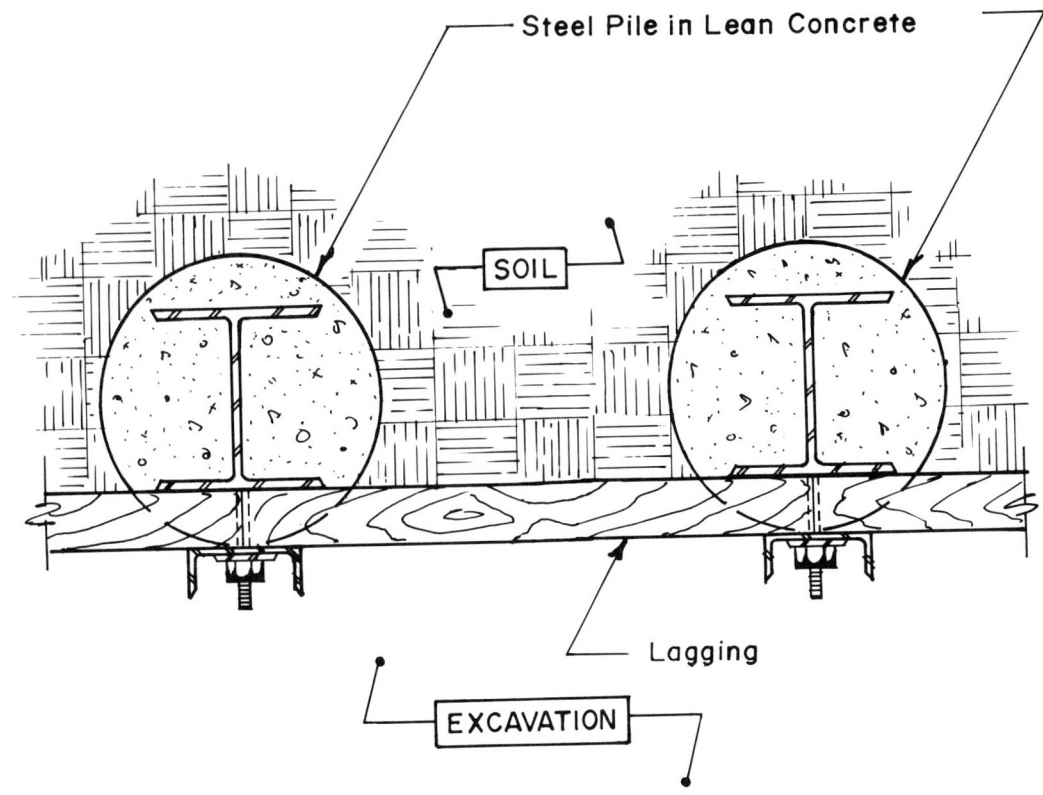

Figure 3.3 Soldier Pile and Lagging

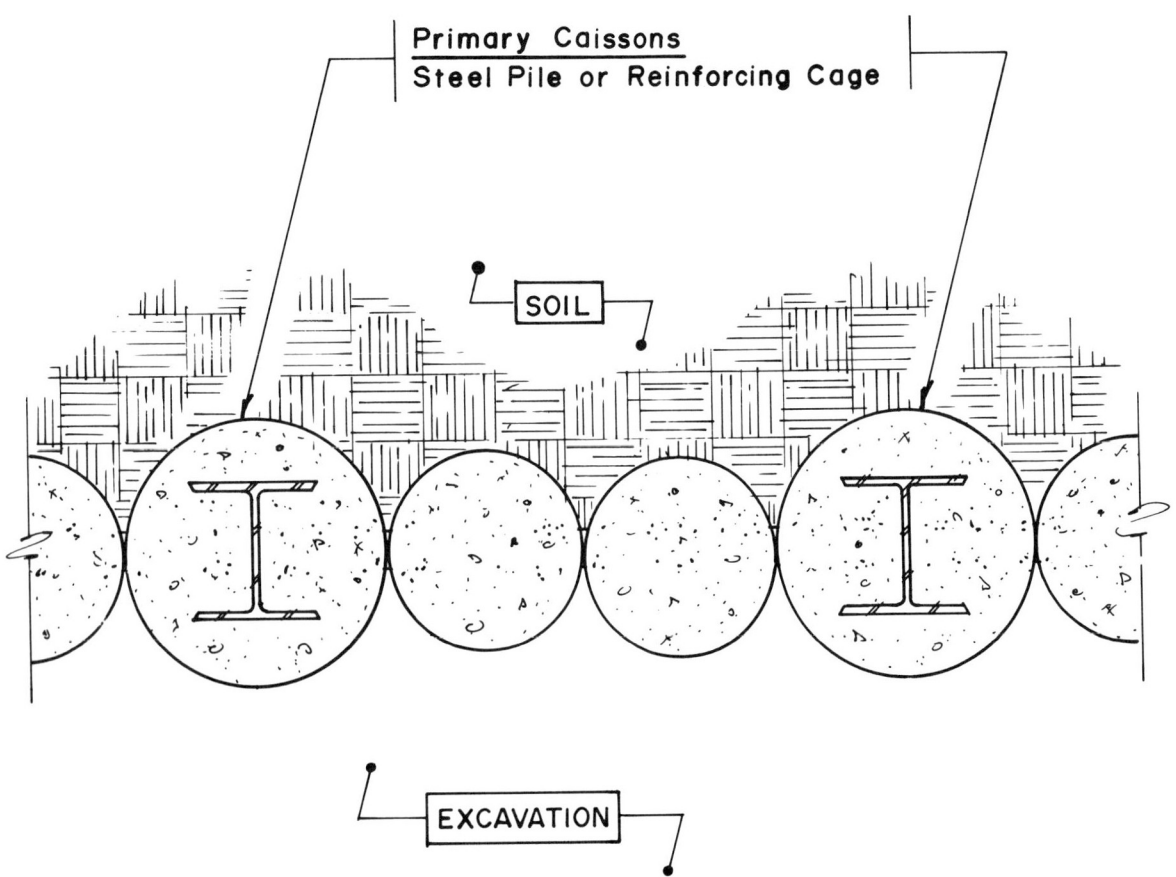

Figure 3.4 Tangent Pile Wall

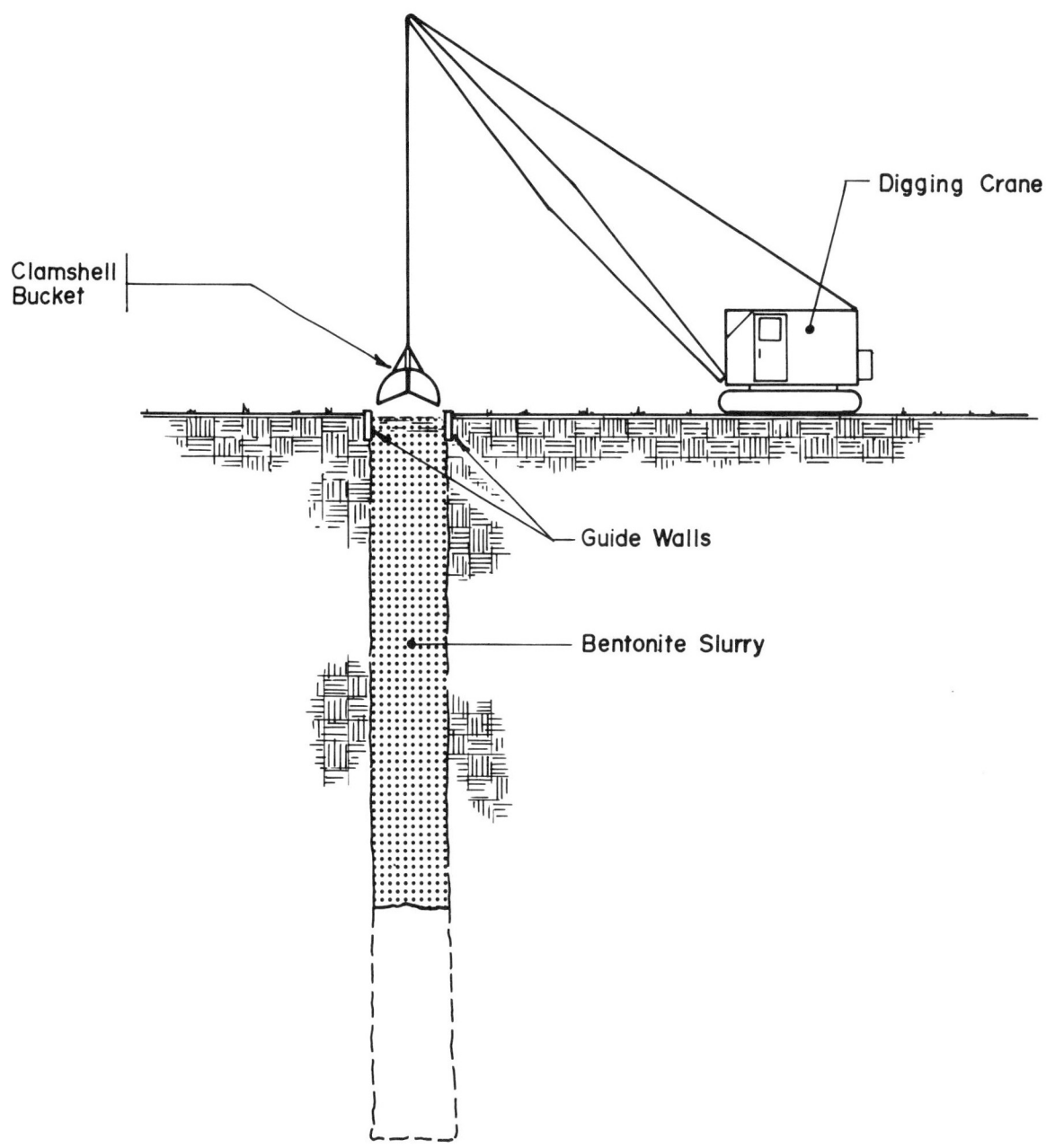

Figure 3.5 Slurry Trench Wall

ture but by its nature relies upon some soil movement to develop an internal "arching" support between the soldier piles while lagging is being installed. As a result there is usually some settlement behind the wall, the extent dependent upon the nature of the soil and the care taken in the installation of the lagging and associated backfill.

A pile and lagging system will not work in wet or sloughing soils. It is very susceptible to major settlement of the retained earth if an unexpected pocket of wet sloughing soil is encountered during excavation.

A continuous row of drilled caissons (tangent piles) can be used as a face support structure. Although these tangent pile walls take many forms, a common one is to install primary or soldier caissons containing steel sections or bar reinforcing, then to place one or two caissons between, thus forming a continuous barrier to support the excavation face as shown in Figure 3.4. As this system has less risk of soil loss and is generally more rigid than the soldier pile and lagging system, it has less potential for allowing settlement. It is therefore recommended for use in some problem soils. Under good conditions it has been successfully used to support foundations of adjacent buildings, thus eliminating the need for underpinning. It is also readily adaptable as a permanent wall with some or all of the caissons acting as foundation units to support the vertical load of the new structure.

Bentonite-water slurries have long been used in the oil drilling industry to support the sides of the drilled holes, to cool the cutting bit and stem, and to bring cuttings to the surface. In Europe in the 1950's this technique was adapted to the construction of subsurface walls by excavating within a trench kept full of bentonite slurry. The most frequently used excavating tool is a clamshell bucket allowing close tolerance excavation of the trench. Excavation is commonly to a width of one-half to two metres and up to 60 metres deep. By carefully selecting the properties of the bentonite slurry or mud, its gel nature will prevent caving of the trench wall and the hydrostatic pressure will prevent movement of the adjacent soil. After excavation, a permanent concrete wall is constructed by placing a reinforcing bar cage into the slurry and pumping concrete to the bottom of the trench, displacing the lighter mud upward as it is filled. The displaced bentonite slurry is collected and re-used. With proper detailing of the panel joints, the concrete wall poured in the slurry trench can form a permanent water retaining basement wall.

While the slurry trench wall is usually the most costly face support system, it is also the least risky, providing positive support to the adjacent soil. It can even support modest adjacent foundation loads virtually without settlement.

Shotcrete or gunite, a pneumatically applied concrete, can be used as a face wall when the excavation walls are able to stand temporarily without support. Weathered rock and stiff clays have sufficient strength to remain unsupported in a vertical cut for several days. Shotcrete soil retention can be used in place of lagging between soldier piles or, more commonly, with tieback anchors set in a grid pattern (approx. 1.5 metres square). Some movement within the soil is inevitable while the face gunite is placed. The positive contact with the excavated face after the gunite is placed partially compensates for this movement. This method is susceptible to pockets of loose soil and is therefore not feasible for all situations.

Driven sheet piling is comprised of special steel shapes, precast concrete or timber. It forms a relatively flexible face support system most applicable to loose, wet granular soils such as those encountered in marine environments. Because of its flexibility and the problems encountered in driving the relatively light shapes in other types of soil, it is not widely used in building applications.

For relatively shallow excavations (normally less than 5 metres) in good soils the face system may be allowed to cantilever for lateral support. Generally the required embedment length must be equal to the depth of the excavation. The system must be allowed to move to develop its support. The resulting settlement behind the wall and the susceptibility of the system to abrupt failure makes it unsuitable to a site where a heritage building sits adjacent to the excavation.

A more common method of providing horizontal support to the face structure is to brace it to the opposite side of the excavation using horizontal struts. Another method is to place raking struts (rakers) down at an angle to the base of the excavation. Using such struts may be the least costly support system but they hinder construction. Some inward movement of the face will occur during the strut installation. Further movement will occur as the struts pick up the load of the retained soil unless the strut is preloaded.

The use of tie-back anchors is perhaps the most efficient means of providing lateral support to the face structure. The required horizontal reaction is transferred, by a tie of high strength steel bar or strand, to an anchor located behind the wall which then transfers the load to the soil by friction or bearing. Anchors can be straight-shaft friction or bell-bearing. They are formed by injecting grout or concrete into a drilled hole. The performance of each anchor is verified by testing to approximately 125 per cent of the design load prior to permanent anchoring. With proper design and care in installation, movement of the shoring face is eliminated by the use of tie-back anchors. The clear excavation site that results may offset the higher cost of this type of support, but a tie-back system also requires space outside the excavation area to place the anchors. If these tie-backs encroach on other property or easements, the permission of the owner must be obtained. As well, the agreement should specify if the tiebacks will be permanent, de-stressed and abandoned, or removed upon completion. Adjacent structures or utilities may prevent the use of tie-back system. Perhaps the most common cause of problems with these systems is a face wall that does not have adequate bearing capacity to support the load induced by angled tiebacks. Even a small downward movement of the face allows the ties to shorten. They release their load, the face moves inward, and settlement occurs behind the wall.

Another technique related to excavation shoring is

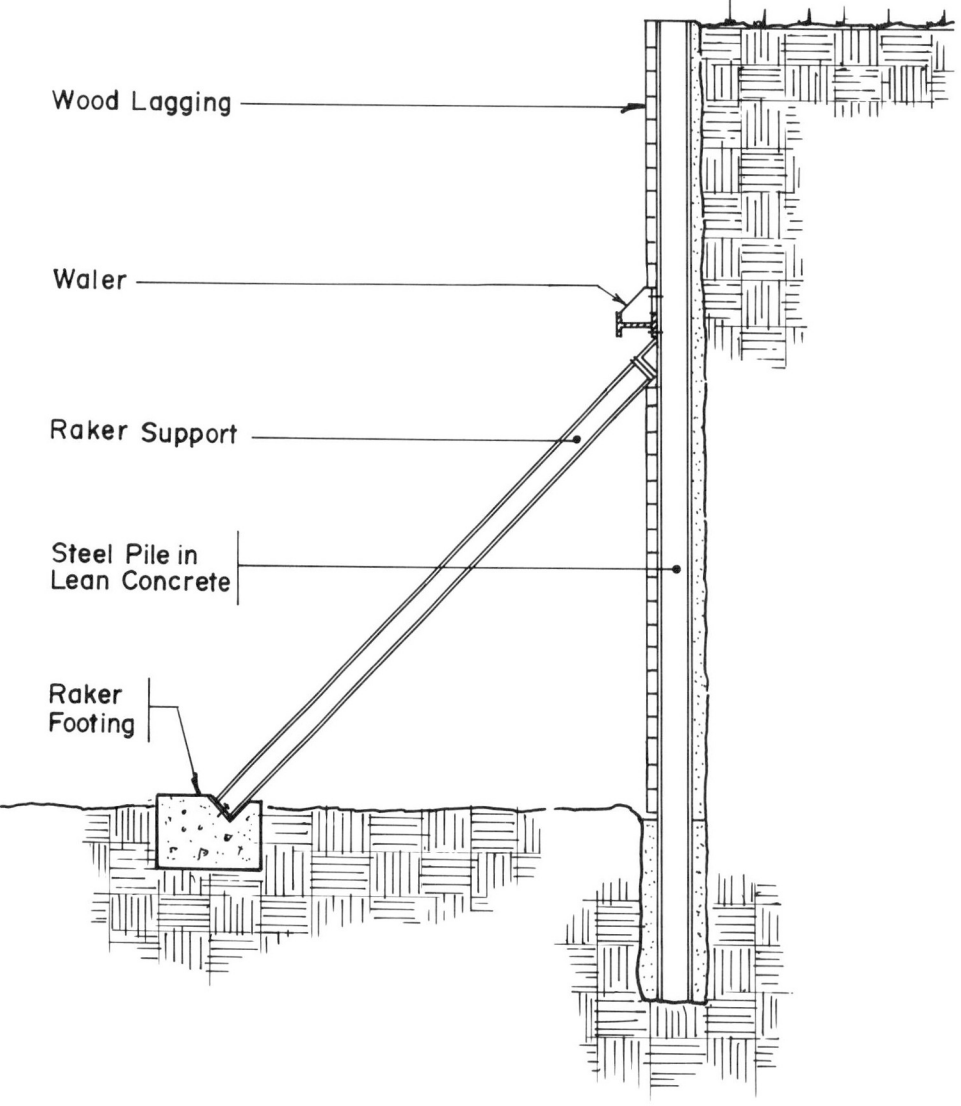

Figure 3.6 Raker Shoring

the use of ground freezing, chemical grouting, or root piles to stabilize and strengthen soils so they become self-supporting. Ground freezing - pumping liquid nitrogen or calcium chloride brine through buried pipes - is expensive and relatively difficult to control but has been used successfully, most often in situations associated with tunnelling. Chemical grout stabilization has similar limitations. Soil stabilization using root piles will be discussed in the following section on underpinning methods.

In any situation involving excavation adjacent to a heritage building, both the building and the shoring system must be regularly monitored for movement to give problem warnings. In its simplest form, monitoring involves recording the horizontal and vertical movement of the top of the shoring system at each stage of excavation and at least weekly thereafter. In more sensitive circumstances, slope-deflection indicators should be placed at intervals down the face structure to detect movement.

Before beginning excavation, the affected heritage structure must be carefully examined to determine and record all significant defects and deformations. Particular attention must be paid to defects that result from movement of the building components. In addition, a system must be established to monitor and record movement of the building on a regular basis during the adjacent construction. Benchmarks must be placed so they are not affected by movement related to the excavation. Remember that natural forces, such

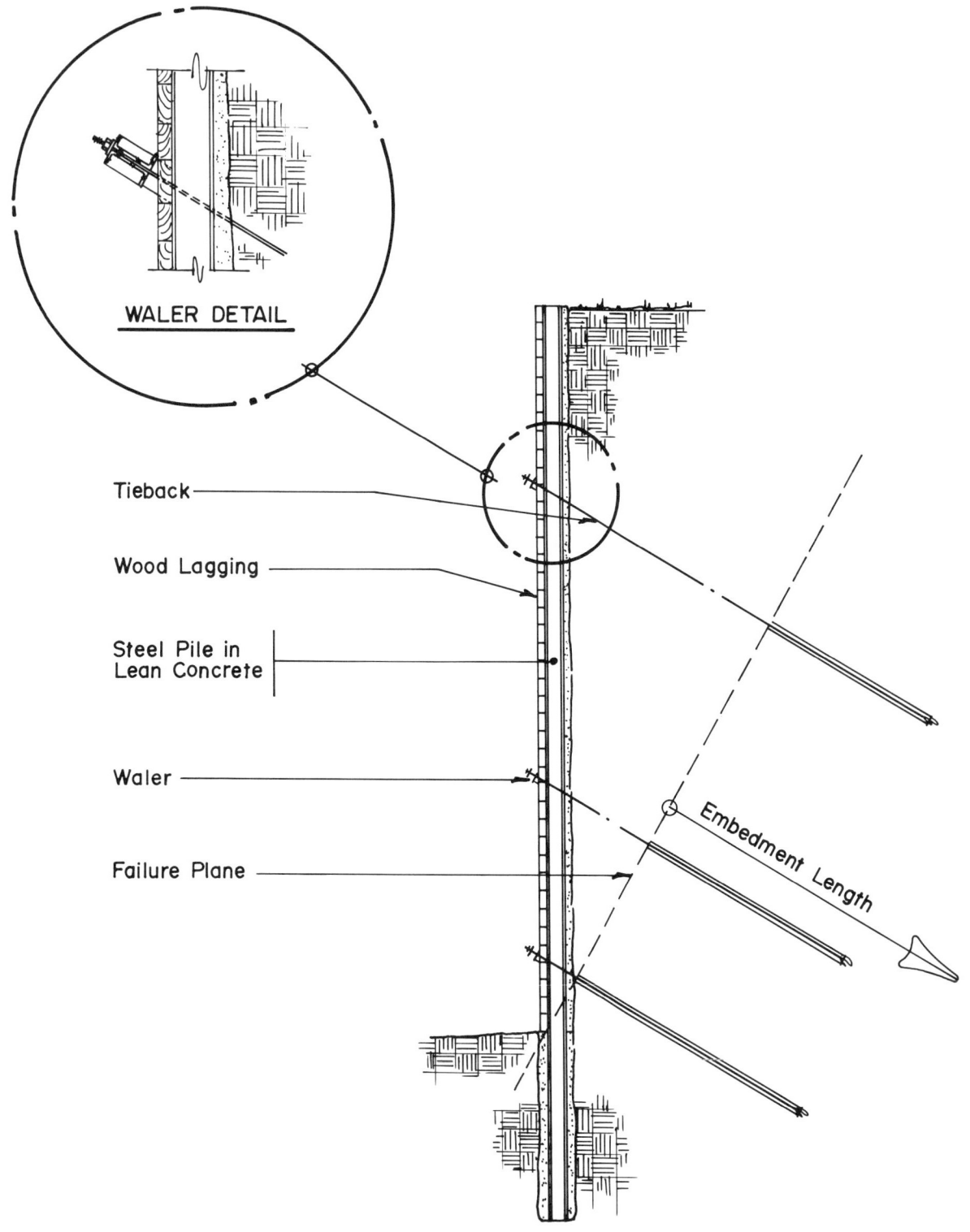

Figure 3.7 Tieback Anchors

as temperature, will continue to cause movement in the building during the construction period. These effects have to be isolated so movement due to adjacent construction can be clearly identified. The use of photographs or a related technique known as photogrammetry, which is discussed in a later chapter, can be a valuable aid in recording "as-found" conditions and subsequent building movement. The pre-work examination report and monitoring system should be accepted and approved by the owners of the affected

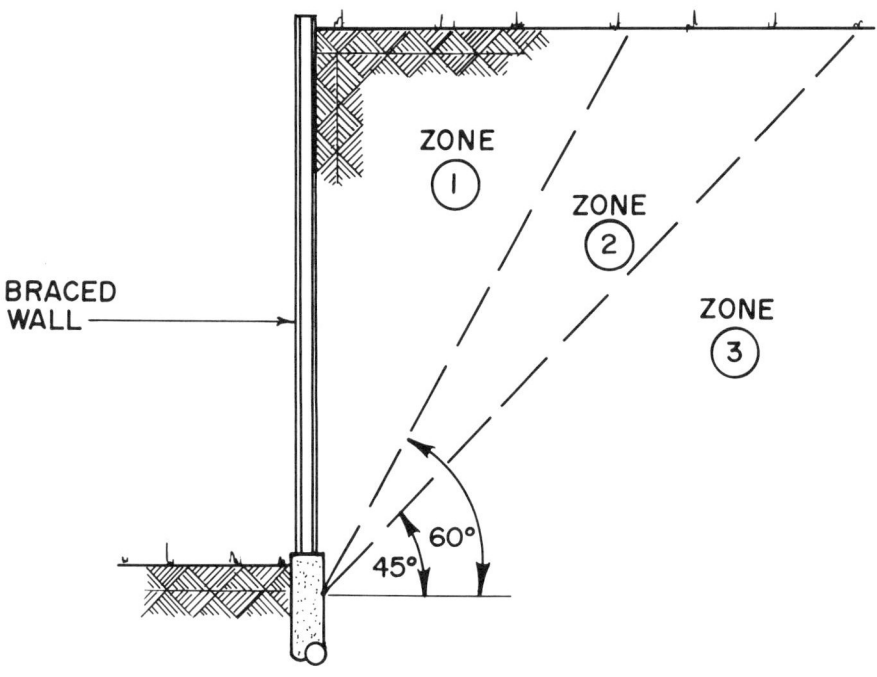

Figure 3.8 Influence Zones for Underpinning

structure prior to commencing work.

Excavation at a site with a high water table will often require dewatering; a temporary lowering of the groundwater level. Building regulations state: "Where proposed construction will result in a temporary or permanent change in groundwater level, the effects of this change on adjacent property shall be fully investigated and provided for in design." The removal of ground-water results in increased effective soil loads which may cause settlement in some soil types. A watertight shoring system such as the slurry trench wall can be used in such cases to eliminate the need for dewatering the adjacent property. Dewatering settlement may also occur due to loss of soil removed with the water. This can be prevented by proper design and execution of the dewatering process.

In frost-susceptible soils, freezing behind a shoring system can create ice lenses which exert enormous horizontal forces. This can cause damage to the shoring system and uplift of soils and structures behind the face. Excavation shoring in frost-susceptible soils must be tarped and heated, or insulated to prevent this occurrence.

UNDERPINNING

The restoration or adaptive reuse of a heritage property or new construction often requires the use of underpinning. This technique can be generally defined as the construction of new support elements beneath an existing foundation. The most obvious need for this technique is to correct a settlement problem due to defective foundations. Underpinning is also used to provide increased load capacity by adding new foundation elements, by increasing the size of existing footings, or by constructing new elements to transfer the load to a more competent-bearing soil strata. Underpinning can be used to solve problems caused when adjacent excavations remove the support for the foundations of existing structures.

Figure 3.8 illustrates the critical zones of influence in soil masses supporting building loads adjacent to an excavation. Generally foundations in Zone 1 have to be underpinned. Zone 2 foundation elements can be left without underpinning, but the design of the excavation shoring will have to accommodate the resultant pressures. If underpinning is to be provided it must terminate within Zone 3.

Final selection of which underpinning system to use depends on a number of factors including: the soil type; the sensitivity of the structure to settlement; and details of the existing foundations. A particularly critical factor in assessing underpinning schemes for heritage buildings is the availability of materials and technology to repair the structure should the underpinning not perform as expected.

In the previous section on excavation shoring, the potential for settlement behind different types of shoring systems was discussed. Figure 3.9 can be used as a general guide in determining the necessity of underpinning. Together, soil consultants, owners and design consultants for all the affected properties must determine which construction methods to employ.

Lateral Support System	Face System	Granular Soil	Stiff Clay	Soft To Firm Clay
Cantilever	—	Moderate to Large	Moderate	May Collapse
Strut	Soldier pile & lagging	0.5 to 1.0*	0.3 to 0.8	>2
Preloaded Strut	Soldier pile & lagging	0.2 to 0.5	0.1 to 0.6	1 to 2
Tieback Anchor	Soldier pile & lagging	0.2 to 0.4	0.1 to 0.5	1 to 2
	Concrete slurry wall	<0.2	<0.1 to 0.5	<1 to 2

*Movement expressed as a percentage of excavation depth

Figure 3.9 Guide to Vertical Movement Behind Shoring Systems

Placing significant amounts of fill or a new building adjacent to existing foundations can cause new settlement. A typical zone of influence is illustrated by Figure 3.10. This problem is especially common when relatively soft clays support a foundation. In this case, underpinning can be used to transfer the existing building loads to a bearing level below the susceptible strata. The potential for settlement due to excavation dewatering or pile driving was discussed in the previous section. Underpinning can be used to transfer the foundation loads to a level below the soils affected by the de-watering or pile driving.

Common types of underpinning are excavated piers, panel underpinning, drilled piles, and jacked piles.

Perhaps the earliest form of underpinning was the excavated pier, constructed by temporarily supporting a building column and then hand-excavating a pier beneath the existing footing. The sides of the excavation were supported by horizontal wood lagging more commonly called "well cribbing," or by the "Chicago well method" using steel rings and vertical wood lagging. Some piers were belled or enlarged to provide greater load capacity when the desired bearing elevation was reached. The pier was then filled with concrete (or masonry in earlier cases). The space between the new and the old foundation was then wedged tight using steel wedges. The last step required the grouting of any voids to provide corrosion protection and pre-

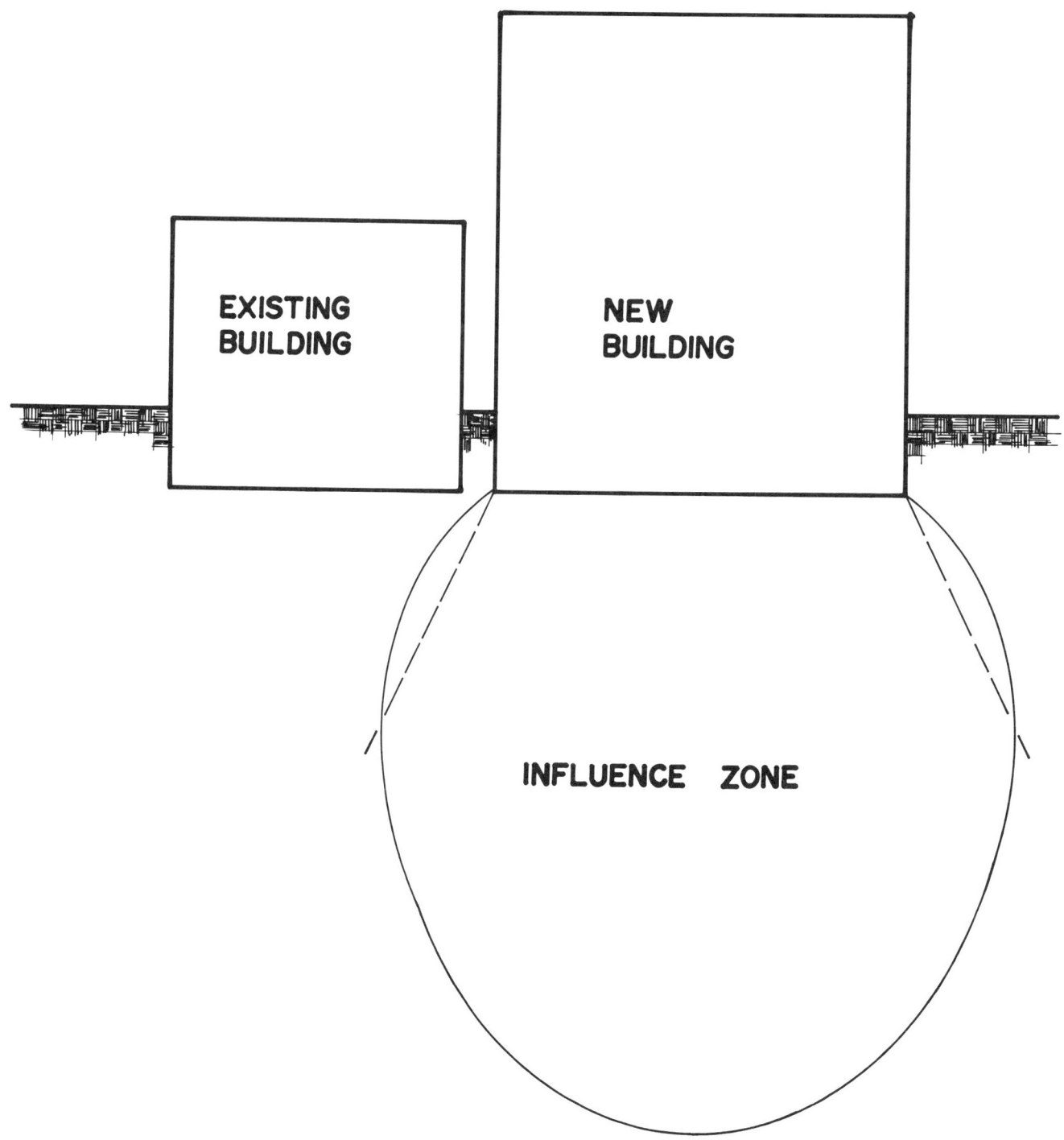

Figure 3.10 Load Influence Zone In Soil Under A New Building

vent ground loss. Many such piers have been constructed to depths of over 30 metres in Chicago. The method is labour intensive and presents considerable risk of cave-ins in some soils.

Panel underpinning, a variation of the excavated pier, is a common method for lowering a wall footing to a maximum depth of 3 or 4 metres in relatively competent soils such as clay or till. As illustrated by Figure 3.11 a series of spaced pits or slots 1 to 1.2 metres wide are excavated beneath the footing, filled with reinforced concrete, and wedged to the underside of the existing footing. The panels are constructed in a specific sequence. First the panels marked 1 are installed. The panels marked 2 and 3 are then con-

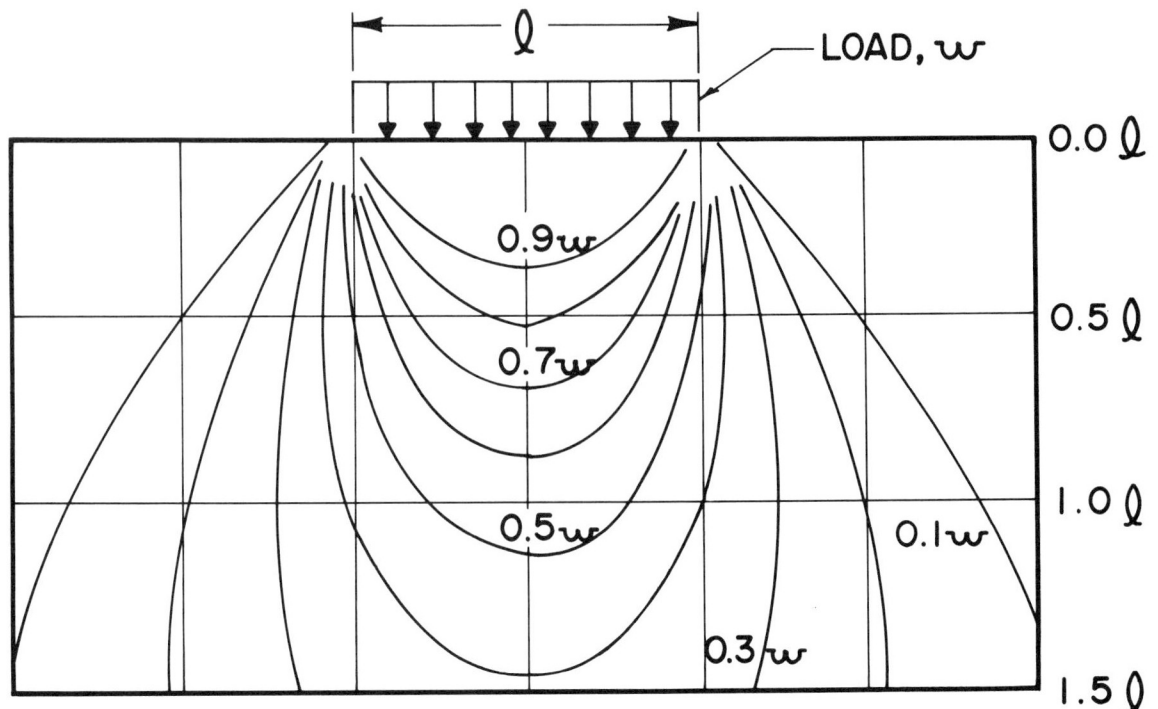

Figure 3.10 Load influence zone in soil under a new building

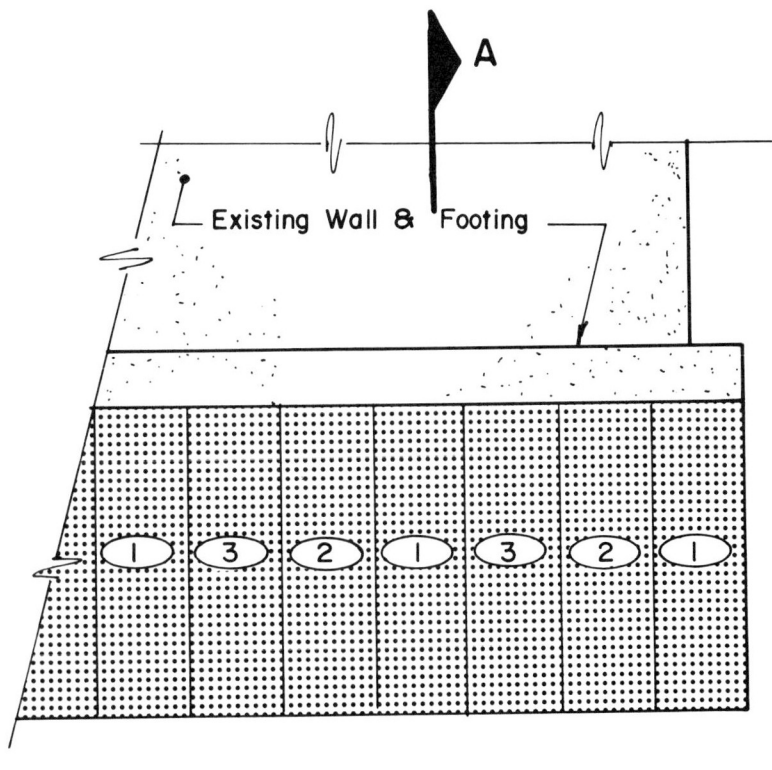

ELEVATION

Figure 3.11 Panel Underpinning

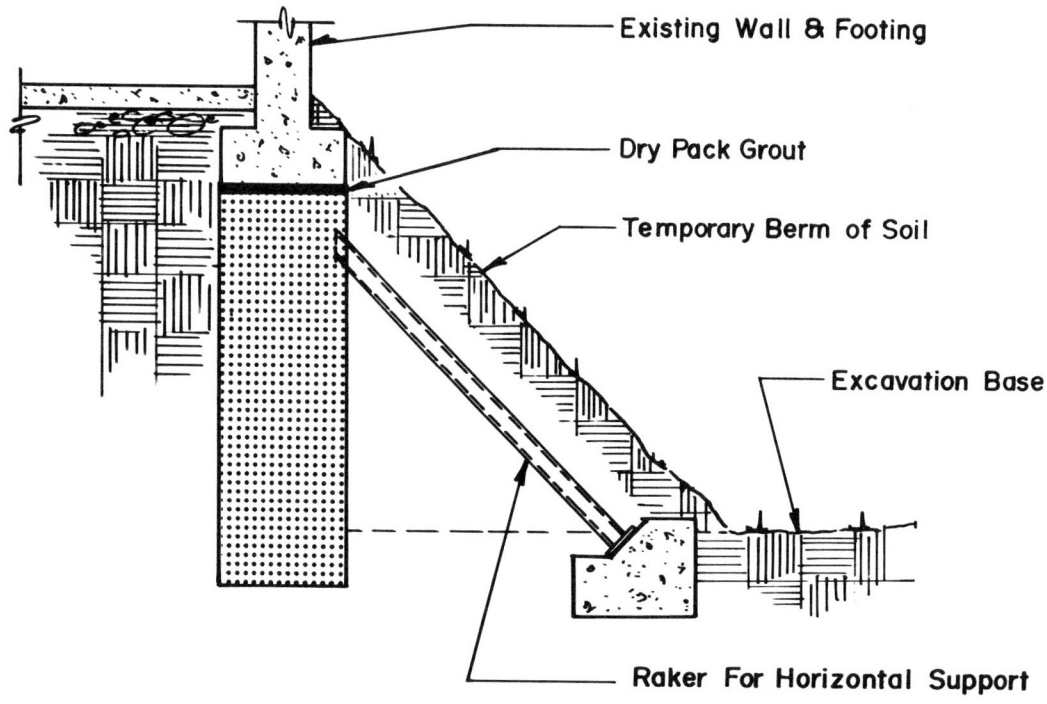

SECTION - A

Figure 3.11 - Panel underpinning

structed in sequence. Raker struts or tiebacks may be required to provide horizontal restraint to the pressure of the soil and other loads behind the underpinning wall. This method is simple and relatively economical. Its major drawback is the time required for the sequential installation. It may also result in some settlement of the soil retained behind the underpinning, the total amount depending upon the care taken during the underpinning operation and the type of soil involved.

A number of underpinning methods use drilled piles of a relatively large diameter. In one type, a hole is augered at a slight angle to the structure to be underpinned. The hole is then reamed out to allow placement of a steel section vertically beneath the existing footing. The load transfer zone at the base of the steel section is filled with concrete and the remainder of the hole filled with a lean concrete mix or sand. Finally the pile is preloaded and wedged to the existing footing. A full height reinforced concrete caisson can be used instead of the steel section. These piles are often installed at a spacing that allows them to carry the required underpinning load and act as a support for the lagging required to shore the adjacent excavation.

Underpinning piles are sometimes placed parallel to existing walls. A bracket is provided to transfer the existing building loads to these piles. The new piles can then be used as foundation units for new construction. It may be necessary to use an adjustable connection to the existing wall so that any added settlement caused by the new construction can be accommodated.

Another form of drilled pile underpinning uses small diameter piles, from 100 to 200 mm in diameter. These piles are placed in a three-dimensional network in order to reinforce the structure of the soil and increase its load bearing capacity. The individual piles are usually formed by drilling a hole, installing a steel reinforcing bar, and pressure grouting. This system, commonly referred to as root pile underpinning, uses the soil as the continuing foundation support and does not require a transfer of load to the piles themselves. A change in the soil state caused by adjacent excavation may still cause some settlement of the building. The economical use of root piles is restricted to certain soil types.

A widely adapted solution to the need for underpinning employs segmented piles forced into the ground by hydraulic jacks. Working from a small excavated area

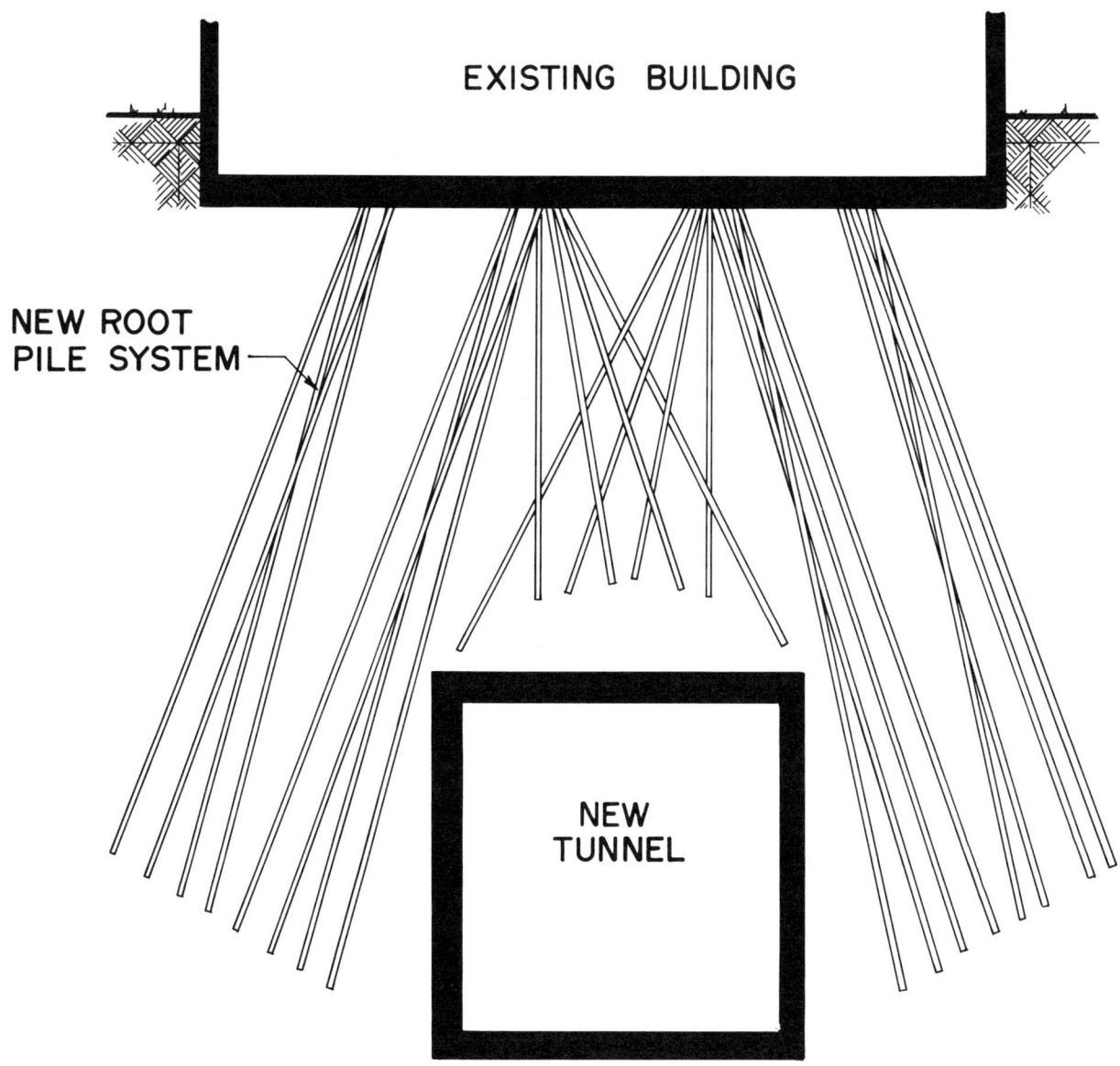

Figure 3.12 Root Pile Underpinning

beneath the footing or wall to be underpinned, short lengths of round steel pipe are welded, one on top of the other, to form a continuous pile as installation proceeds. The dead weight of the existing structure itself serves as the jacking reaction. If the underpinning must transfer the foundation load to a specific bearing strata or elevation, it may be necessary to pre-drill a slightly undersized hole to receive the pile. Another option is to remove the soil from within an open ended pile as it is installed. The completed pile is filled with concrete and its capacity proven by applying an overload, often to 125 per cent of the design load. The last step involves the installation of wedges tight to the existing foundation while the design load is maintained. This method works well in many difficult soils and where access is restricted, such as within a tunnel beneath a building. Jacked-pile underpinning is slow and expensive, but is a very safe technique if properly executed.

Although underpinning is often employed because of potential settlement problems, some settlement will nearly always accompany the underpinning work itself. The amount will depend on the design of the underpinning, the conditions that exist at a particular site, and the care and excellence of execution. Local differential settlements are often more damaging than greater uniform settlements. Preloading of the underpinning elements will eliminate much of the poten-

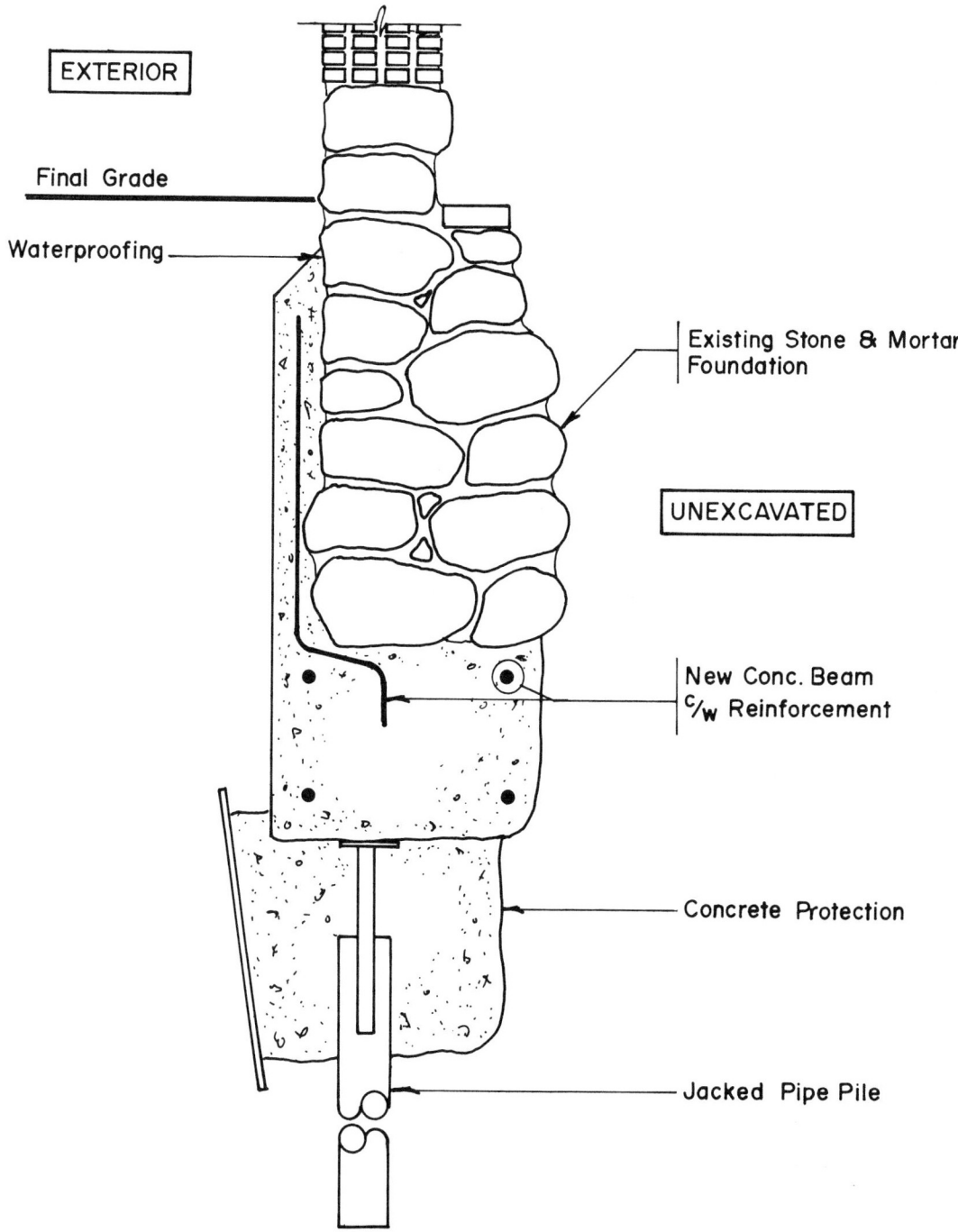

Figure 3.13 Grandin House Underpinning

tial settlement. The preloading technique uses hydraulic jacks to hold the design load on the new element until it is permanently connected to the existing structure. This permanent connection is made using welded steel sections, wedges, dry-pack grout, or some other permanent means. It is important to consider the stability and deformation characteristics of the connecting medium to prevent load release when the hydraulic jack is removed. Recording the as-found state of the structure and establishing a monitoring system is an essential part of any underpinning operation.

The underpinning of a structure required because of adjacent new construction is the responsibility of the party undertaking the new construction. However,

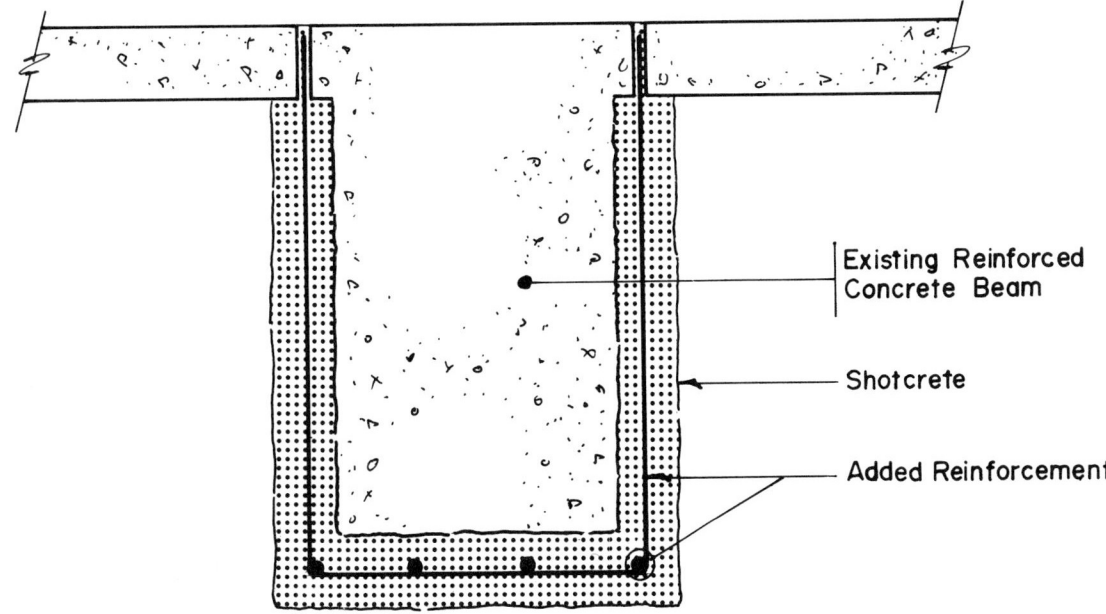

Figure 3.14 Shotcrete Beam Repair

the entire underpinning operation must be accepted by the owner of the existing structure. Contracts, agreements, and related drawings and specifications must clearly define all construction that encroaches on the neighbouring property as well procedures to be used.

An interesting example of jacked pile underpinning was recently undertaken at the Grandin House in St. Albert, Alberta. This masonry and wood framed building was constructed in 1863. The walls bear on rubble stone foundations which had undergone considerable settlement. A reinforced concrete beam and containment wall for the rubble foundation was cast in segments prior to installation of the underpinning piles as shown in Figure 3.13.

Underpinning installed to prevent further settlement of a heritage building can also be used to straighten or level portions of the structure. This lifting process requires a series of hydraulic jacks with safety devices to compensate for the potential failure of any individual component. Perhaps the most spectacular example of lifting a settled building is the Capuchines Shrine in Mexico City. This eighteenth century church, weighing 12 million kilograms, was raised 3.5 metres using a carefully executed plan employing piles and hydraulic jacks.

In an example closer to home one wing of the Saskatchewan Legislature Building (See Chapter 5) was levelled and raised using this technique.

SHOTCRETE

Shotcrete is a relatively dry mortar or concrete mixture pneumatically conveyed through a hose and sprayed onto a surface at high velocity. It is also known as gunite or sprayed concrete. An excellent bond is established between the shotcrete and other sound materials. This adhesion allows the application of shotcrete to vertical and overhead surfaces without sagging or sloughing. In view of the specialized nature of the process, an experienced applicator is necessary for a successful project.

Shotcrete is used in new construction to devise curved and folded roofs without extensive formwork, to make linings for reservoirs, swimming pools, tunnels, and sewers, and as part of excavation shoring systems. It can also be used to encase structural steel elements for fireproofing or to strengthen or repair slabs, beams, columns, and walls of reinforced concrete or masonry. Due to the nature of the material and the readily obtained intimate contact with the existing element, a superior bond can normally be achieved on a clean and sound surface without bonding agents. Surface preparation requires some chipping to remove unsound material, followed by a sandblast cleaning.

Although steel wire mesh is the most common form of reinforcement for shotcrete, conventional bar reinforcement can be used for the repair or strengthening of structures. The size of bars should be limited to 15 mm diameter and adequate spacing maintained to ensure proper bonding of the shotcrete. Larger bar sizes can be used with exceptional care in shotcrete placement. Fibre reinforced shotcrete incorporates short fibres of steel, plastic, or glass in the projected mixture. These fibres substantially increase the tensile strength of the finished product.

Gunite is best used in thin sections where the finished appearance is not critical. Although it is possible to trowel fresh gunite, it is not recommended, as the bond to the sub-strate may be broken.

Shotcrete does not have the freeze-thaw durability of conventional concrete because of its lack of air entrainment. Therefore it should not be considered a permanent material in a severe freeze-thaw environment.

Deteriorated or fire-damaged reinforced concrete elements can be restored to full structural capacity by the use of shotcrete repairs. This is often accomplished within the original dimensions of the member. In Figure 3.14 for example, a beam with damaged reinforcement was chipped back to sound concrete and cleaned by sandblasting. Reinforcement bars were then fixed near the existing concrete surface. The shotcrete was applied to bond the reinforcement to the old concrete and to provide required fireproofing. In a similar manner reinforcement can be added to existing elements to enhance their load capacity.

Members needing repair or strengthening must be temporarily supported or shored to remove the applied loads. Proper sharing of the design loads then occurs between the new and old elements once the load is re-applied.

Masonry walls that have deteriorated or require additional capacity to resist wind or earthquake loadings can be strengthened by applying a backup wall of reinforced concrete. Shotcrete is the preferred technique because it can be applied against the existing wall without having to construct another form face. Also the risk of damage to the wall from the fluid pressures of fresh concrete is eliminated. This technique has been used extensively in upgrading buildings to meet the earthquake requirements of present building codes. The Carnegie Library in Vancouver (see Chapter 5) exemplifies this type of application.

Another recent innovation in the use of shotcrete involves the panelization of important elements of heritage properties. (See Chapters 5 and 7)

DISMANTLING AND REASSEMBLY

Redevelopment of a site may not allow the retention of a heritage structure. Preservation by dismantling and reassembly may be the only acceptable alternative to destruction. As implied, this method requires careful "unbuilding" of the structure piece by piece. The pieces are removed, stored and reassembled at a new location.

An accurate and detailed record of the as-found building is an essential first step in this process. This record may be created by hand measurement and recording of physical details, combined with conventional photography or photogrammetry. The plans, elevations, and detail drawings thus created are then combined with a marking system identifying each component of the structure to be dismantled. The use of record documents combined with the identifying marks permits easy reconstruction of the various pieces.

One aspect of this component marking bears watching. The piece marks are usually shown on an elevation view of the building facade. There have been a number of cases where the contractor took this notation literally and marked the exposed face with an indelible material which later proved almost impossible to remove.

During the dismantling process various hidden aspects of the building construction are exposed and subsequently destroyed. These details must be recorded to ensure that all aspects of the reconstruction are compatible. For example, the properties of the mortar used to rebuild a masonry wall must be consistent with the masonry units themselves. The properties of the original mortar should be noted and determined, by test if necessary, as a guide for designing the new mortar. Other important factors are the location of metal ties and provisions for ventilation and drainage of air spaces in masonry walls.

The loss of some building components due to theft is a high probability in addition to the risk that some parts may be damaged beyond repair in the dismantling process. The storage site chosen must be secure from theft, vandalism and damage due to infrequent but plausible natural hazards such as floods or earth slides. The design of a storage system must facilitate the identification of components for orderly retrieval upon rebuilding. It must also provide protection from damage by vermin and weather. The careful disassembly of the cast iron Laing Stress Building in lower Manhattan to make way for the World Trade Center is a case in point. Some components were taken from the initial storage yard and all the remaining pieces disappeared after being moved to "secure" storage in a warehouse.

The shotcrete panelization technique used on Edmonton's Rothesay Apartments (see Chapter 5) offers a remedy for many of these problems.

POLYMERS

Polymers have found widespread application in the construction industry and are commonly used in coating, patching and repairing building elements of concrete, masonry, wood and steel. They are able to prevent the entry of moisture and dissolved salts which can cause deterioration. Polymers resist chemical attack, provide barriers to heat and electric current and protect against radiation. Also, their ability to bond to almost any surface, wet or dry, their high strength, their excellent creep resistance and their fast curing rate has made them very attractive as a repair material.

There are a multitude of different formulations of polymers, each designed specifically for its end use. The newest coating has a high carbon dioxide diffusion resistance, providing protection from industrial pollutants including sulfur dioxides, hydrochloric acid, oxides of nitrogen and other diluted acids and alkalis found in acid rain. Without protection, these chemicals enter concrete elements and reduce the Ph, or alkaline level, to a point where the corrosion of embedded reinforcement occurs. Although the deterioration of concrete takes much longer than that associated with the familiar effects of de-icing salts on vehicle parkades, the ultimate results are as severe. Polymer applications can assist in the preservation of stone monuments and structures that are rapidily being eroded by the "manmade" components in our atmosphere.

When considering the rehabilitation of heritage structures, it is important to retain the maximum amount of original material. The total replacement of deteriorated structural members is not necessary. The use of polymers, although not always least expensive, is often the best method of repair. It is possible to fully restore the strength of a member using polymers and yet retain a maximum amount of the sound portion of the member.

Polymers useful for the construction industry may be divided into two general groups: additives that modify cement mortars; and reactive thermosetting resins.

The first group improves the performance of cement mortar as a concrete repair material. The polymer latex modifies the mortar in several ways. It serves as a plasticizer, reducing the water requirements or increasing the workability. Also the permeability of the mortar is reduced, providing increased resistance to penetration by water and oils, as well as greater protection from attack by corrosive agents. Finally polymer latex improves the bond between the repair mortar and the original material. Common polymers used as additives include styrene butadiene, acrylic and modified acrylic latexes.

The second general group of polymers are reactive thermosetting resins which may be further subdivided into epoxy resins and polyester resins. Both of these are two or three component systems made up of resins, hardener and fillers. The primary components, resin and hardener, are odourless solutions of low viscosity. When they are mixed together a chemical reaction takes place producing a thermoset material. This material has high strength, low creep, strong resistance to numerous chemicals, excellent adhesion and good electrical insulation properties.

In comparing epoxy and polyester resins, several points emerge. When combining the components for epoxy resins proper proportioning and complete mixing is much more critical than for polyester resins. Therefore greater control is required in the mixing process for epoxies. The change in volume between cured and uncured epoxy resins is low. In addition, the maximum heat evolution due to the chemical reaction occurs when the epoxy is still in a fluid state. These two factors combine to minimize the residual stress caused by thermal and volumetric changes in epoxy resins. In contrast, polyester resins set before maximum heat evolution and also change volume during curing. These resins therefore may only be used in small areas to reduce residual stresses.

By careful selection of the properties of the resin and hardener, it is possible to obtain a polymer that will perform as required in the conditions which occur during mixing, placing and curing of the repair, and the lifetime of the structure. The properties of the polymer may also be modified by the addition of inert fillers such as silica and aluminum.

Polymers are very versatile and may be used in several ways to rehabilitate heritage structures. Before repairing begins, however, it is important to fully understand and eliminate the cause of the deterioration.

Polymers in the form of epoxy resins offer both a high strength and bond plus a fluid nature prior to curing. These properties allow the rejoining of cracked materials, making them function again in a monolithic manner. Epoxies can be pressure grouted into concrete

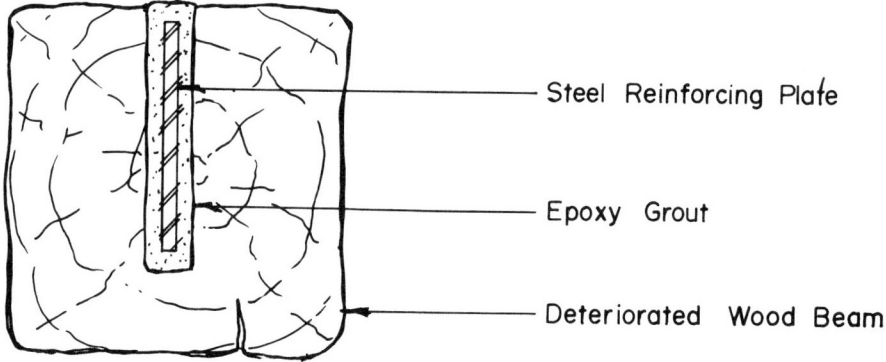

Figure 3.15 W-E-R System Beam Repair

cracks as small as 5 microns.

Where deterioration has occured in the cross section of the structural member through spalling of concrete or rotting of wood, it is possible to replace the defective material using polymers. As mentioned previously, if large areas need to be replaced, polyester resins are not suitable. Epoxy resins or polymer modified cements could restore the cross-section of the member once all unsound material is removed.

The high strength and bond of epoxy resin makes it feasible to increase the load capacity of a structural element. This is done by "gluing" a reinforcing plate to the existing surface. This technique is equally applicable to concrete, masonry, wood or steel. Load testing of laboratory specimens has shown it is possible to yield a steel reinforcing plate bonded to the side of a hardened concrete beam without breaking the epoxy bond.

Once repairs are complete it is desirable to provide increased protection of the repaired and original sections. This can be accomplished by the application of a polymeric coating. When the cause of the original deterioration is determined a suitable protective coating can then be selected.

In the case of metal corrosion the application of a non-breathing type of paint would be an appropriate final step in the rehabilitation process. A sealer which allows the passage of moisture - a breather coating is more appropriate for porous materials such as wood.

This highlights the basic steps in the repair process: determine the cause; repair the damage; eliminate the cause.

The repair of concrete using polymers is straightforward. It is important to remove all deteriorated concrete and steel. New steel may be added by welding to old steel that is sound. The replacement substance, whether polymer or polymer modified concrete may be injected into cracks, cast-in-place or sprayed over the area to be repaired.

Masonry is also easily repaired using polymers. Cracks in the brick or mortar may be repaired in a similar manner to those in concrete. If mortar is seriously deteriorated it may be replaced entirely by an epoxy grout. If the damage is extensive, it might be necessary to fill the cavities of the masonry and possibly insert reinforcing. This is done most effectively by using polymer-modified mortar with its increased workability and reduced shrinkage.

The use of polymers in wood repair has become important because it can be used to rebond cracks, splits, or delaminations in timbers. New wooden members can also be bonded to the remaining sound portions of timbers ravaged by dry rot.

Epoxy resins also offer a means to carry out inconspicuous repairs to wooden structures, monuments and works of art. Steel reinforcement can be concealed in slots and holes cut in the wood member. A composite bond between the two elements is provided by epoxy grout. Figure 3.15 illustrates the reinforcement of a beam by the WER-System, one of the epoxy bonded systems available for the same purpose.

When steel or iron members have been damaged or need to have increased load capacity, polymers again are useful. The member can be encased in a polymer or polymer modified concrete. Depending on the type used, a polymer concrete may also increase the fire resistance of the member. To increase the load capacity an oft-used method is to attach an extra plate of metal to increase the cross-sectional area. Traditionally it is bolted or welded to the original member. If this is not feasible the extra plate may be glued to the member using an epoxy adhesive. As discussed previously, the resulting bond is strong enough to assure composite action of the two parts.

Unfortunately, there are several disadvantages to specifying polymers as a repair material. These must be taken into account when considering their use.

These products offer an almost infinite variation depending on the proportioning of the different resins, curing agents, modifiers, solvents, accelerators, and fillers. This presents a problem in selecting the most appropriate product for a particular application. Each variation can have properties that respond to changes in temperature, moisture content, or load differently. When one adds the variations possible in the materials to be patched, the selection process becomes complex.

In many buildings sealing the outer surface may trap moisture within the exterior shell, causing additional problems. Some recently developed acrylic sealants allow water vapours to pass while excluding free water. The products have a limited life-span and are not fully proven in service. However, they offer the potential to overcome problems that occur when dealing with exterior walls.

Quality control of the rebonding process is difficult. The epoxy itself can be sampled to verify proportions and make laboratory test specimens. Samples thus produced can give false readings compared to materials installed in actual field conditions. In-situ conditions can only be determined by full scale load tests of the completed repair. These large scale tests can be supplemented by laboratory testing of samples removed from the structure. The best assurance of quality is the employment of knowledgeable and experienced workmen.

When polymer-based products are used in masonry work, their hardness and density must be compatible with the original mortar. The epoxy can form damaging moisture barriers and cold bridges within the masonry. The result may be a rather costly "repair" if the repair itself must be replaced within several years.

Currently available epoxies are sensitive to heat and will fail early in a fire. Even exposure to temperatures near 40 degrees Celsius for extended periods can cause loss of strength. Their use near heating ducts, hot-water or steampipes, and floodlights should be avoided. In addition, exposure to sunlight may cause the deterioration of some epoxies over extended periods of time.

Although epoxy-bonded reinforcing elements can fail in a fire, the original structural element may be sufficiently safe to ensure temporary stability and public safety. In buildings requiring relatively low fire resistance, the use of intumescent or heat-insulating paints may provide the necessary fire protection for exposed members. More conventional and less expensive sprayed or trowelled-on fireproofing materials can be used to protect members which will be concealed in the finished building.

An aid to the proper selection of polymers for concrete repair is provided by specifications such as "ASTM C881-79 Epoxy-Resin Based Bonding Systems for Concrete" and related publications by the American Concrete Institute (see bibliography). Unfortunately tables of equivalents for applications to masonry and wood do not exist at this time.

TRANSFER SYSTEMS

Integrating a heritage structure into a new development can bring about conflicts. The new space plans and the existing vertical load-carrying members are often incompatible. One solution may be to change the location of some of the vertical elements - a task accomplished with a transfer system.

A transfer system can be as simple as a small shift in the floor to floor location of a column, using a beam as the transfer medium. With heavier loads, a transfer column accomplishes the same end result. The transfer column illustrated in Figure 3.16 uses the floor systems to resist the horizontal thrusts generated by the offset loads.

A more complex transfer system can allow a complete change in column locations from one floor to another. This extensive transfer usually requires a full storey-high two-way structural grid. Such a system was used in the adaptive re-use of the Queens Quay Terminal (See Chapter 5).

Transfer systems can also be used to great benefit in underpinning heritage structures. The Canadian Im-

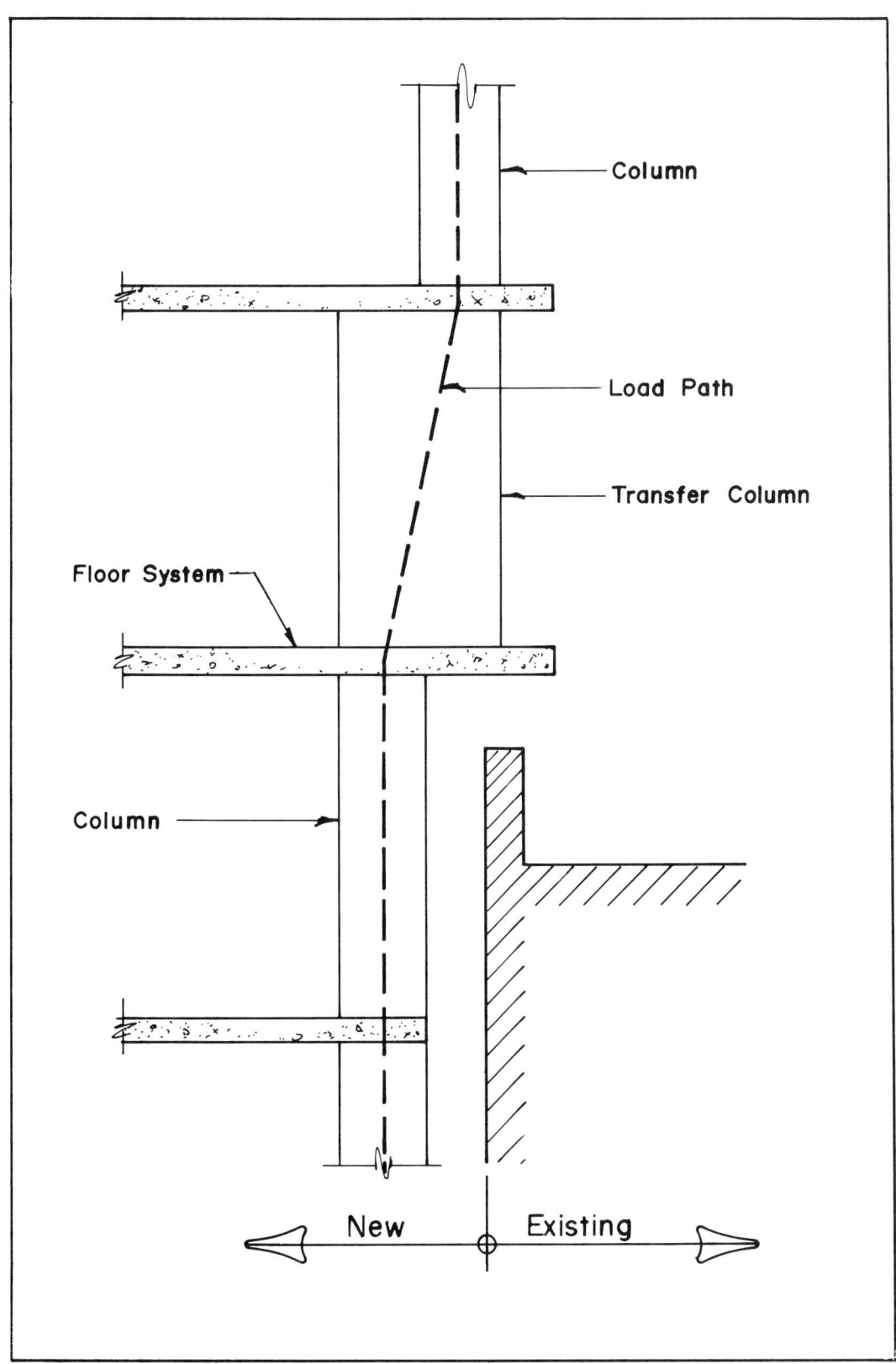

Figure 3.16 Transfer Column

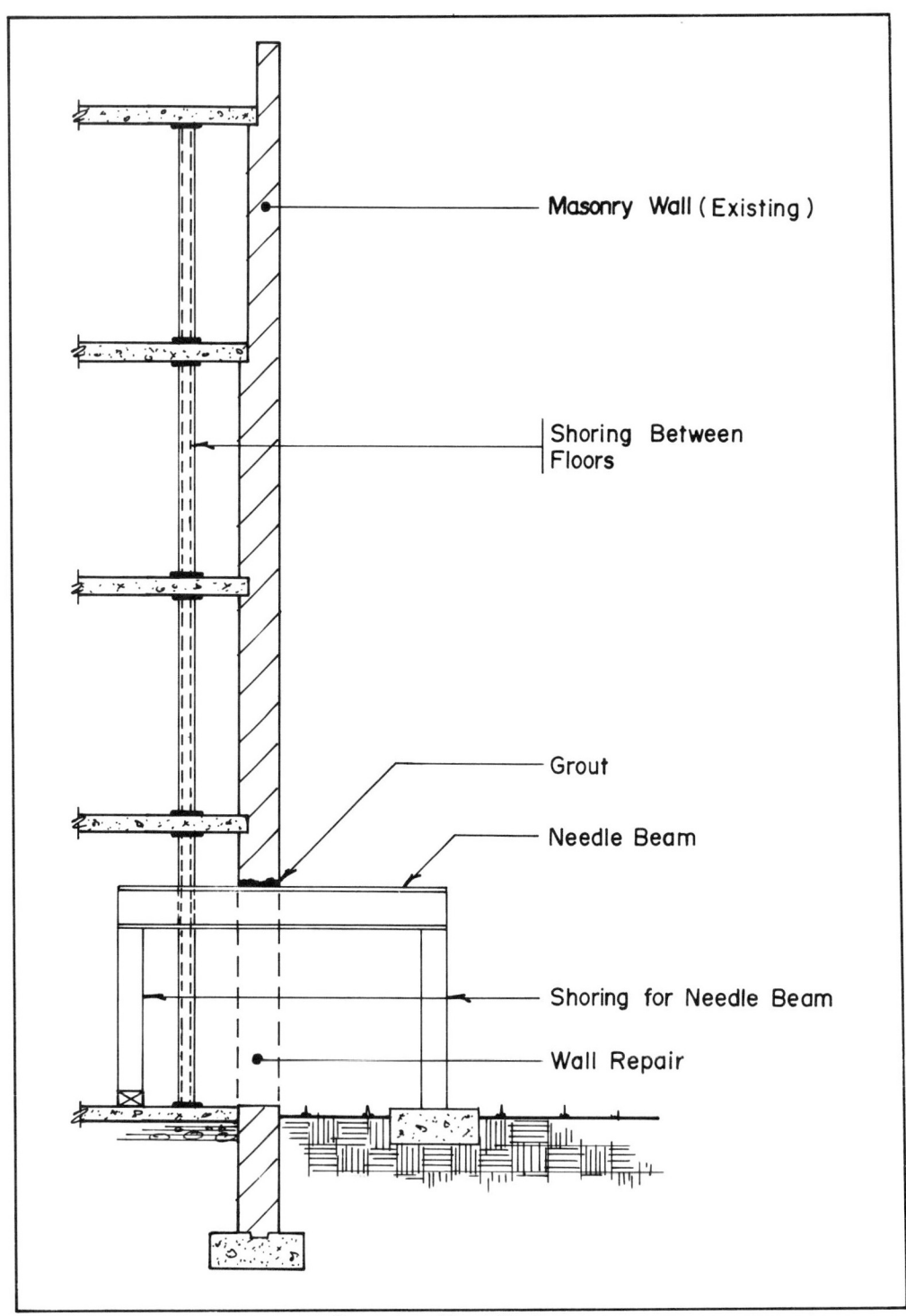

Figure 3.17 Dead Shoring

perial Bank of Commerce Building in Edmonton (also studied in Chapter 5) used a post-tensioned reinforced concrete transfer system. The load balancing nature of post-tensioning allows a designer to reduce long term deflections due to the creep phenomena in the concrete. This system made it feasible to tunnel a dual track transit line diagonally under the site without disruption to the bank's operation.

There are several important considerations in the design of transfer systems. The transfer must be considered equivalent to a foundation for the structure which it supports. Tolerable limits of deflection, and

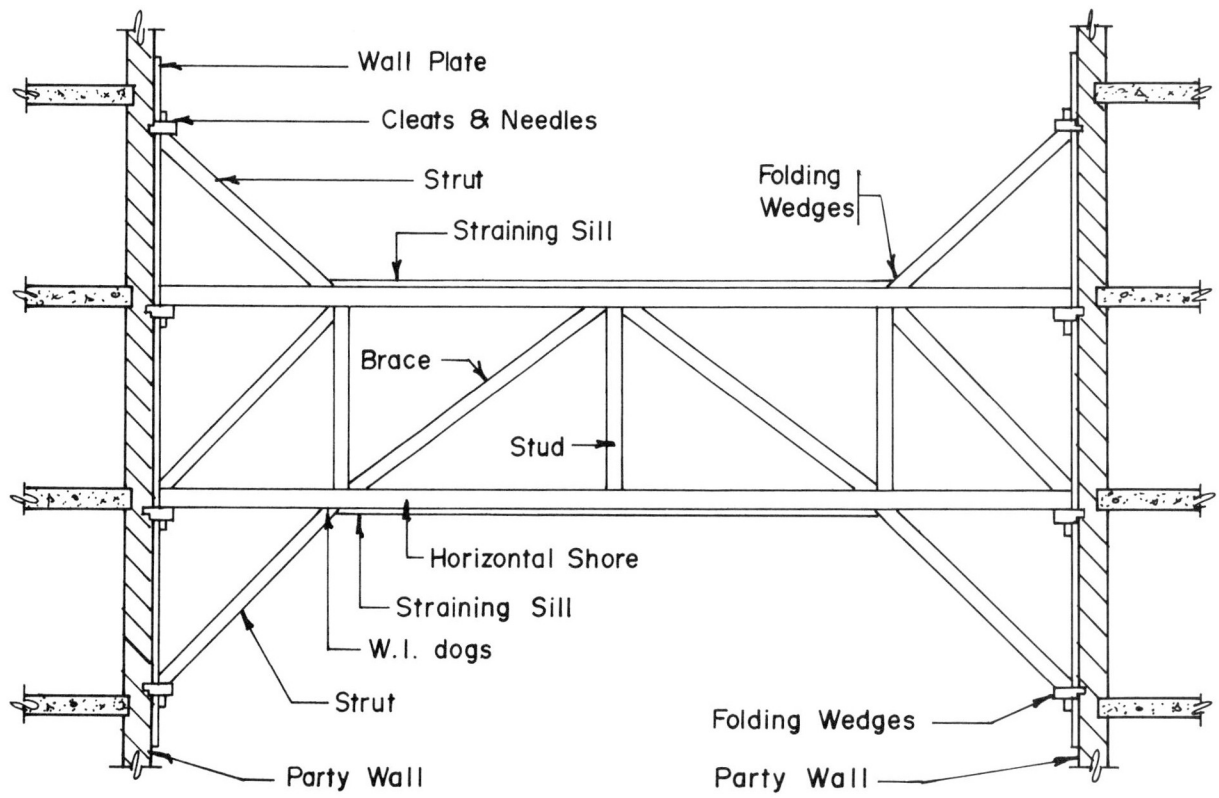

Figure 3.18 Flying Shores

the consequences of exceeding them, are similar to those applied to differential settlement of foundations.

Pre-loading of a transfer system, usually by jacking, is the best way to reduce the risk of settlements. The pre-loading must be calculated, and not determined by jacking the structure until it moves.

It has been stressed that condition surveys and on-going monitoring are important for most structural conservation techniques. This is especially true for transfer systems because instabilities in the system could lead to a total loss of the existing and new construction

TEMPORARY SUPPORTS

Construction work involving structural repair, alteration or demolition usually requires some form of temporary support to ensure its integrity. A prerequisite for the selection and design of a temporary support system is a thorough understanding of the structural system to be supported. The provision of temporary support is not a simple undertaking. Loads must be calculated, the size, location and connection details of all components determined, and erection procedures clearly defined. Construction safety regulations require that temporary structures be designed by an engineer. CSA Standard S2691.1 "Falsework for Construction Purposes" provides rules and requirements for falsework materials and components used in the construction, alteration or repair of buildings and other structures. The importance of temporary support is proven by the collapse of numerous buildings which stood in a damaged condition but collapsed during repair attempts.

Temporary support systems used in heritage conservation work can be as simple as scaffolding or as complex as in-situ trusses. Scaffolding is used to provide working platforms and as a form of lateral bracing for the structure itself. The use of tubular component systems is widespread today as it is very adaptable and readily available. However, accidents are not uncommon when this type of scaffolding is used. Construction safety regulations and the manufacturer's directions must be strictly followed. If scaffolding is used as a temporary support as well as a working platform, its design and detail should be verified by an engineer.

Dead shores are members that carry vertical loads only and rely on the structure or added bracing for

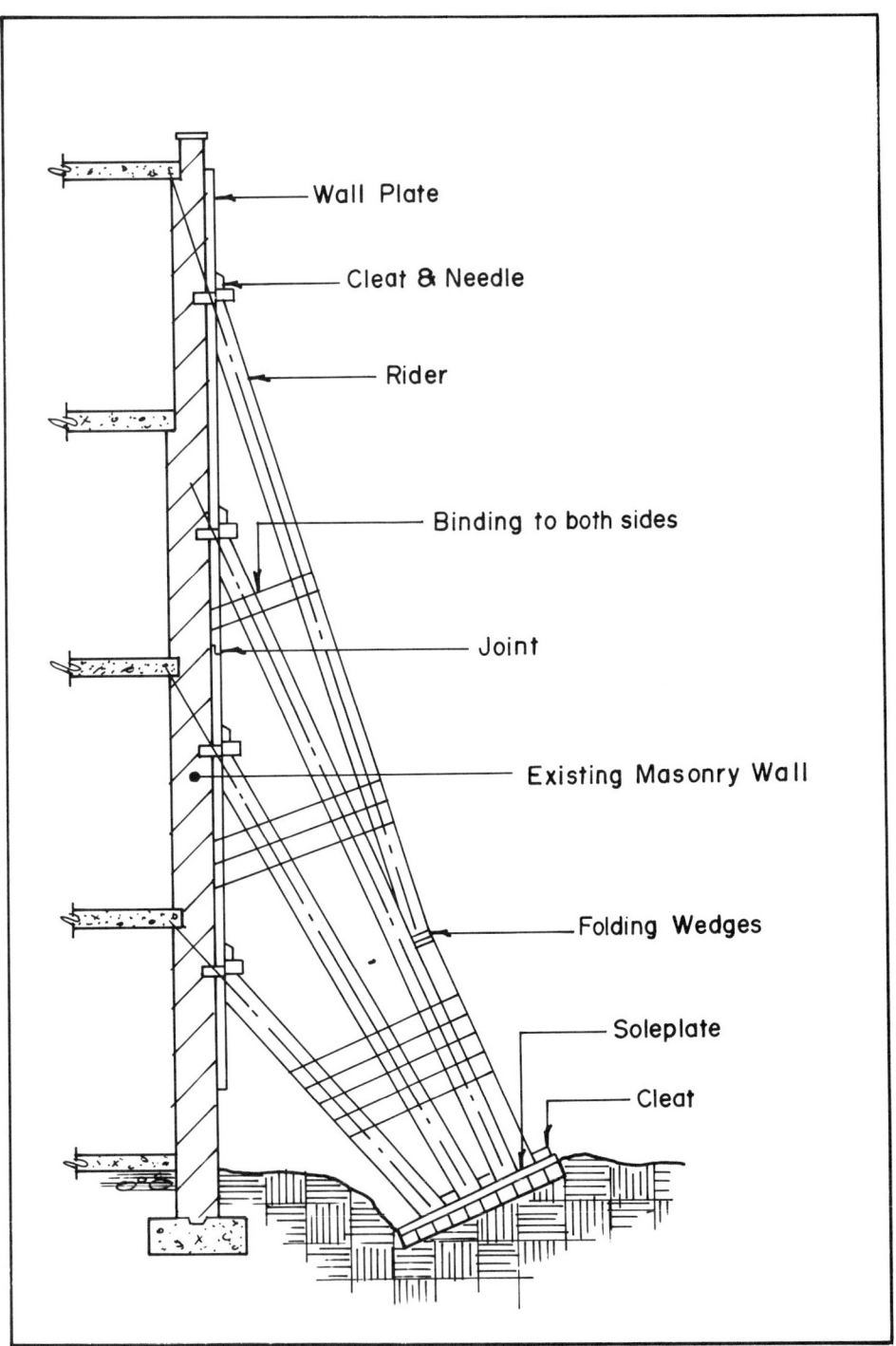

Figure 3.19 Raking Shore

stability. Some provision for tightening or pre-loading must be included. This ensures that loads are carried by the shores and not by the structure and can be achieved using wedges, screw jacks or hydraulic jacks. In analysing any structural system - temporary or permanent - it is essential to determine the weakest point. In dead shoring the weakest point is the base of the lowest level of shores. These shores usually rest on earth or a slab-on-grade. Settlement of the soil in either case is common. This can lead to a total redistribution of the load paths in the shoring system and in the building frame. The solution is to provide regular monitoring and adjustment of the shoring system. Particularly sensitive systems may require installation of instruments to monitor the sustained loads at critical locations in the system. Any change in loadings can be compensated by the application of counteracting forces through hydraulic jacks.

After installing a series of shores between floors to relieve the wall load, needle beams are inserted

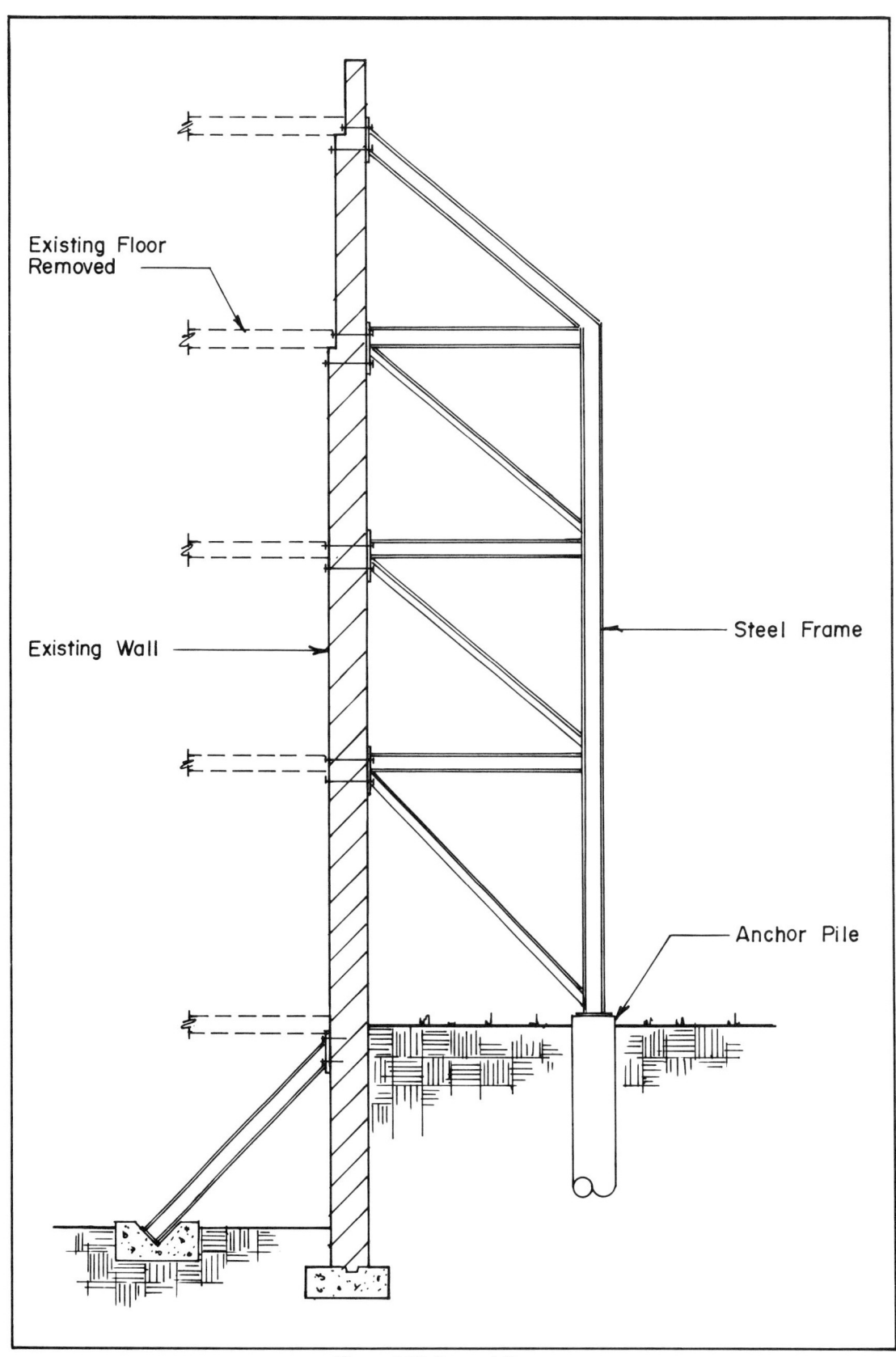

Figure 3.20 Support Frame

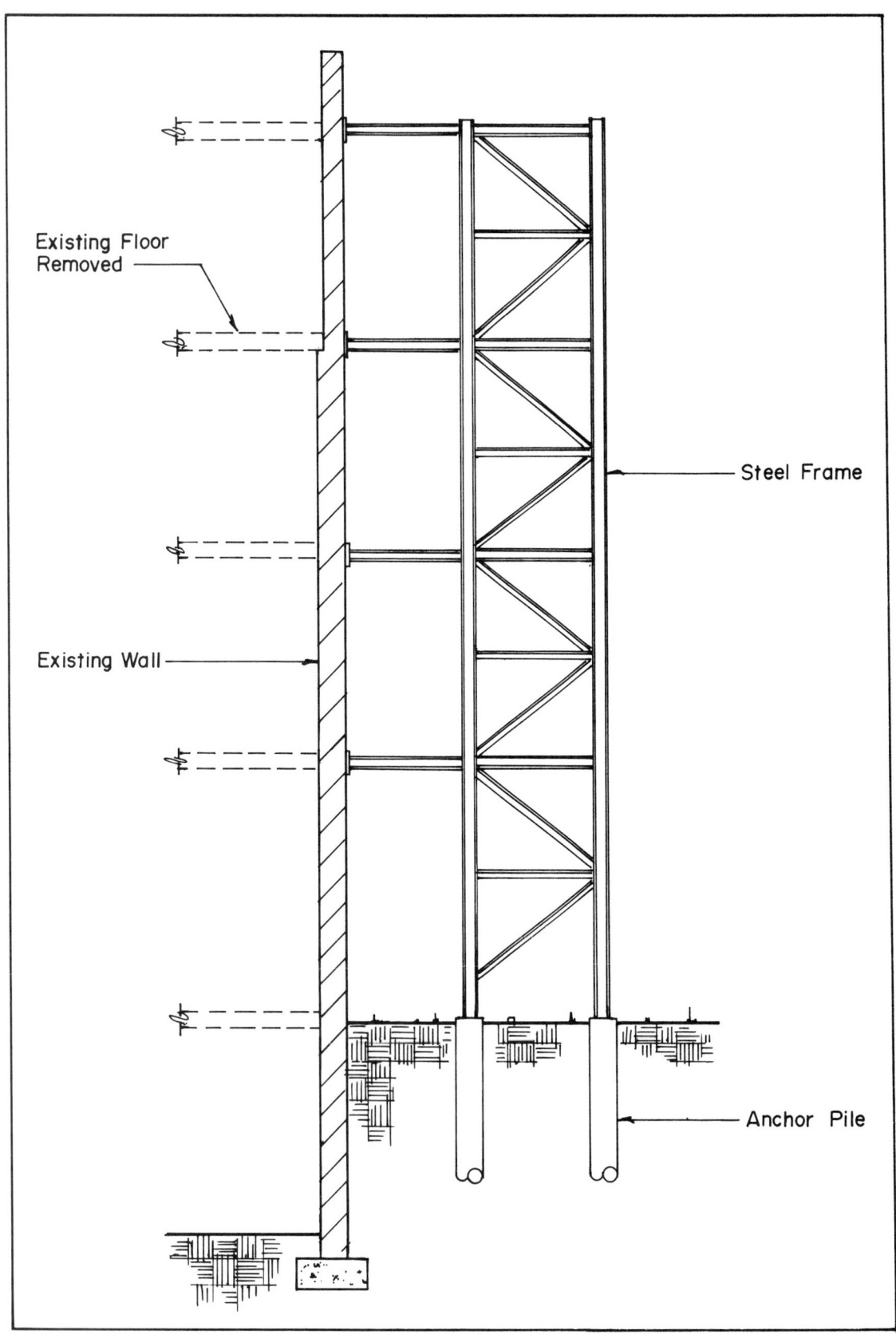

Figure 3.21 Support Tower

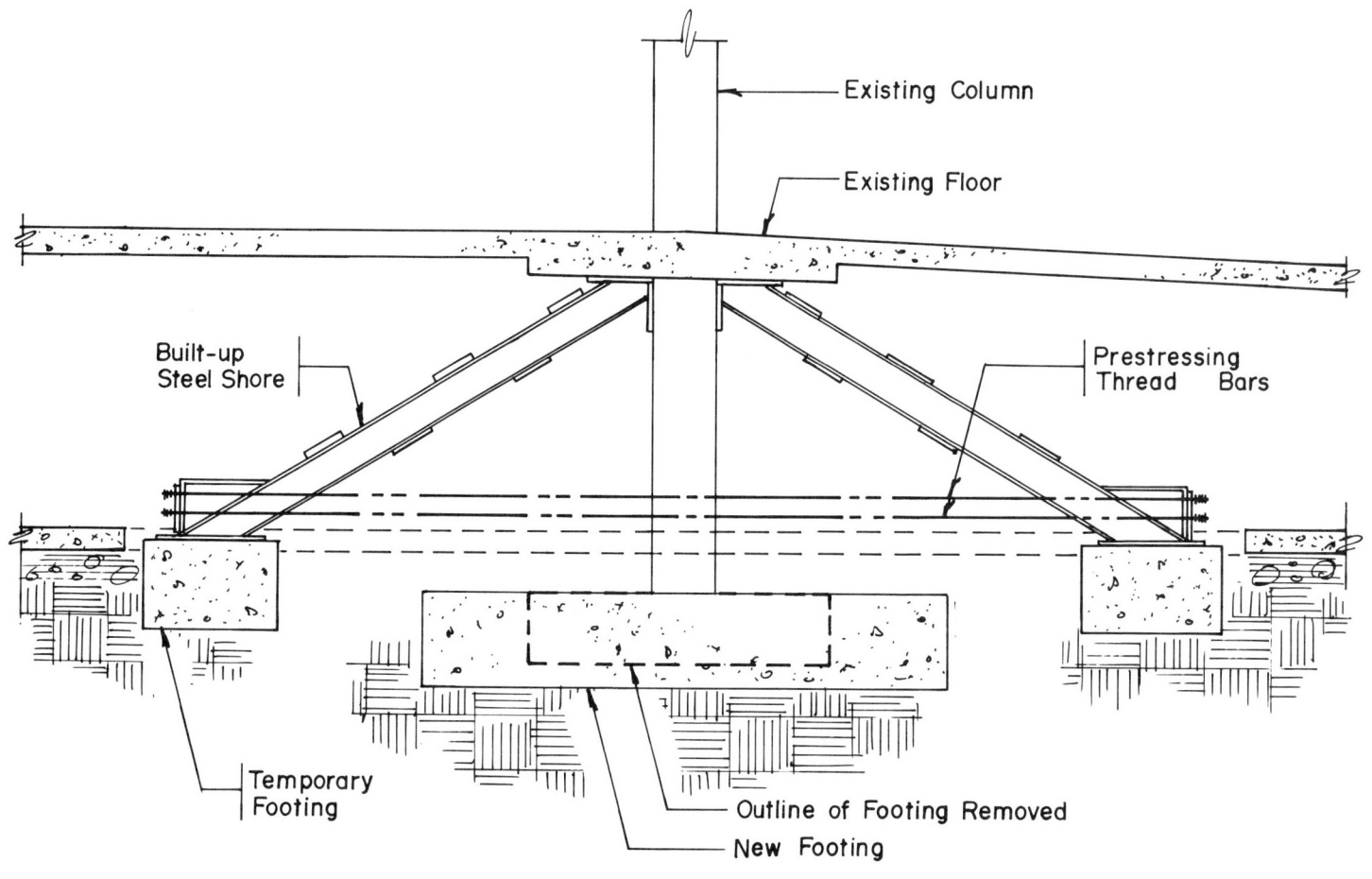

Figure 3.22 Temporary Column Support

through holes pierced in the wall. The spacing of the needle beams is determined by the safe distance the wall can span without support. These beams are supported on shores, grouted to the wall, and then loaded by tightening the shores. In this manner the portion of the wall below the needles can be removed to create a new opening or make repairs.

Horizontal or flying shores span wall-to-wall to provide temporary lateral support. This type of shoring is often used to support the shell of a building while the floor structure is replaced, or to support party walls as in Figure 3.18. Diagonal or raking shores may also be used to provide lateral support to a wall or building. As they provide support from the ground they should include a means of compensating for settlement. A heavy duty raking shore is illustrated in Figure 3.19.

Space restrictions can rule out the use of raking shores. An alternate means of support is a tower to provide lateral support to a tall wall. The details of such a tower will vary rather widely, dependent upon the type of wall, the frequency of support it requires, and the space available. Frame support as illustrated in Figure 3.20 may be the most cost effective method. It requires a sound wall capable of withstanding tension and compression as the wall forms an integral part of the system. If the condition of the wall does not allow it to be safely loaded in this manner, a tower support as shown in Figure 3.21 must be used. A tower is a stable free-standing structure, tied to the wall in a manner that transmits only lateral forces. Both types of shoring require positive anchorage of the base to prevent overturning. This is accomplished by providing a massive concrete footing or by the installation of tension piles.

In some situations, a unique shoring system is devised for a particular problem. In the example illustrated in Figure 3.22, a temporary column support was installed to enable enlargement of a footing. Alternately, an underpinning support such as that illustrated in Figure 3.23 could have been used. In both cases, the load

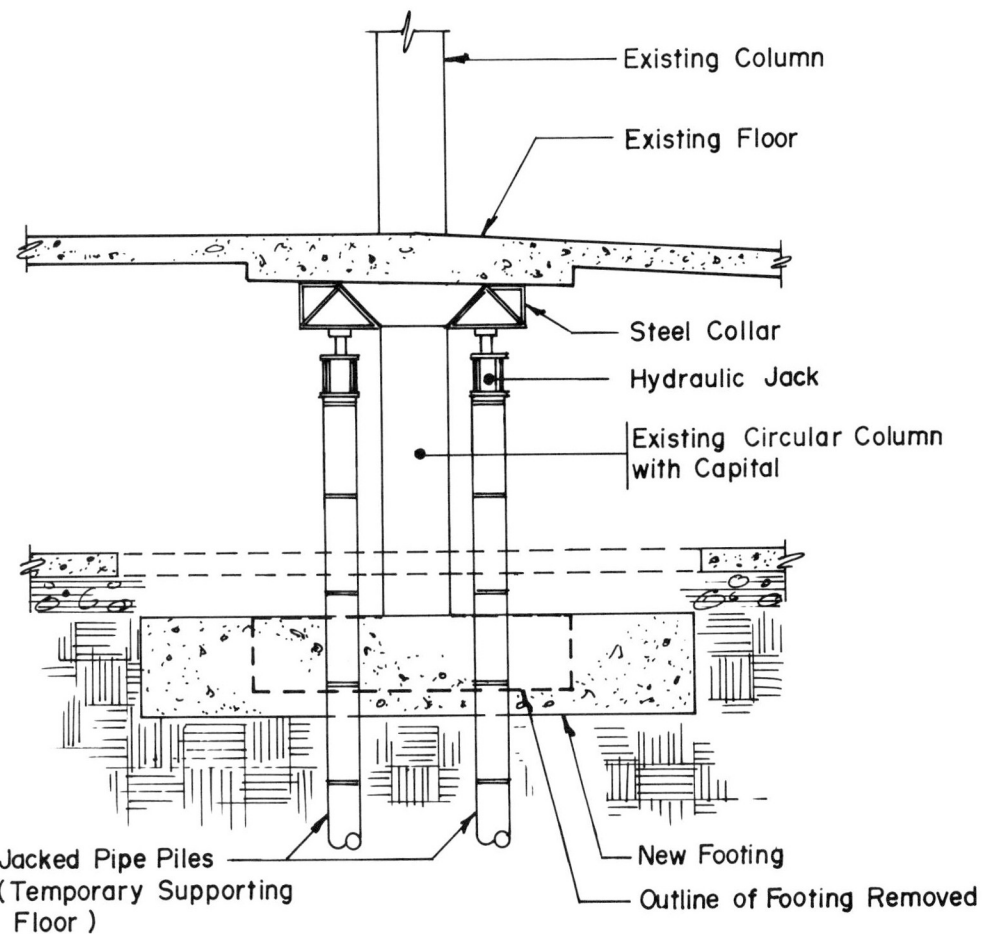

Figure 3.23 Column Shoring

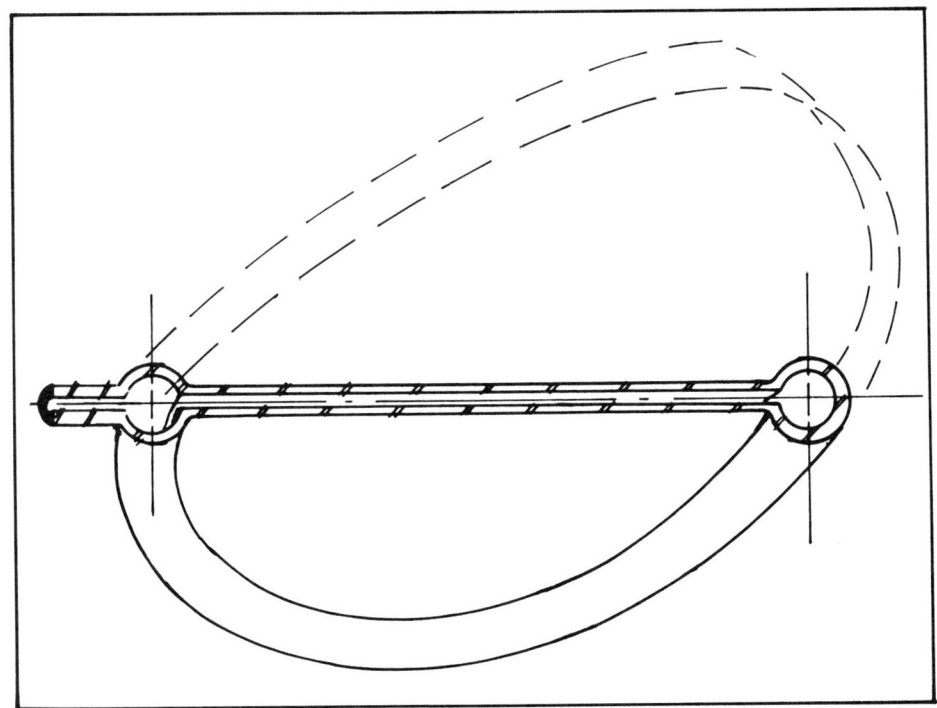

Figure 3.24 Flatjack

capacity of the floor-to-column junction must be strong enough to transfer the column load. In temporary supports of this type, some means of pre-loading is required before the column can be cut. In Figure 3.22 this is done by tightening the pre-stressing rods and thus raising the column. In Figure 3.23 wedges or hydraulic jacks can be used.

Hydraulic rams are well adapted to use in temporary support systems. They allow prestressing or pre-loading of supports. They are easily monitored and adjusted to maintain a particular load or support position. Flat jacks comprised of two steel plates joined by a flexible ring are well suited to limited spaces and load monitoring (See Figure 3.24). The load is applied by inflating the jacks hydraulically or pneumatically. Sand jacks are also available to provide static support. These jacks are positioned and filled with sand after the structure has been raised by hydraulic rams.

Again, with temporary supports as with other types of construction, establishing a system for detecting support movements is good practice.

OTHER TECHNIQUES

Relocation

Historic buildings are often endangered by their proximity to planned transportation corridors. The possibility of moving such structures should not be overlooked. Many large masonry buildings have been successfully relocated. The process involves the careful computation of wall and column loads and the design of shoring, internal bracing and a runner system attached to the base. Finally, a suitable moving medium must be selected and the track designed.

For a short distance relocation, a light building can be pushed on soaped or greased timber skids which rest upon timber cribbing. A heavier structure requires structural steel runners with steel rollers as the moving medium. These then roll on steel tracks supported by temporary concrete footings. Longer distance moves require the use of wheeled dollies and sometimes, a specially prepared roadbed.

A five-storey concrete and brick building in southern Norway, constructed in the 1920's was recently moved some 5 metres to allow a road widening project. The Russians have moved stone buildings twice this height.

Chemical Mixing

The bearing capacity and stability of soft, sedimentary soils can be improved by in-place mixing with a solidifying chemical slurry. A specially designed mixing machine can do this without removing the soil. As soil is not removed this process does not endanger adjacent soil or foundation units. This can be a valuable alternate to shoring and underpinning for heritage structures.

Slabjacking

The term "slabjacking" or "mudjacking" is used to describe an operation whereby a cement grout is pumped beneath a slab-on-grade to restore uniform support. Mudjacking can also lift a settled slab back to its original position. Holes are drilled through the slab in a predetermined pattern. Grout is then pumped between the slab and soil, creating pressure sufficient to raise the slab. The grout hardens to form a new base for the slab. Slabjacking is certainly not a precise science and an experienced contractor is required to determine the spacing of grouting holes, composition of the grout, and pump pressure to be used for a specific application. Pumping grout beneath a slab can cause surprises, such as the unintentional lifting of nearby elements or even buildings. The operation should therefore be closely monitored. It is particularly important to compare the quantity of grout injected to the calculated requirement.

Photogrammetry

Photogrammetry is the art and science of obtaining measurements and other information about physical objects using photographs. Perhaps the most familiar application is the use of aerial photographs to produce topographical maps. Close range photogrammetry is used in building construction to record dimensions and details of building facades and their components. Information obtained from these photographs can then be used to produce drawings showing the elevations, plans and sections of a building. A series of photographs together with suitable benchmarks are helpful in monitoring settlement and other movements of a building, with an accuracy up to 0.5 mm. They can also record progressive deterioration in a long term monitoring program for a heritage building.

The advantages of close range photogrammetry include its speed of recording, the ease with which fragile or complex and detailed objects can be measured, and the permanent record produced without creating drawings at the time. The choice of a dimensionally stable negative is important for archival recording. The early standard negative was glass, but other types of film for this specific purpose have now been developed.

Photogrammetry was used to monitor the settlement and raising of the Saskatchewan Legislature Buildings during underpinning work and the settlement of the First Presbyterian Church in Edmonton during construction of an adjacent high-rise office building. In another application, record and bidding documents for the restoration of the sandstone facade of the Canada Permanent Building in Edmonton were produced using photogrammetric techniques.

Painted Fireproofing

When a particular epoxy paint is subjected to elevated temperatures, it expands up to three hundred times its initial thickness. In the process a dense honeycombed insulation is formed. This swelling action is called "intumescence." The resulting insulating coat can be used to encapsulate combustible materials. It can also increase the fire rating of exposed steel, aluminum, concrete or timber members. This application is particularly useful in heritage structures where the structure is exposed. It is much easier to paint an ornate cast iron column with this special paint than to remove and replace it with an ersatz, fireproof replica.

Subliming materials similar to the tiles protecting the space shuttles are also available to provide fireproofing. These space-age materials will not see widespread use in conservation work for some time due to their prohibitive cost.

Chapter 4

RESIDENTIAL CONSTRUCTION

FOUNDATIONS

The factors most likely to influence the performance of residential foundations are design, cold, coal and water. They are interrelated to some degree.

Design

Residential construction seldom has the benefit of detailed foundation or soils engineering. This is true for contemporary housing as well as historic residences. Foundation designs for this type of housing are usually based on standards developed over the years. The standard designs evolved from their successful performance for the prevailing soil conditions in a given community. Unfortunately, soils are known for their wide variation, often over a very short distance. Thus the standard design may not apply everywhere in a given community.

Historic buildings existing today were some of the first buildings erected in frontier Canada. Thus no local experience or standards relating to foundations were available to early architects and builders. Many of our early buildings were damaged beyond repair by faulty foundations and have since been demolished. Those remaining usually have reasonably sound foundations and exhibit only localized distress due to foundation movements. On investigation it is often found that a heritage building has been shored up at some time in its history, most often using some variation of the techniques presented in Chapter 3 of this book.

Cold

Frost heaving of soil under foundations is a common occurrence in older buildings in Canada. The change of groundwater from liquid to solid state results in an increase of water volume as ice is formed. This increased volume fills the pores of the surrounding soil and ultimately causes it to swell. The freezing process can also cause water to be drawn to the frozen zone, thus increasing the size of the frozen mass. Under certain conditions this cumulative freezing action results in the formation of an ice lens, so called because its cross section resembles a glass lens.

This soil expansion is an irresistable force, pushing the foundations upward. The vertical movement causes cracking in masonry walls. It also creates fissures in other types of construction. These cracks and fissures allow the entry of water into the structure, resulting in progressive deterioration of other building elements. Of course, when spring arrives the earth thaws and the structure tries to return to its original position. Generally, the freeze-thaw action decreases the soil's bearing capacity. Settlement may result from the reduced bearing capacity, causing further flexing of the structure. Over the years this annual cycle leads to serious deterioration of any historic building.

Frost cover from exterior ground level to the underside of footings can vary from 1,000 to 1,500 mm for heated buildings in Southern Canada. In sub-arctic areas, frost penetration can reach 3,000 mm while in arctic zones the soil remains frozen to great depths throughout the year. During the life of an historic residence, several circumstances can result in the depletion of this protection. A change in use of the lower level can result in the removal of heat, possibly for energy conservation, with frost penetration resulting below the founding level. A change in exterior grade level due to some misdirected changes in landscaping could similarly reduce frost cover. Localized frost heaving is often found at entrances to basements where a stairwell is excavated outside the basement walls. Wells were often excavated for coal chutes in the era of coal heating. The following drawings illustrate these conditions.

Coal

Many of our western frontier settlements grew up

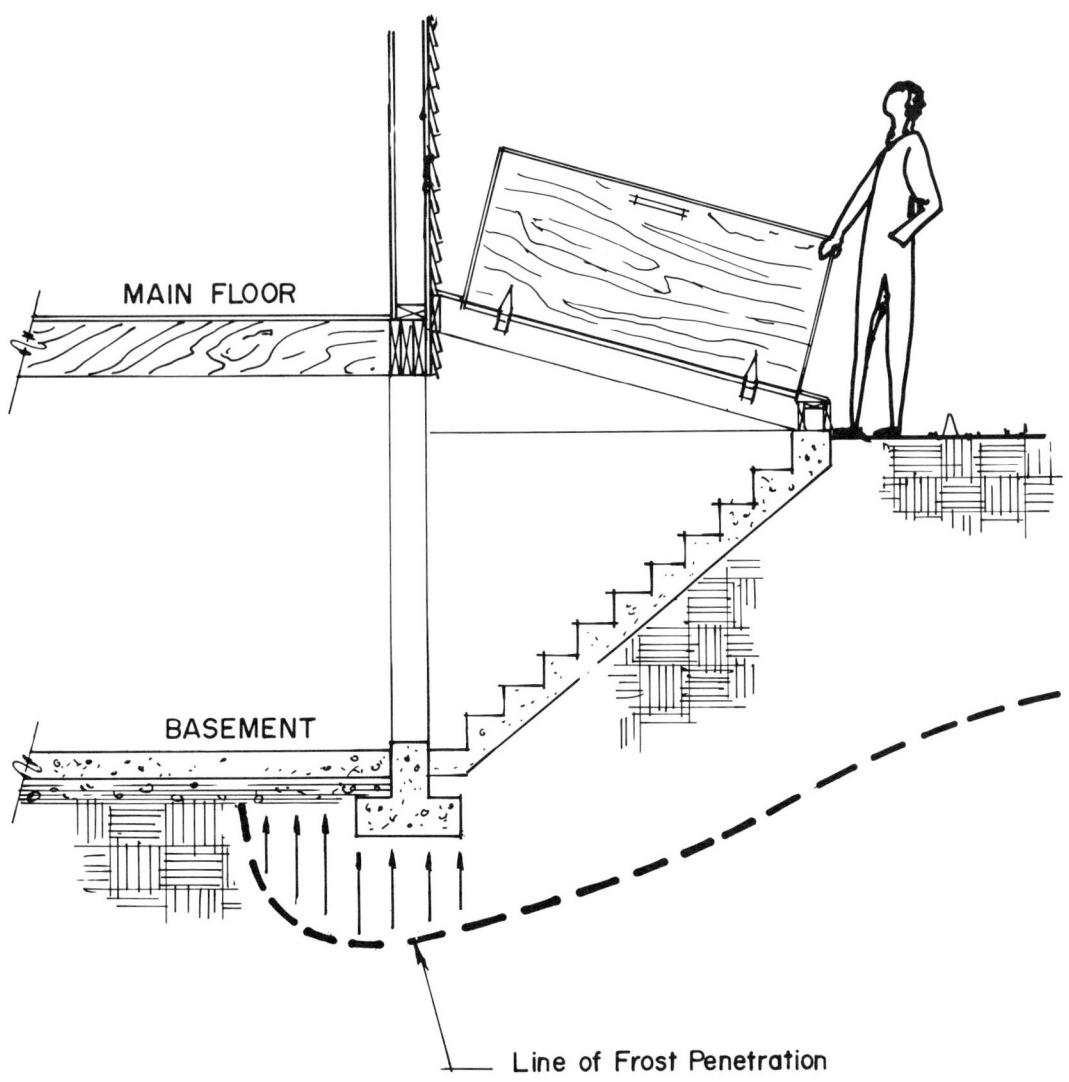

Figure 4.1 Coal Chute

around coal deposits. Coal was required as fuel for home heating as well as rail and steamboat transportation passing through. In the early days most coal was mined underground. The massive equipment required for surface strip mining had not yet been developed. The propagation of underground tunnels was completely haphazard, following a coal seam here and there until the seam became too thin to mine. The network of tunnels often spread out directly below the town. As the mines were exhausted, the tunnels were sealed off. The timbers supporting the tunnel roofs eventually rotted and the ground subsided, squeezing the tunnels shut and causing serious changes in ground surface contours. The surface disturbances undoubtedly caused the demise of a number of our early residences in coal towns and some earth movements to this day can be traced to early mining activity.

Movements and settlement of historic residences in areas with a coal mining history may be traced to this mining. Qualified soils engineers often have access to charts of coal mines and can advise if further ground subsidence can be expected at a given location. Regardless if further settlement is expected, the foundations of an historic residence can be shored up using the methods described in Chapter 3. If additional movement is expected from the mining activity, the foundation repairs can be designed to allow leveling of the structure on an on-going basis.

Coal may also contribute indirectly to the deterioration of concrete basement walls in older homes. While coal was in use as a heating fuel, prodigious quantities of cinders were generated. Cinders from certain types of coal contain a very high sulphate concentration. These sulphates attack normal Portland cement, even-

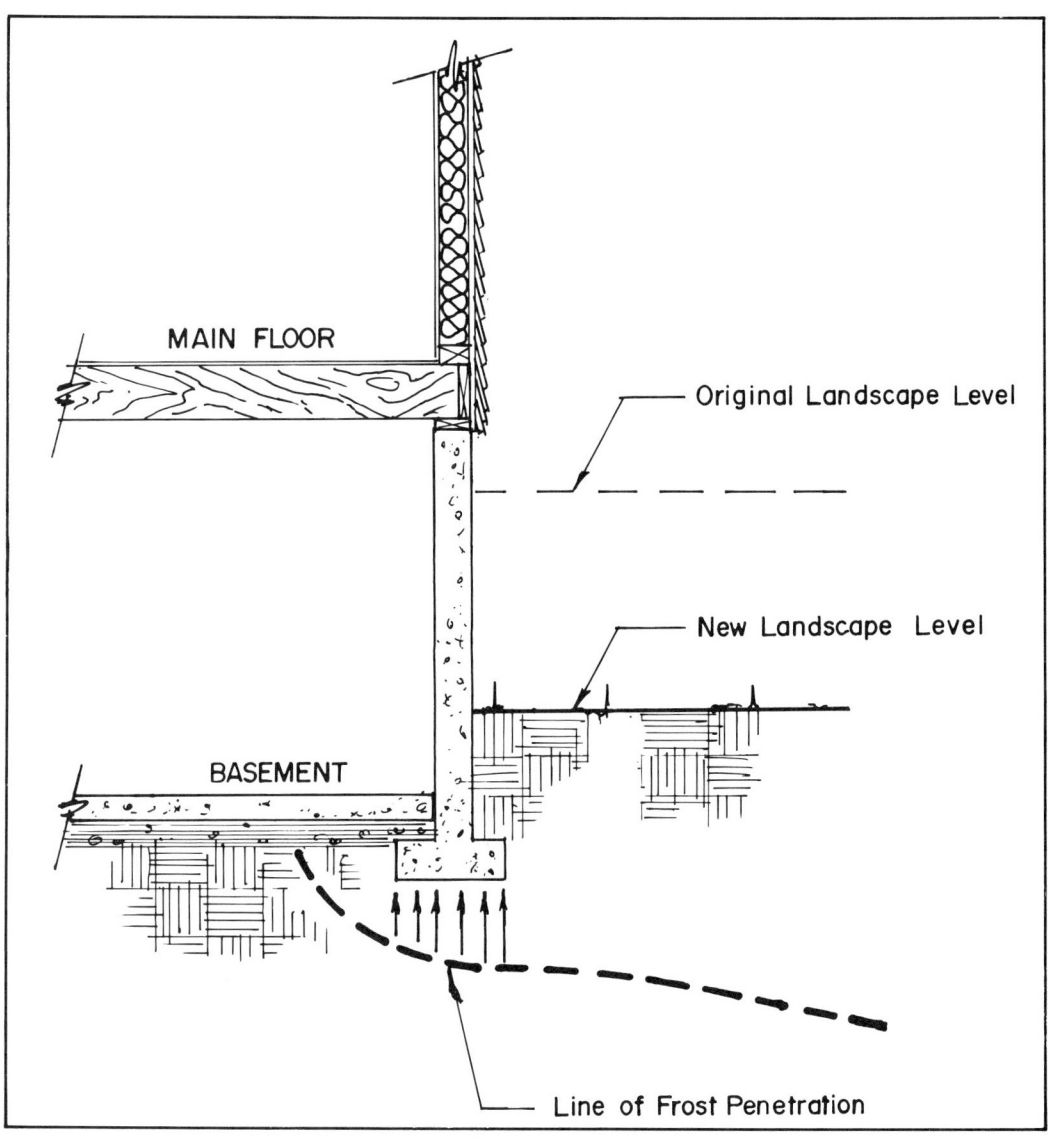

Figure 4.2 Lowered Landscaping

tually leading to the complete disintegration of those concrete elements in contact with the cinders.

The author was asked to investigate the apparent crumbling of a house basement in Ottawa. The house was approximately seventy years old. The concrete in the basement walls had the appearance, strength and texture of weak chalk. The new owner had discovered this condition in attempting to install shelving. Further investigation revealed that the exterior of the foundation walls had been backfilled with furnace cinders, leading to the irreversible deterioration of the foundation. The repair process for this type of problem is very costly, but fortunately can be carried out without disturbing the historic elements in the upper parts of the structure. Possible solutions are shown in the following sketches.

Water

We saw above how the presence of water can contribute to foundation problems during cold weather. An equally damaging phenomenon can occur in hot weather.

Ground water occupies the spaces between the mineral particles in soil. In certain types of soil, particularly clay, the water may occupy all free spaces, creating a "pore pressure" in the soil. This is fine if sufficient water is present. Should the water disappear however, the pore pressure becomes zero, the soil compresses and any structure supported on the soil settles. This desiccation can occur for a number of reasons. The most common cause is the inevitable lowering of the natural water table in urban areas. This

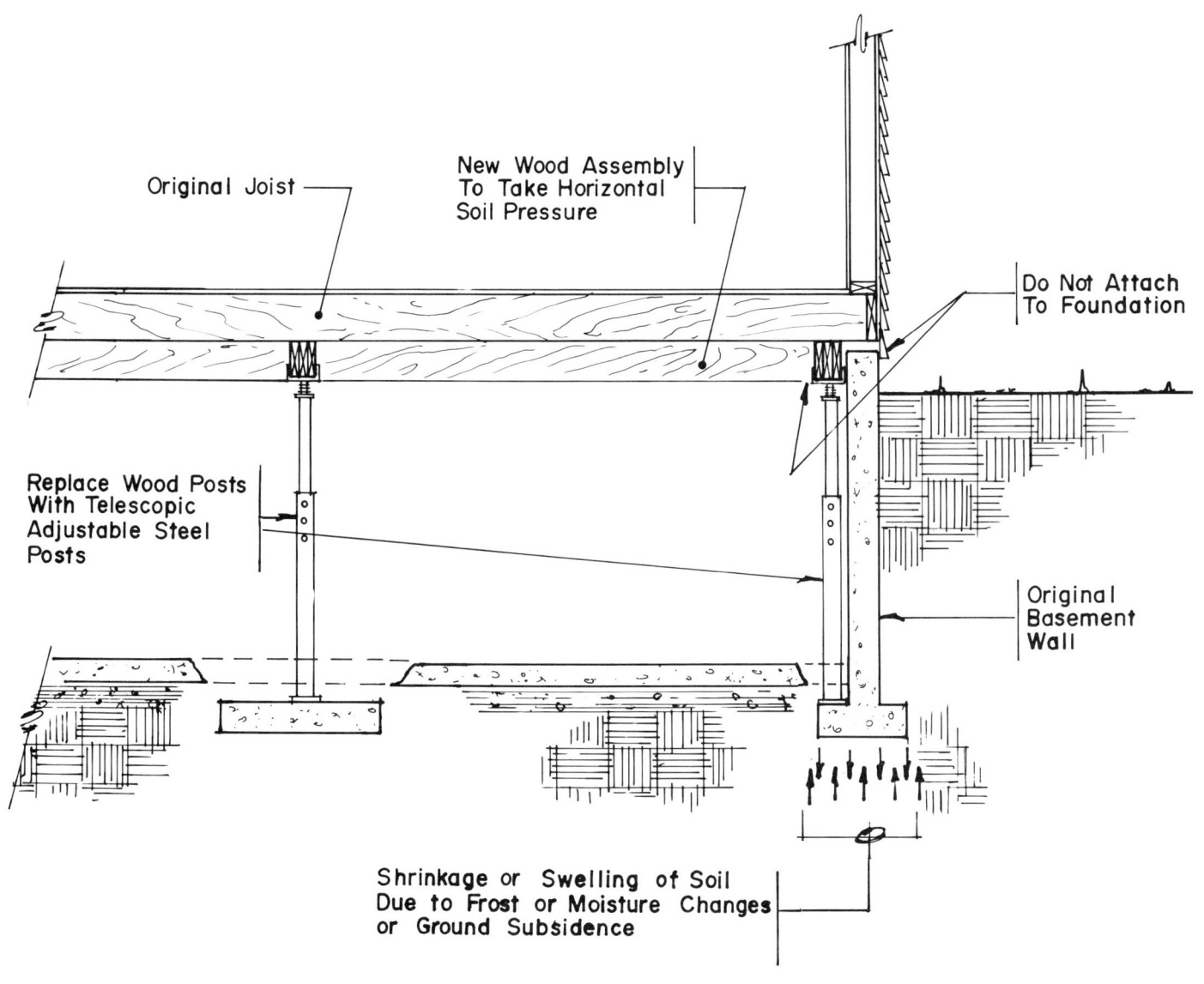

Figure 4.3 Adjustable Foundation Support

is a result of large paved areas and storm water systems cutting off replenishment of ground water by rain water.

Reduction in soil moisture can also result from leakage into old, deteriorated sewers. Ornamental trees with extensive root systems and prodigious thirsts are often found to be the cause of reduced soil moisture.

Increased soil moisture content can cause an increase in the soil volume as a result of increased pore pressure. The condition is only prevalent in clays, known quite logically as "swelling clays." Thus the soil supporting some of our historic houses have the potential to swell and shrink several times during the year and any building frame supported on these soils will deteriorate.

Water is the most plentiful solvent. The passage of water through soil adjacent to building foundations can dissolve naturally occuring chemicals in the soil. These chemicals, particulary sulphates, can have a serious effect on concrete used in basement walls and footings. The best protection is the use of sulphate resistant cement in the concrete and the provision of good waterproofing on the walls. It is not possible to replace the cement in existing concrete, which, in a heritage property may already be seriously corroded. Several solutions for this were illustrated earlier in this section.

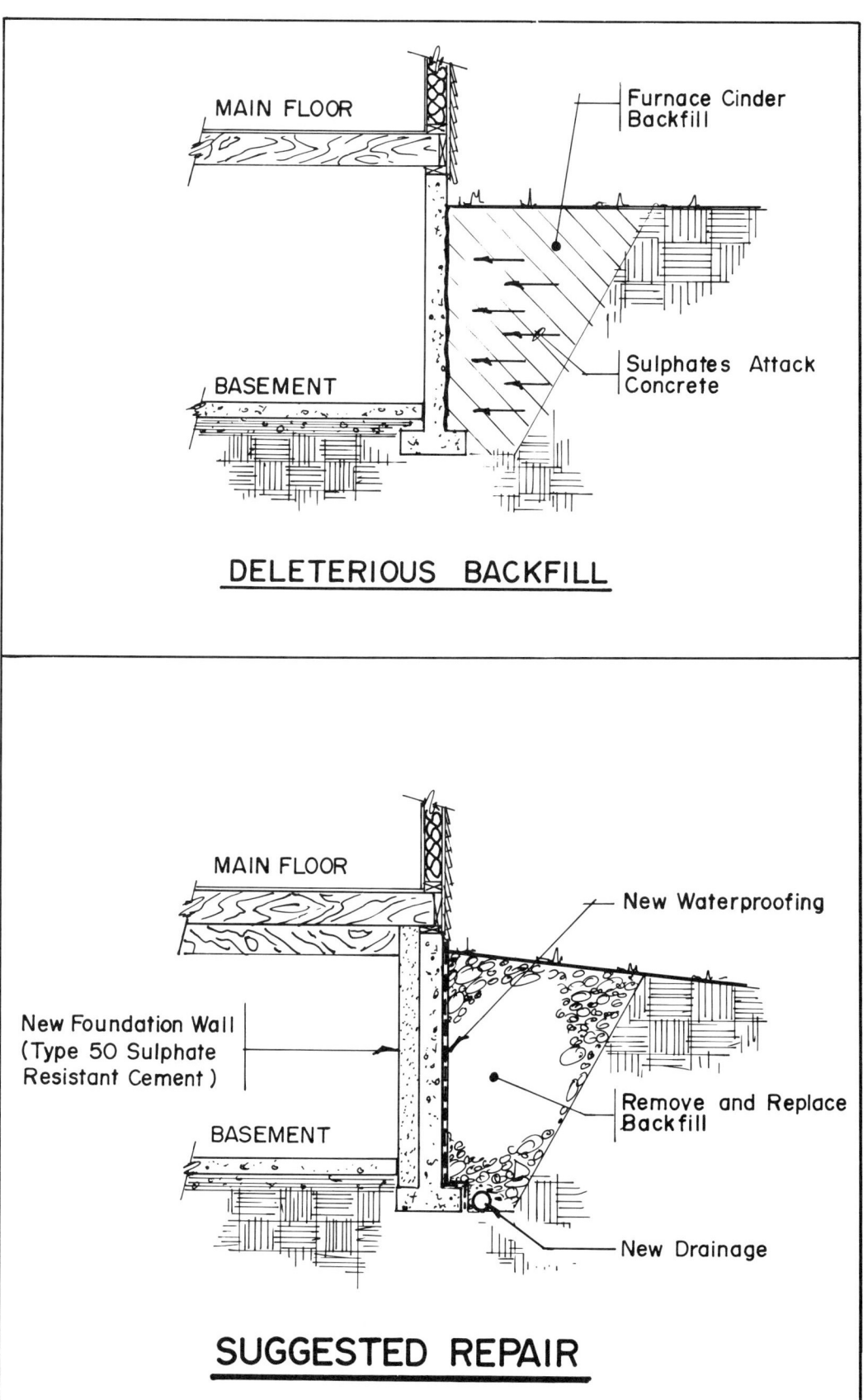

Figure 4.4 Repair for Corroded Walls

Figure 4.5 - Range of termites and carpenter ants in Canada

DETERIORATION OF WOOD FRAME

Wood is one of the oldest and most universal of building materials. It is also, unfortunately, one of the least durable. Wood is an organic material and thus is susceptible to attack from an extensive array of living organisms.

Bacteria

Bacteria is very common in wood that has a high moisture content, however its presence does not affect the strength of wood except over long periods of time. Initially bacteria subsist on food reserves stored in the soft parenchyma cells and on easily digestible membranes of pits. Their preliminary attack causes a marked increase in the permeability of the wood and a slight decrease in toughness. The increase in absorption contributes to the decay of the wood by allowing other agents - fungi and insects - to infest the wood.

The long term effects of bacterial attack are very important when considering older buildings. The bacteria secrete enzymes which decompose liquefied wood substances and significantly reduce strength properties such as bending strength; stiffness; specific gravity; compressive strength; and modulus of elasticity.

Fungi

Fungi are plants without flowers, leaves or chlorophyll, and they reproduce through the propagation of spores. It is the microscopic filaments that grow from these fruiting bodies which cause damage. Individual strands called hyphae grow into and through the wood cells. These hyphae destroy individual cells of wood tissue by inducing a biochemical attack.

Depending on the species, fungi has the ability to survive extended periods of dryness. The absence of fruiting bodies on the surface wood that has dried does not indicate the elimination of spores and fungal fragments. They may become active again in favourable environments.

The prime requirement for fungal growth is water. At least a film of water must be present on the surface of wood cell walls. Wood is safe from attack if its average moisture content remains lower than 20%. Decay may become serious if the moisture content is above the fiber saturation point (approximately 30%). While the fibre structure of the wood may be saturated, there can be sufficient oxygen in the pores of the wood to support growth of the fungi. When both the fibre structure and the pore structure of the wood are saturated, fungi growth ceases. This explains the preservation of wooden antiquities over many centuries in a submerged location.

There are two major forms of decay caused by fungal species. The first is brown rot, also confusingly classified as dry rot (the wood must be damp to decay). Often, a few fungi send strands into surrounding wet soils and transport water into dry wood where they can moisten and rot it. In brown rot, only the cellulose is removed. The wood, which turns slightly browner due to the increase in the percentage of brown lignin in the residue, will crack across the grain, shrink and collapse. The darker colour and the cracks create the impression of dryness.

The second major form of decay is white rot. In this case, the cell as a whole is attacked and both lignin and cellulose are removed at the same rate. The remaining wood consists of whitish areas surrounded by black zone-lines consisting of masses of hyphae. The wood does not crack across the grain and retains its outward dimension without contracting or collapsing until the decay is severe. The decay begins from the cell cavity and works towards the middle lamella between cells.

Due to the nature of these two forms of decay, brown rot will cause the most rapid decay of the wood's mechanical properties. Brown rot decay is more easily detectable and preventative measures may be taken before extensive collapse has occured. With white rot, the potential for damage is greater because significant decay may occur before the rot is noticed.

There are other forms of fungi, such as soft rot fungi, molds and stains but they do not cause structural degradation of the wood.

Insects

Wood may be used as food or shelter by countless species of insects with varying requirements of moisture. They generally live the longest part of their life as larvae which grow in wood. Most damage is done at the larval stage although in some species the adults bore out of the wood to mate. Termites and carpenter ants are exceptions. They do most of their damage while in the adult stage.

Termites

Termites use the wood as a food source, causing extensive decay. They swallow wood fragments, which are then broken down into water-soluble components by micro-organisms in their digestive systems. The species of termites that are of concern in Canada are the subterranean termites found only in southern Ontario and British Columbia.

Subterranean termites develop their colonies in the ground near the wood they need as food. They first attack the wood where it comes into contact with the ground. They reach it on foundations above ground either through cavities in the foundation, such as occur in concrete block foundations, or by building earthen tubes or runways on the surface of the foundations.

In addition to the presence of shelter tubes there are other signs of termite activity. Termites construct galleries in timber leaving a shell of sound wood which conceals their activities. In the spring and fall, new queen and king termites migrate to begin new colonies. The presence of these winged termites should serve as warning. Futher evidence is the appearance of blisters or dark stains in flooring.

Marine Borers

Marine borers attack wood in salt or brackish waters. They may use the wood in several ways: as shelter, obtaining their food from the water around them; as food source, digesting the wood itself; or as hunting ground, feeding on micro-organisms in and on the wood.

Marine borers are typically very small and the entrance holes they create never grow larger than 5mm. Some species may completely honeycomb the interior of a pile and leave very little evidence on the surface. Other species may attack only the outer surface to a depth of 25 to 50 mm. If present in large numbers their

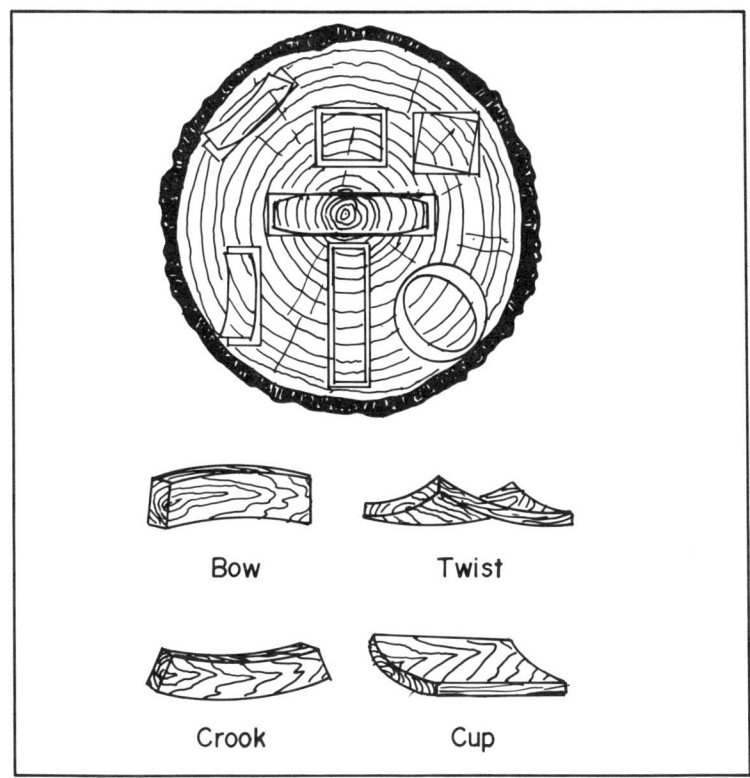

Figure 4.6 Shrinkage Effects in Wood

burrows will severely weaken the outer wood layer, making it susceptible to erosion from tidal action or damage from floating objects. This allows the borers to continue attacking deeper wood until an hourglass shape is formed in the intertidal region.

Ants and Beetles

Carpenter ants are so named for their ability to attack wood and use it only for shelter and nesting. They prefer wood that has been softened by decay or that is naturally soft. The immature ants need high humidity to survive, therefore carpenter ants generally require wood that is nearly saturated. When carpenter ants are left undisturbed for several years, they may enlarge their tunnels to the point where serious structural damage occurs.

Beetles generally create the greatest damage while in their larval stage. The adults may bore into the soft outer wood to lay their eggs or lay them in open pores. The larvae then bore through the wood making tunnels less than 2 mm in diameter leaving them packed with a fine powder. Some species will complete their development in the wood and bore through it to begin their adult life. Beetles prefer wood that has a 20% to 30% moisture content but may tolerate wood below 10%. The effect of their attack is similar to that of marine borers and carpenter ants.

Shrinkage and Swelling

Wood changes dimension as it gains or loses moisture below the fibre saturation point. Above this point fluctuations in the moisture content do not affect the properties or dimension of the wood. Shrinking and swelling may cause warping, checking, splitting or performance problems such as binding of doors.

Wood exhibits its greatest degree of shrinkage in the direction of its annual growth rings (tangentially). The shrinkage across the rings (radially) is about one-half as much, and the shrinkage along the grain is very light. Depending on the direction of the grain relative to the shape of the cross-section of the wood pieces, several major types of distortion may occur.

Evidence of shrinkage includes: cracks in plastered walls; open joints and nail pops in drywall construction; distortion of door openings; and uneven floors. The only problems of a structural nature that shrinkage will cause are loosening of joints and fasteners, splitting of wood in critical areas or, possibly, a change in the load path of a structure.

A knowledge of the mechanics of shrinkage is important to understand its effects. When moisture migrates out of wood fibre, it leaves the cell walls and causes them to contract. As the cells shrink they become more dense and stronger. The opposite occurs when wood absorbs water. Therefore the drier the wood is, the stronger it is.

As wood dries, water escapes from its surfaces after migrating from the internal regions. Therefore the surface of the wood always dries first. In pieces of wood with large cross-sections, the surface may be below the fibre saturation point while the interior is at that point. If the moisture content decreases further the outer shell will want to shrink while the inner core will not. This causes the development of stresses in the wood- compression perpendicular to the grain in the core, and tension perpendicular to the grain in the shell. When this stress exceeds the tensile strength of the wood parallel to the grain, what is called a seasoning check will begin to develop. As the moisture content continues to drop, the opening will widen and deepen. In members with large cross-sections, the stresses are higher and the checks will be deeper because the core will take longer to dry out. This is why many heavy timber structures have large checks and will appear to be almost split in two.

A similar process is involved in the development of end splits. Due to the nature of wood, water travels much faster longitudinally than transversely. This causes end faces to dry out more rapidly than lateral surfaces. Regions adjoining end sections will not be as dry and will therefore resist the shrinking of the ends causing transverse tension and splitting along the grain.

The presence of longitudinal or end splits may or may not be structurally significant. Splits which are approximately parallel to the grain and located away from connections generally pose no problem. Splits which have a slope that falls within the allowable slope of grain for the grade of lumber, are considered parallel. Splits that occur near connections may cause problems.

Splits may be ignored near connections if the member is loaded in compression parallel to the grain. If a member is loaded in tension parallel to the grain, splits near connections may cause problems. The member may have to be replaced or reinforced, particularly if the split occurs at an end connection.

More serious splits are those occurring at a slope greater than that allowed for a given structural grade. They may considerably reduce the effective section and safety of the structure. Cases may also arise where the splits are parallel to the grain, but where the loading is at an angle to the grain. These cases are similar and require careful consideration.

Another problem which may occur is related more closely to the overall shrinkage and expansion of wood. If wood is restrained against swelling by parallel members or by plates and washers under bolts, it will be put under pressure and compressed. If this situation persists for a long period, a process similar to relaxation in steel will result - the stresses in the wood will diminish and the dimensions and the moisture content will remain the same. If conditions then cause the moisture content to decrease, the member will shrink and pull away from other members, plates or washers. This may, for example, cause a connection to become loose and ineffective. It is therefore important to make a periodic inspection of bolted connnections.

Creep

The time dependent deformation of a material under constant load is called creep. For example, when a beam is loaded it will deflect. There will be an initial instantaneous elastic deflection followed by a slower creep deflection. The duration and magnitude of creep is a function of many variables: moisture content; temperature; magnitude of load; and type of material. With wood, creep varies with the orientation of the grain relative to the load.

Because of the nature of wood, its many species and varied growing conditions, the amount and effect of creep varies considerably. Despite this, it is possible to predict a typical creep history. After initial instantaneous elastic deflection, deformation will continue slowly at a decreasing rate. If creep proceeds until failure occurs, there will be a rapid increase in the rate of deformation just prior to rupture. Otherwise creep will gradually stop.

If the load is subsequently removed, the elastic portion of the deformation will be instantly recovered. In addition, a significant portion of the creep will be recovered, but at a gradually decreasing rate. A certain amount of permanent deformation will remain. Creep therefore, consists of a delayed elastic deformation which is time-dependent and recoverable, and a viscous deformation that is time-dependant, permanent and non-recoverable.

The time required for deformation to reach a stable equilibrium varies considerably, but generally all creep should be complete within one year. However, if at any time, loading, moisture or temperature conditions change, a new equilibrium will have established itself.

Prevention

The key to using wood as a construction material

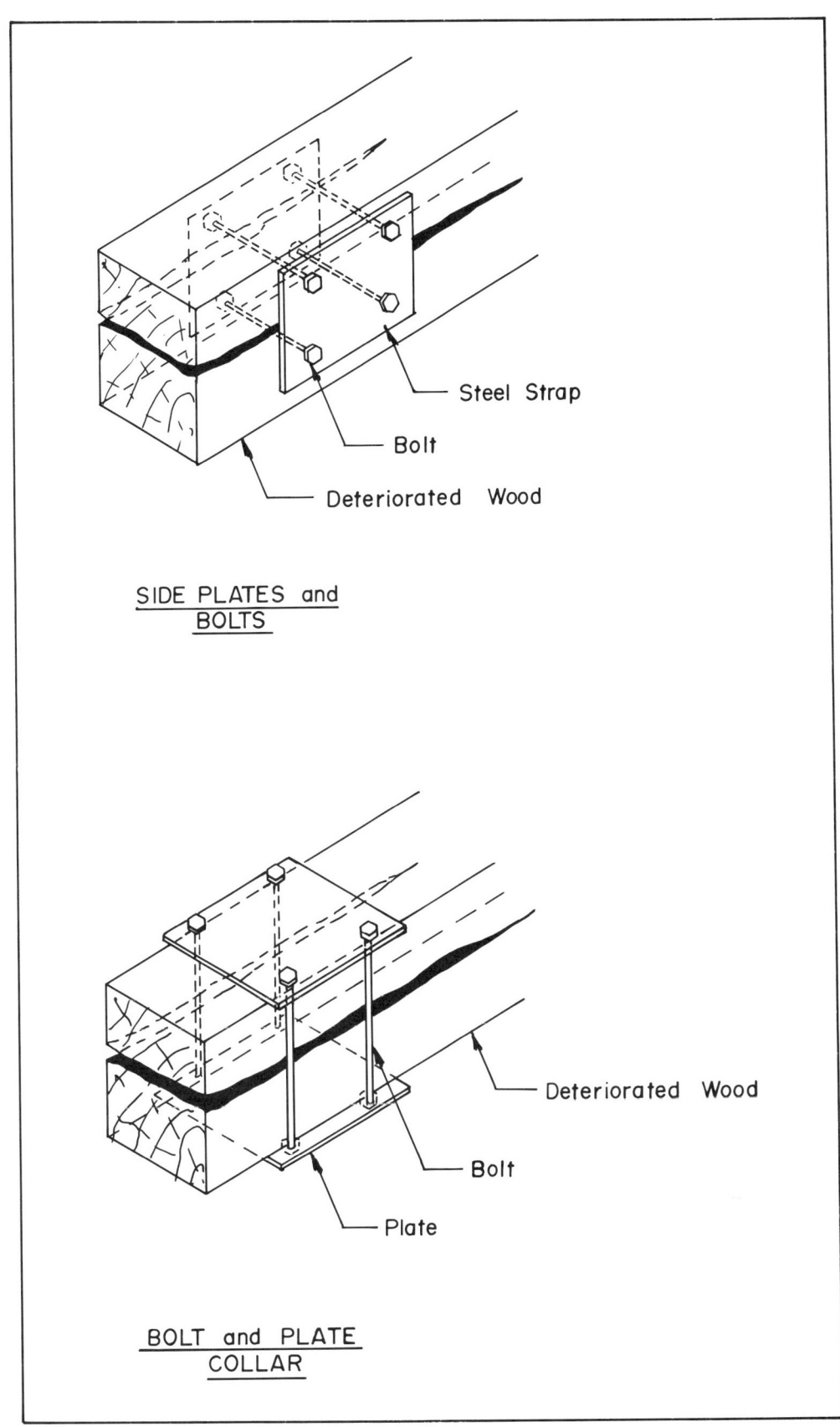

Figure 4.7 Wood Repair - Clamps

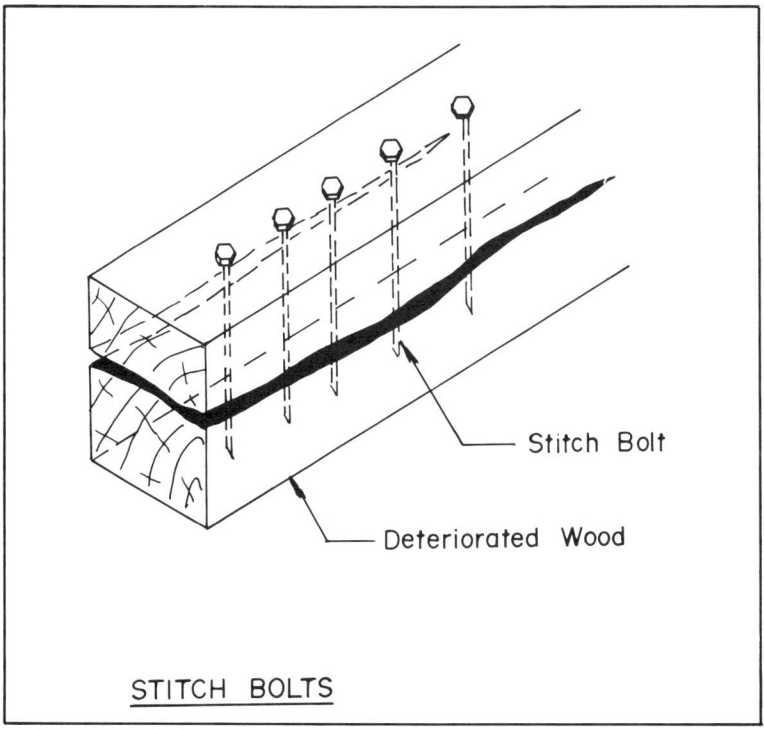

Figure 4.8 Wood Repair - Stitch Bolts

is in understanding the nature of its deterioration and taking steps to prevent it. This can be accomplished by sensible design strategies.

The single most important consideration in preventing deterioration is the moisture content of the wood. Wood that is kept dry will remain strong and intact for many years. When designing or repairing wooden structures, it is important to consider the presence of water and to ensure that wood is protected.

When exposed or in contact with soil the wood should be a decay resistant type, or treated with a preservative. Pressure treated wood is best because of the deep penetration of the preservative. Fungi, bacteria and insects are deterred by preservatives and paint.

In wood above ground, it is necessary to ensure that water is not trapped. In particular, care should be taken at the ends of members where water is easily absorbed.

A program of maintenance is also important in wooden structures. This could include painting, tightening of bolts and connections, inspection for presence of insects or early signs of decay, and detection of water leakage.

In the rehabilitation of old buildings, it is important first to identify and eliminate the causes of decay. This will ensure a successful and enduring structure. Once renovation is complete, the structure can be expected to better resist the attack of nature.

REPAIR TECHNIQUES

The repair of foundations has already been covered in Chapter 3 and earlier in this chapter. Preservation and rehabilitation procedures for wood members were also discussed generally in Chapter 3. This section details the methods available to repair house framing.

Clamping and Stitch Bolts

Two simple methods to stop cracking and splitting are the use of clamps and stitch bolts. If the splits and checks in a wooden member do not impair its strength, measures must still be taken to assure that the condition does not deteriorate further.

Clamps and stitch bolts perform the same function- the application of pressure perpendicular to the split. The clamp is completely external to the member. It is composed of steel straps across two opposing perpendicular faces tied together by bolts. The clamps should be positioned to close the split when the bolts are tightened.

Stitch bolts perform the same function but they are placed inside the wood. This may not be suitable in members where the effective section may be considerably reduced. Bolts are inserted in the member at right angles to the split and tightened to close the stitch.

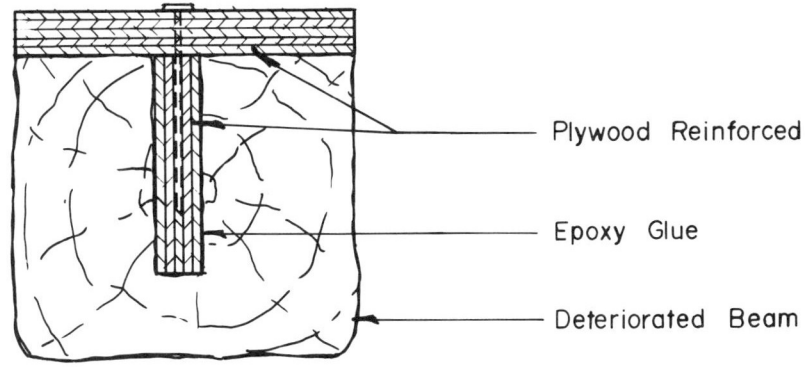
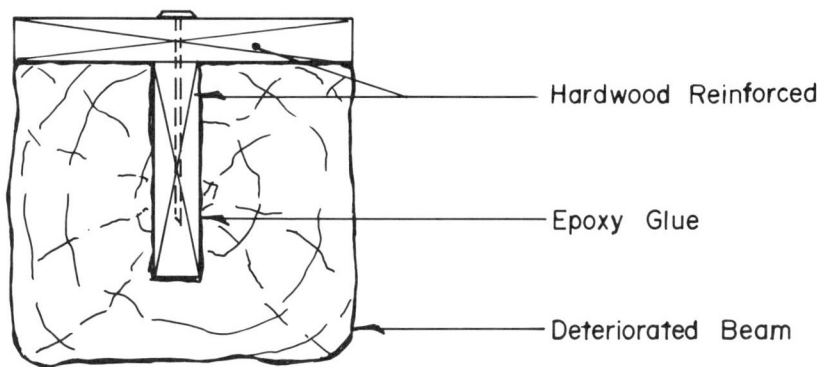

Figure 4.9 Epoxy Beam Reinforcement

Reinforcement

If, as discussed previously, splitting, rotting, insect attack or shrinkage have severely reduced the strength of the member, it may need to be replaced. Since this is often undesirable it is usually better to reinforce the damaged section with wood or steel.

The new section may be added using wooden or steel splice plates, bolted onto the existing member. Care should be taken that the holes for the bolts do not reduce the net section of the member significantly.

If the reinforcement of the member needs to be concealed, this may be done using epoxy reinforcing, as discussed later in this chapter.

Post-Tensioning

In some structures the wood itself may be undamaged but the joints may be loose. Such a case may occur on the tension chord of a truss. This will result in redistribution of forces in the truss and may overstress other members, leading to further deterioration.

These joints can be strengthened using high strength steel rods bolted into steel brackets. By tightening the nuts, the rod may be pre-stressed and the stress on the joints relieved. This procedure must be undertaken carefully to ensure that the correct amount of pre-stressing is used.

When placing pre-stressing rods it is important to ensure that they do not detract from the appearance of the structure. It may be less noticeable if instead of steel rods, pre-stressing strands are used.

Epoxy Reinforcing

Epoxy compounds are very useful for the repair of many materials. They consist of a resin and resin-hardening agent, that are mixed together just prior to use. The properties of the resins can be varied considerably by the addition of various modifiers.

Epoxy resins have a number of advantages:
- a strength two to three times that of sound wood
- they are injected into the wood in liquid form and can flow into voids and cracks
- rapid hardening at normal temperatures
- a high degree of adhesion to clean surfaces
- resistance to cracking

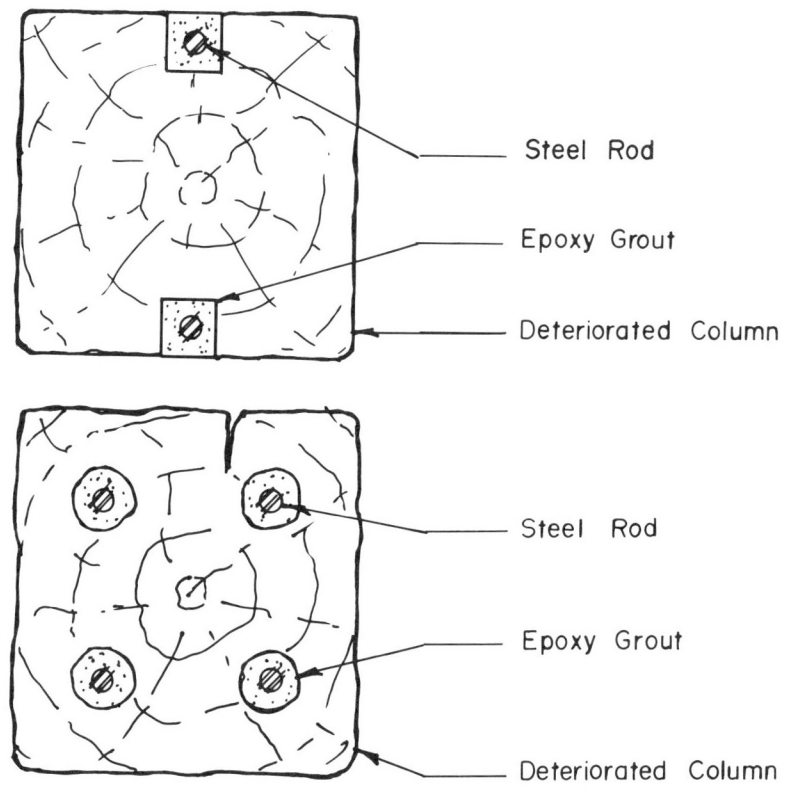

Figure 4.10 Epoxy Column Reinforcement

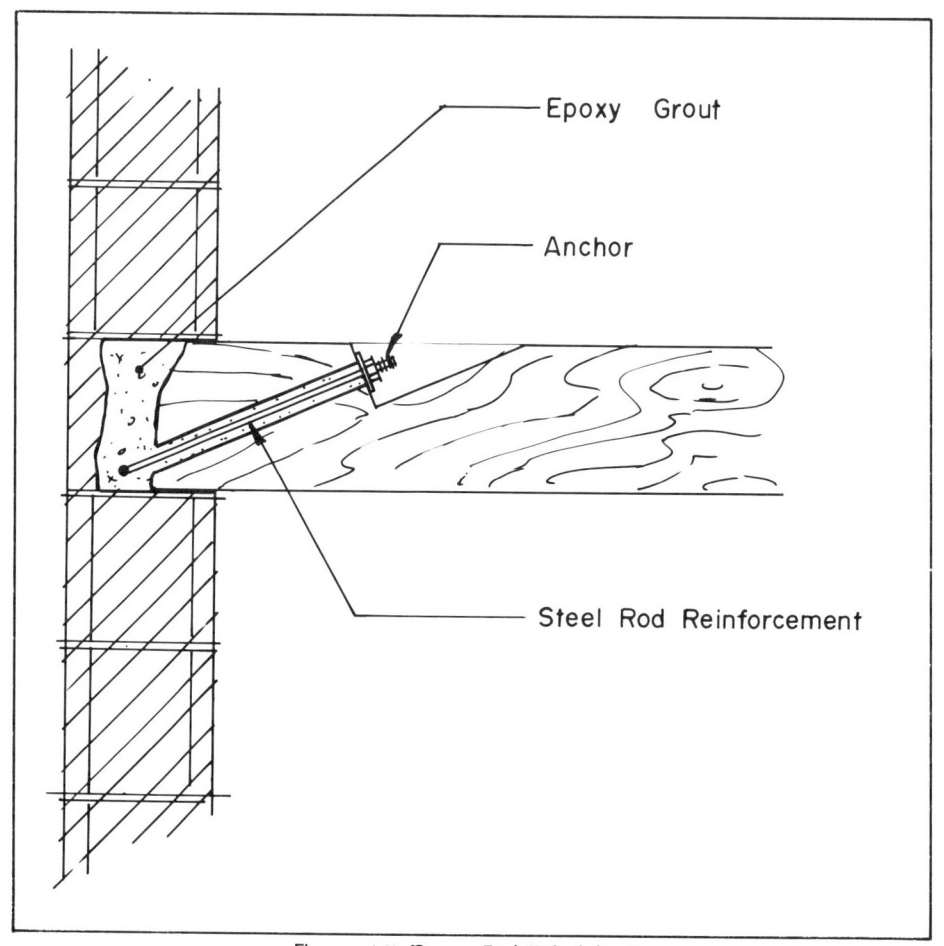

Figure 4.11 Beam End Rehabilitation

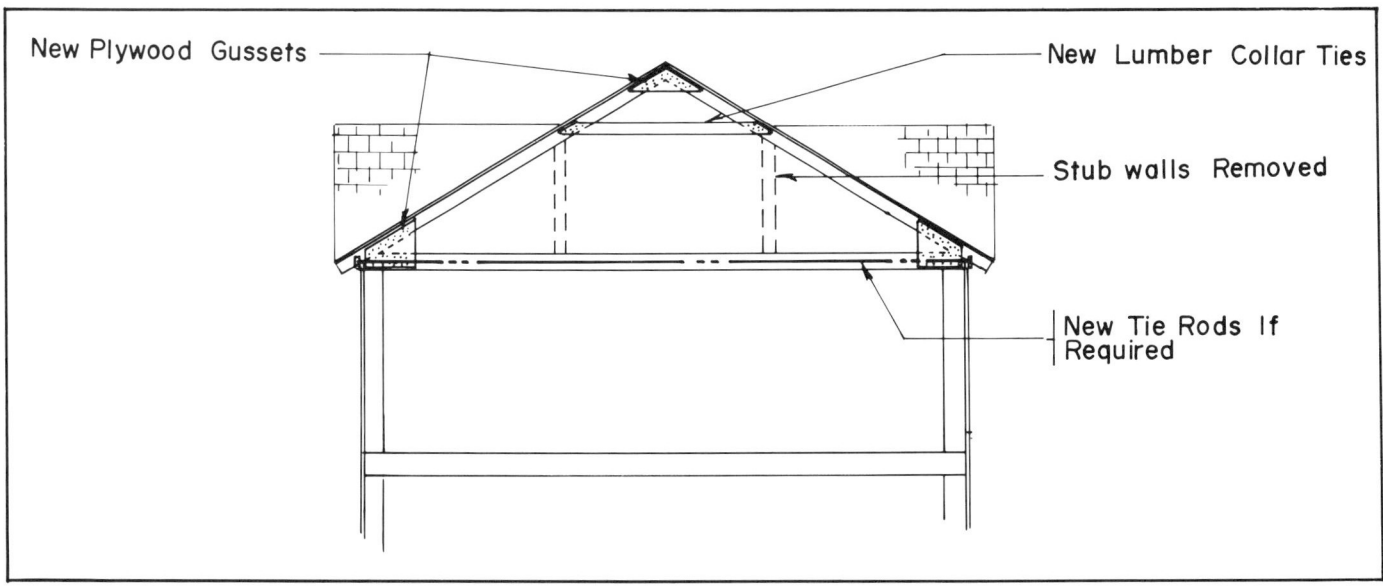

Figure 4.12 Gable Roof - Remove Stub Walls

resistance to acids, alkalies and solvents

The easiest way to use epoxy, is to simply inject it into cracks and voids. Before this is done, the area must be cleaned and all unsound wood removed.

The time required for initial curing of epoxy is less than one hour, with only seven days required to reach its final state. Thus, work must be carefully planned. The more fluid and workable the resin is made, the shorter the time required for hardening.

In cases where the deterioration of wood is more extensive it is usually more suitable to use some form of reinforcing in conjunction with epoxy. Some common reinforcing materials include steel rods or plates, fibreglass or plywood. In this technique cavities are drilled or cut into the member, the reinforcing introduced and the epoxy injected to form a new stronger composite member.

When using epoxies in combination with preservative, great care must be exercised. The preservative should be applied last because it has little effect on cured epoxy. In cases where the preservative must be applied first, it should be selected carefully as it may retard the final set of the epoxy. Preservatives can also lower the adhesive strength between the wood and epoxy.

One serious problem with epoxies is the fact that their strength quickly diminishes above room temperatures. They should not be used in areas of high heat. This includes areas near heating conduits, hot lights and acute sun exposure. If exposed to such conditions, the epoxy will retain its strength for a short period and may appear to be sound. Careful testing should be done to evaluate the strength of the epoxy.

An insulating cover can be placed over the epoxy to prevent deterioration.

Another important consideration with epoxy reinforcing is quality control. It is important to ensure an adequate bond between the epoxy, the wood and the reinforcing materials. If the epoxy is inadequately applied, the repair will be of little value.

STRUCTURAL GYMNASTICS

One of the first steps in renovating a heritage house is to repair the damage caused by the elements and normal wear and tear. Once this is accomplished, using the methods described elsewhere in this book, thoughts may turn to how the usefulness of the structure can be improved. One area usually deficient is the basement. In fact, the basement may be non-existent. The underpinning and shoring methods described in Chapter 3 illustrate how the below grade portions of almost any building can be restored and expanded.

Most historic houses have wood frames. The following sketches illustrate some ways these frames can be modified to improve the interior layout of an older home.

Many historic homes are being converted to professional and association offices (see Chapter 5 - Duggan House). In order to make these conversions feasible it may be necessary to remove some interior walls. In the older house frames, joist spans were relatively short. Some of the walls to be removed may be supporting the structure above. An architect or structural engineer should be consulted before any walls are removed.

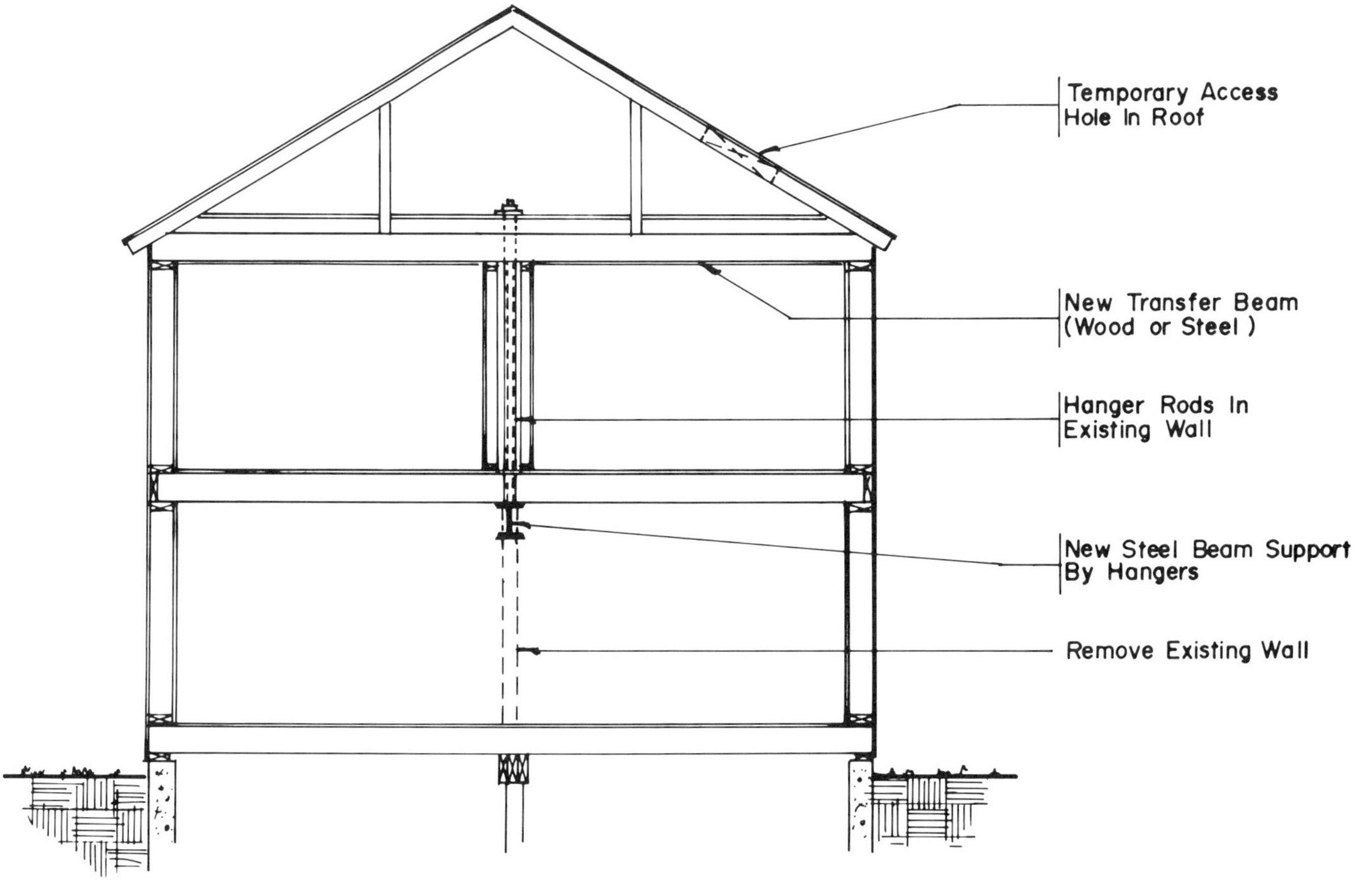

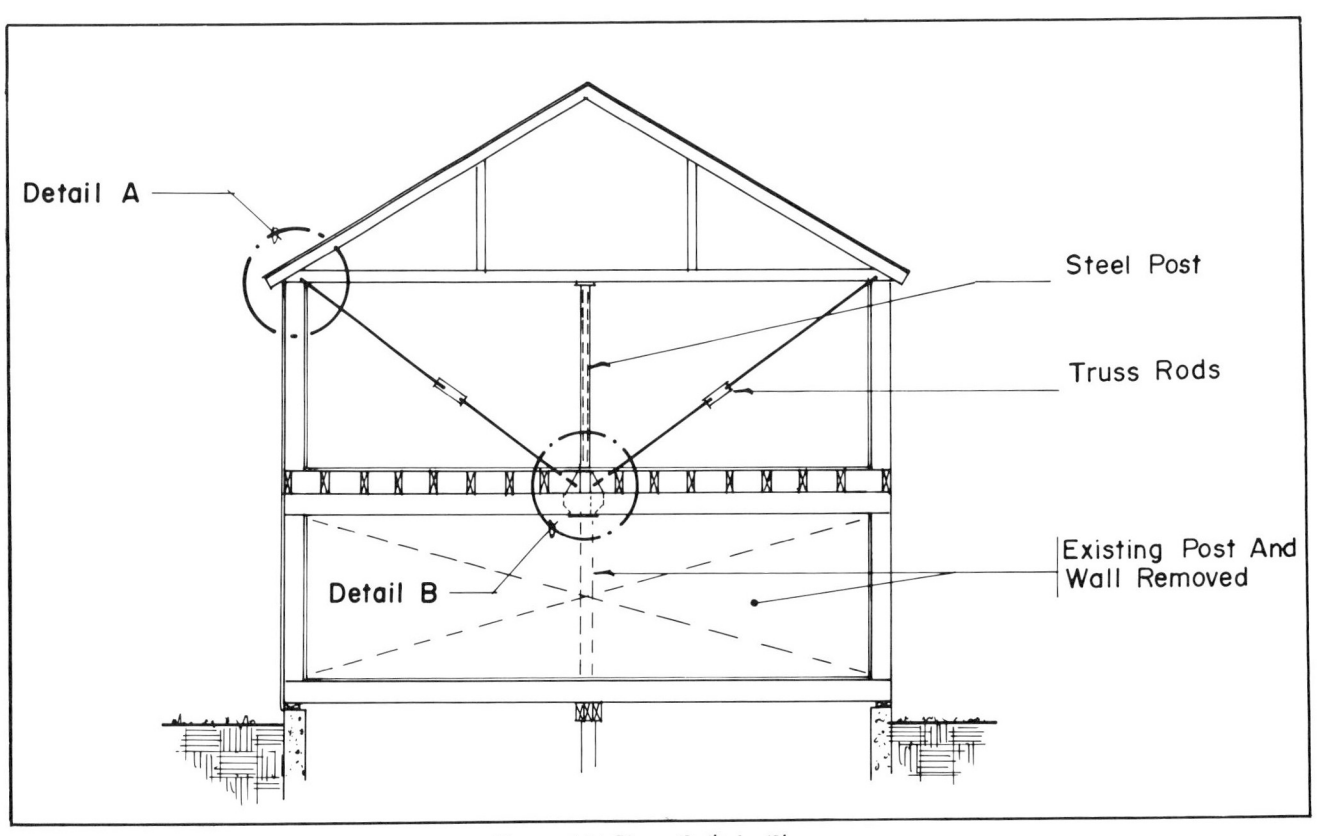

Figure 4.13 Hanger Rod And Transfer Beam

Figure 4.14 Truss Built In Place

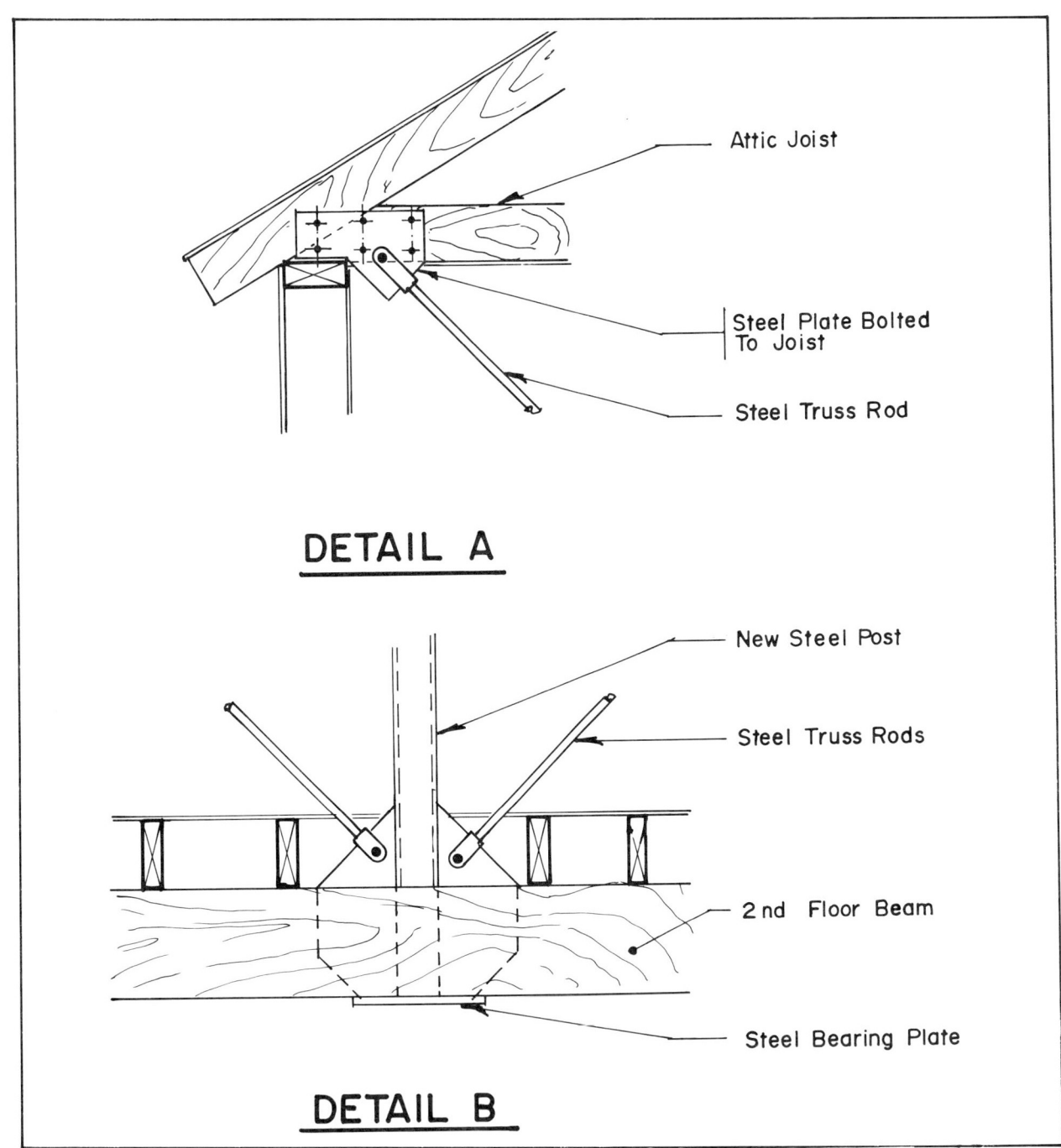

Figure 4.14 Truss built in place

PIONEER STRUCTURES

A group of structures worthy of examination are pioneer structures. They were built by early settlers using the materials and construction techniques readily available to them. Examples include log and sod houses, and heavy timber barns.

Heritage conservationists are often interested in this type of structure. Many historic parks have been developed by relocating, reconstructing and rehabilitating pioneer structures. An important requirement is that these structures be preserved in a condition that closely duplicates the original. This requires special care in rehabilitation. Techniques which alter the appearance of the structure are not acceptable alternatives. The techniques that are feasible tend to be labour intensive and thus very expensive.

These structures were almost exclusively constructed out of wood and soil. Due to the nature of wood, the structures were invariably subjected to severe deterioration. Sod houses in particular did not last very long

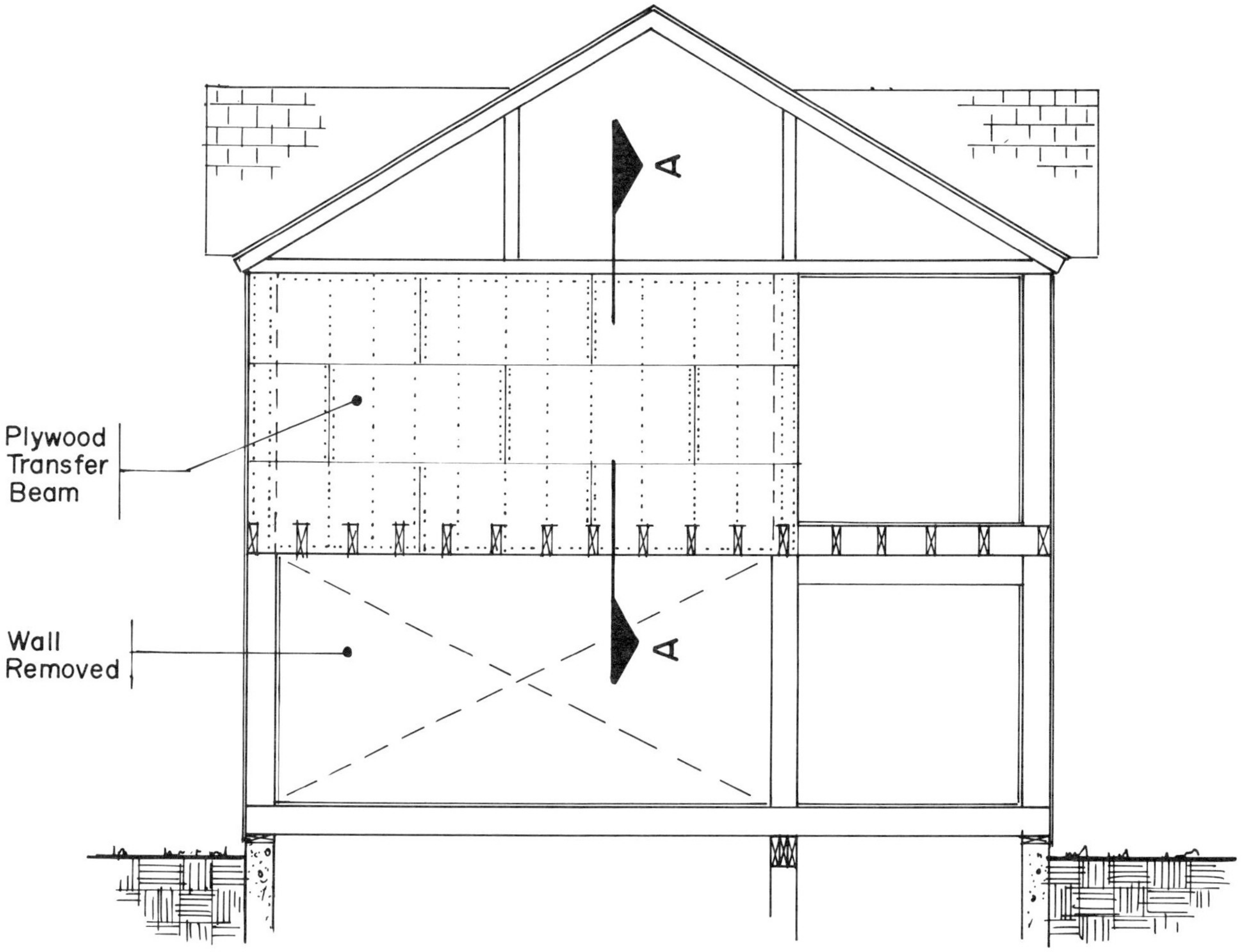

Figure 4.15 Plywood Web Beam

and are therefore very rare. Most sod buildings remaining today are reconstructions of originals.

Log structures are built a little more durably and are able to withstand deteriorating forces more effectively. The most common problem is the deterioration of the bottom sills. Generally, log buildings were built without foundations. The lower logs were laid directly on the ground without protection and were thus subjected to rot and insect attack.

In rehabilitation, the bottom course of logs may be replaced if they are beyond repair provided the new logs are constructed to match the old ones. This requires the use of traditional methods of construction. The logs must be cut, hewn, and assembled using the same procedures used in the original construction. The craftsmen and materials are available for such work, but it may be a lengthy process.

For the less severely damaged parts of the structure alternate techniques may exist. One of the most suitable for this application is the use of epoxy resins. As described earlier in this chapter, epoxy resins may be used to reinforce or splice members that have decayed. This allows the structure to retain its integrity without altering its outward appearance. This method is also faster than rebuilding the entire member. In those areas where the repairs are not visible, other methods may be used.

After the repairs or reconstructions are complete,

Photo 4.1 Log Home - In Disrepair

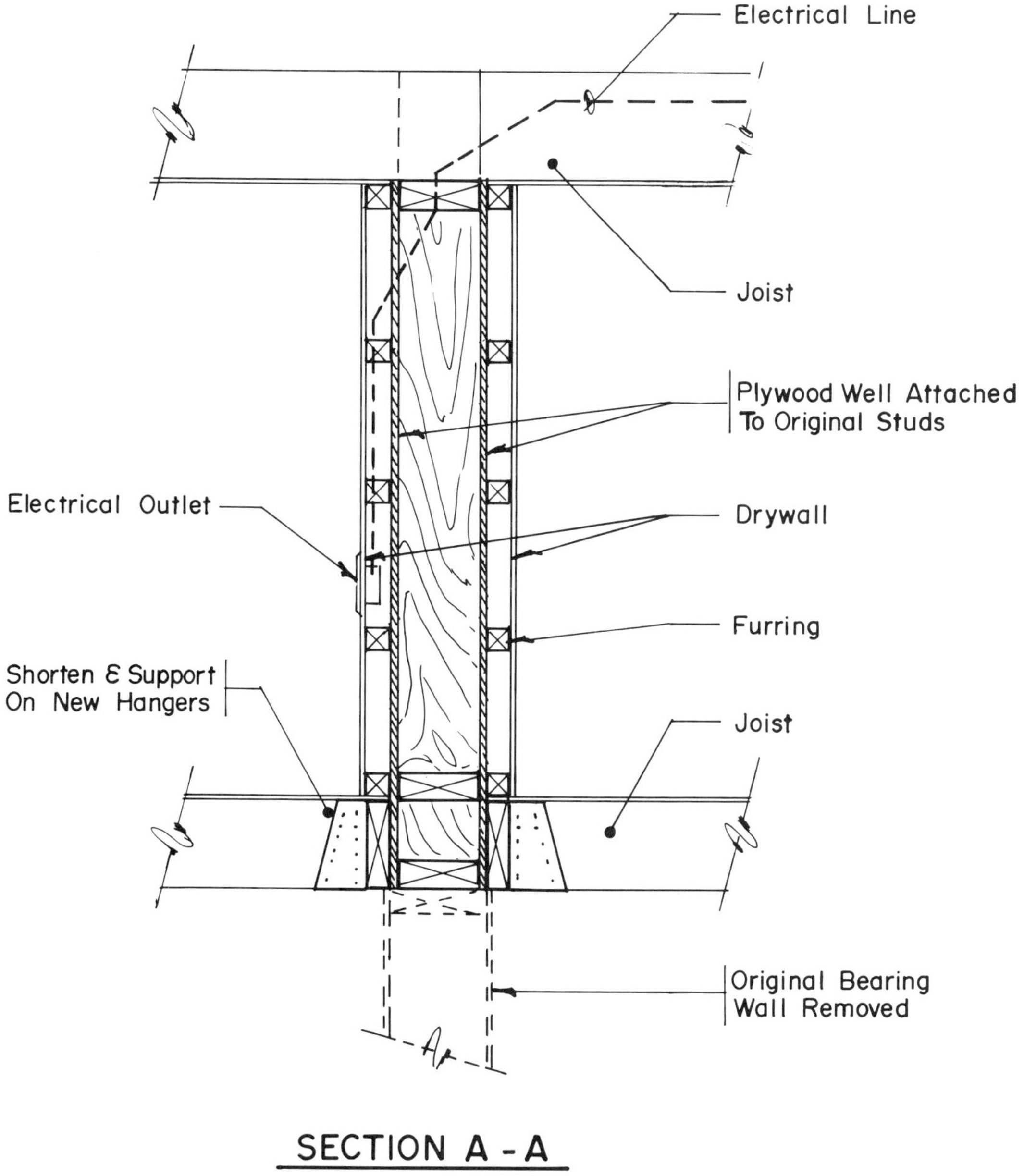

SECTION A - A

Figure 4.15 Plywood web beam

steps should be undertaken to ensure a good environment for the structure. This can include providing an adequate foundation. The bottom course should be protected from direct contact with the ground. If this is not feasible or desirable, it may be sufficient to treat the wood with preservatives and paint.

It is also important to reduce the presence of water by providing adequate drainage. If water is not present, as discussed previously, the opportunity for decay is greatly reduced.

Photo 4.2 Log Home - Restored

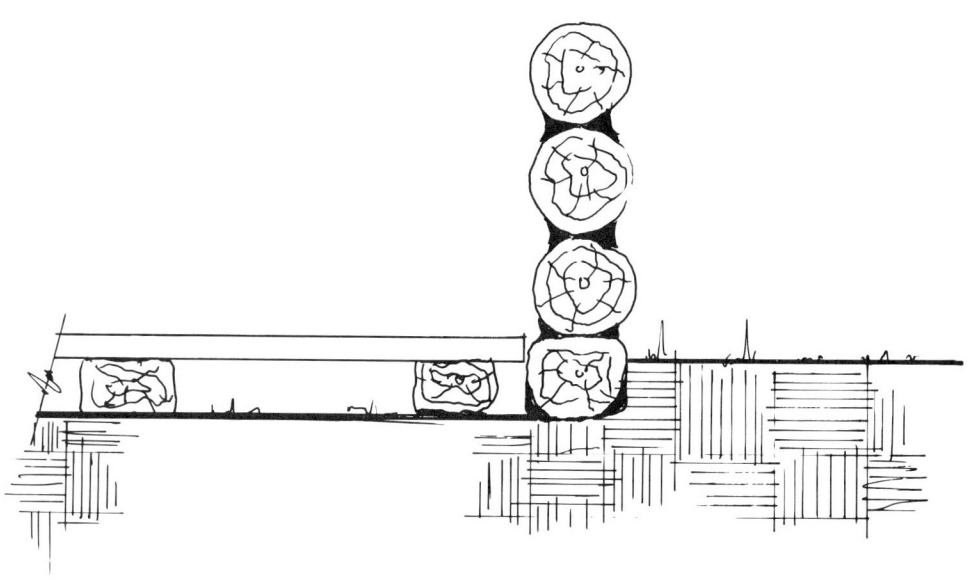

ORIGINAL CONDITION

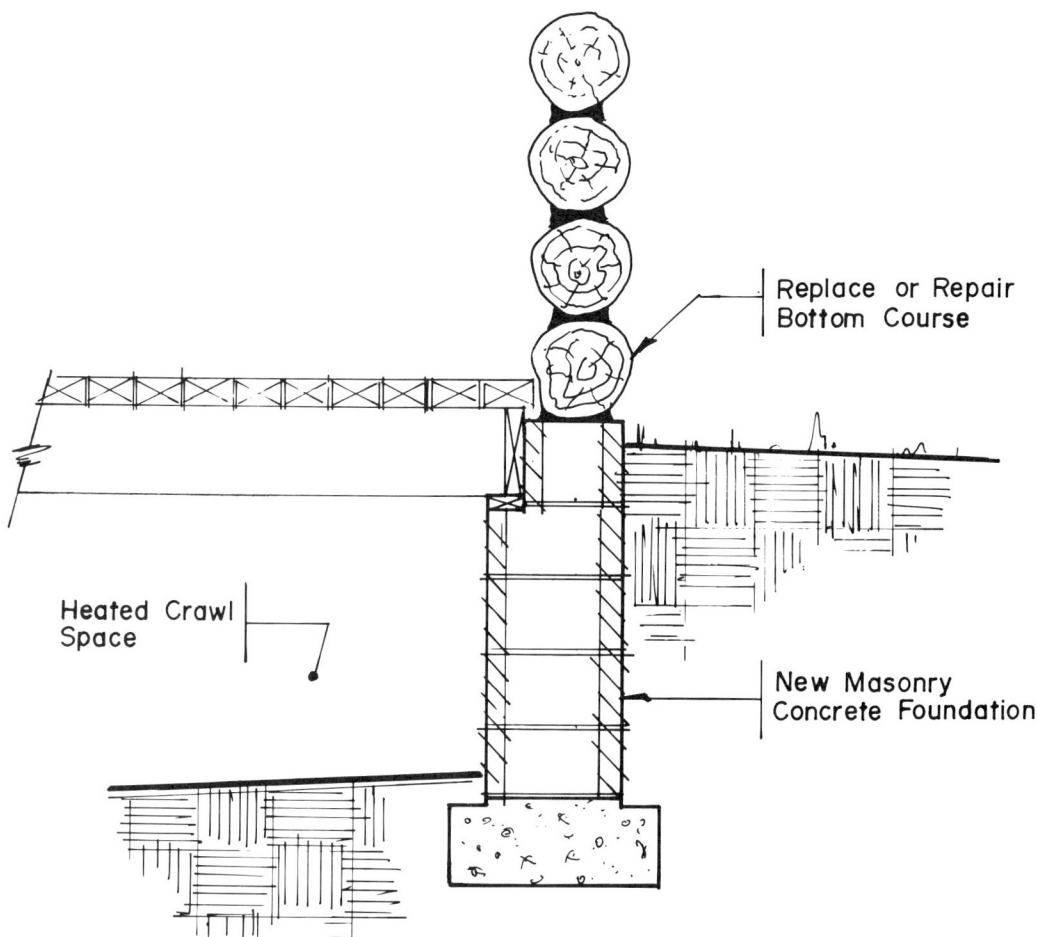

SUGGESTED SOLUTION

Figure 4.16 Log House Foundation

Chapter 5

PROJECT STUDIES

1. DUGGAN HOUSE, EDMONTON

This rehabilitation of an historic residence demonstrates the feasibility of undertaking smaller renovation projects. Duggan House is a two and one-half storey brick structure with a complex roof line and irregular facades. When originally built Duggan House had a front veranda which was an important visual element. The veranda had been supported by timber piles. When these rotted due to inadequate protection, the veranda was removed. The new veranda, designed to duplicate the original, is now supported on concrete piles.

At some point, an entrance was built directly into the basement. This created an opening in the foundation wall near a corner. The structural effects of the alteration were obviously not considered. When the opening was created, a lintel beam was not used-rather the brick work was left to span the doorway on its own.

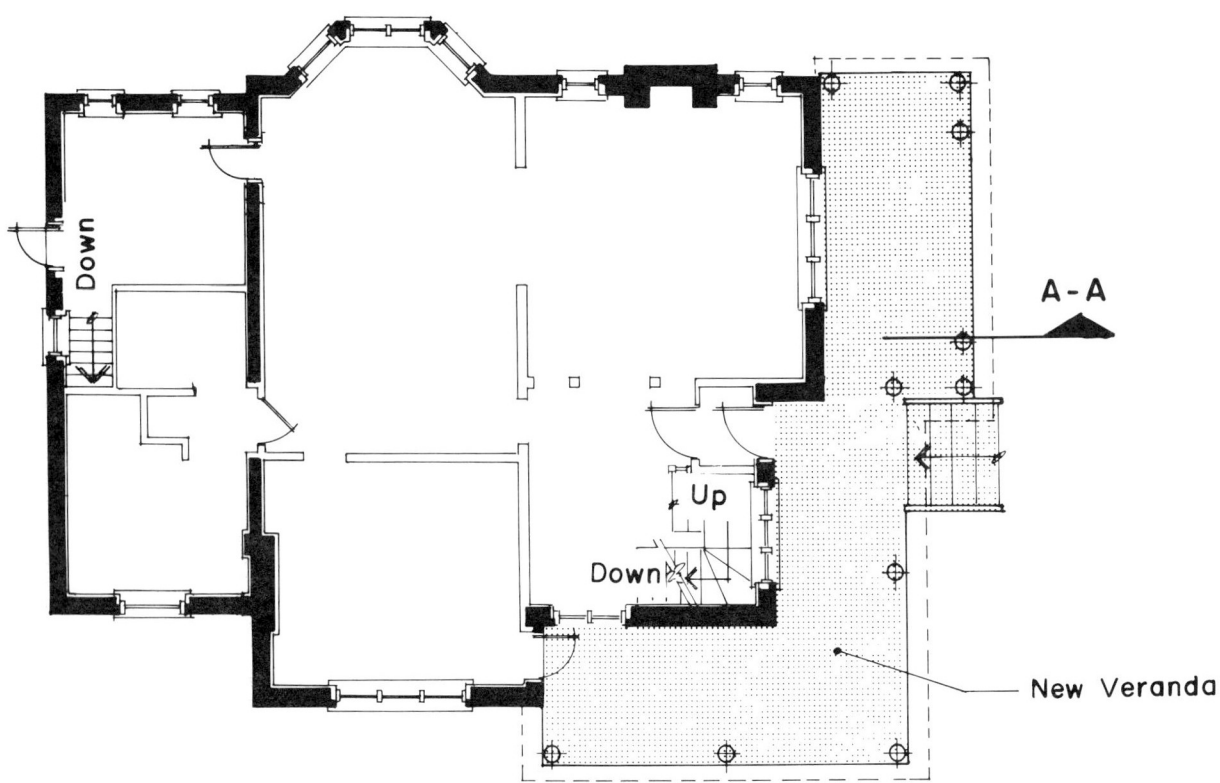

Figure 5.1.1 - Main Floor Plan

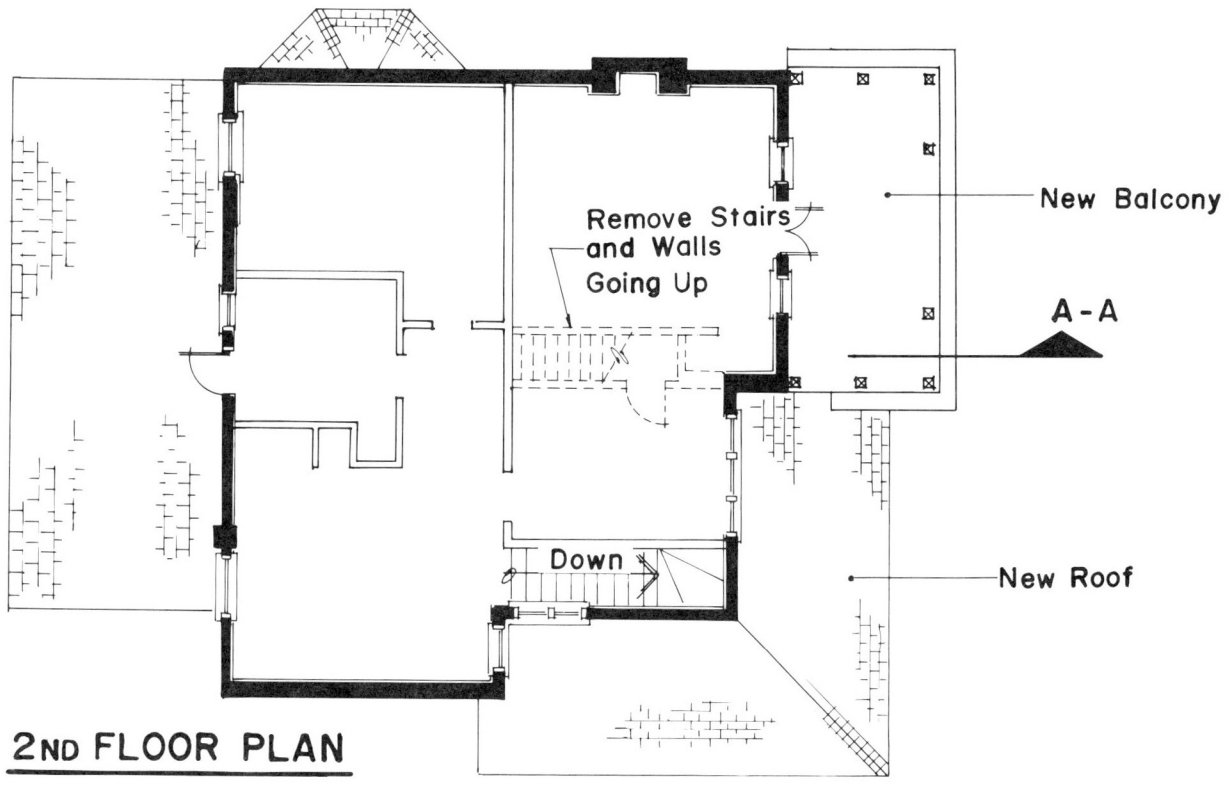

Figure 5.1.2 - Second Floor Plan

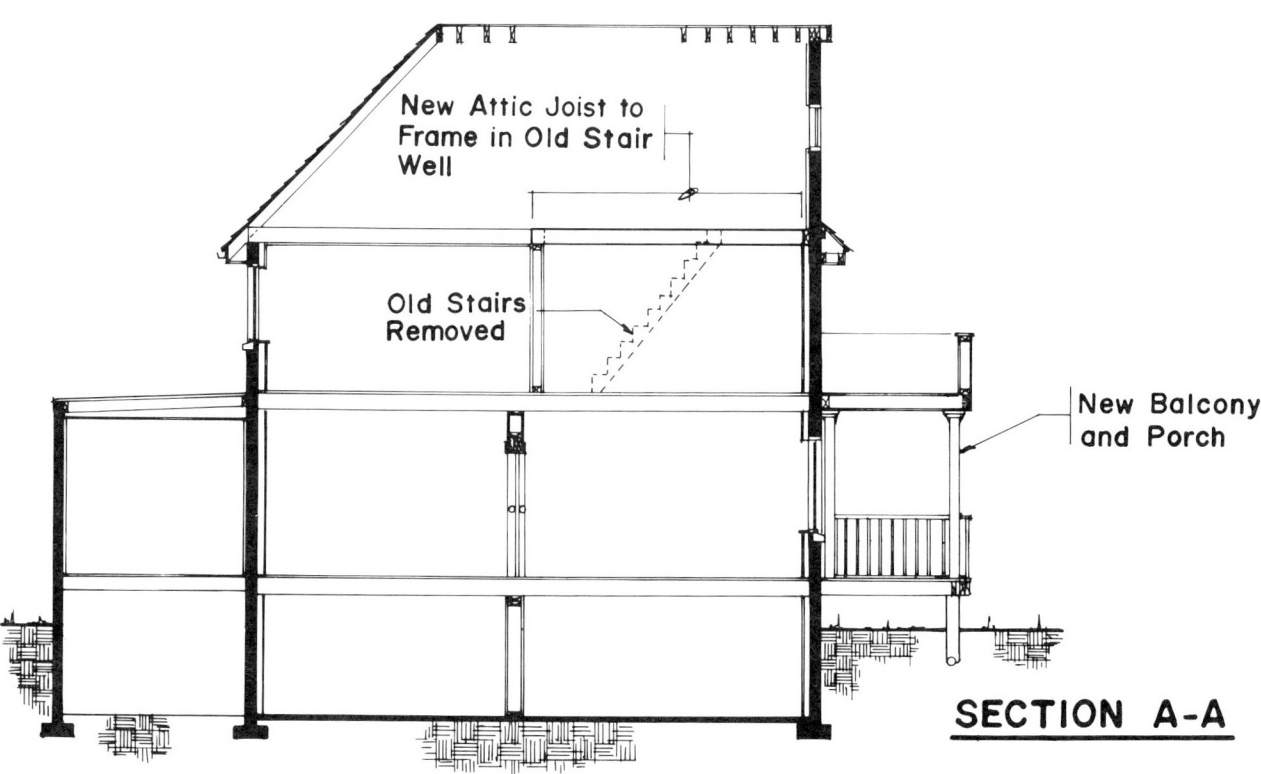

Figure 5.1.3 - Building Section

Photo 5.1.1 Duggan House-Before Restoration

In addition, a very poorly insulated shed was built around the door which allowed the cold to penetrate into the building and foundation. As the soil beneath the foundation was subjected to cold and warm temperatures over the years, it passed through numerous freeze-thaw cycles causing the foundation to heave and sink repeatedly. This action, combined with the weakened wall, caused severe deterioration of the corner.

The door was removed and the foundation wall repaired with concrete. The brick wall itself was rebuilt, re-using the old bricks wherever possible.

A concrete lintel over a basement window at the rear of the building had cracked, causing distress in the wall above. This was replaced with a steel lintel and the brick work repaired. A door in the rear was built without a lintel and was repaired in a similar manner.

Project Information

Original Construction

Built:	1907
Owner:	J.J. Duggan
Redevelopment	
Owner/Developer:	Alberta Association of Architects
Architect:	Holland Cummins Partnership
Structural Engineer:	Read Jones Christofferson Ltd.
Contractor:	Tri-Lin Construction
Completed:	1982
Duration:	Five months
Cost:	$160,000.00 including all structural, mechanical, electrical and architectural renovations.
Conservation Techniques Used:	Foundation Protection Masonry Repair Reconstruction Adaptive Re-use

Photo 5.1.2 After Restoration

Photo 5.1.3 Masonry Repair

2. ST. BRIGID CHURCH, OTTAWA

In the mid-sixties structural deformations were noticed in the walls of this load-bearing limestone and heavy timber framed church. The movements were caused by a lowering of the ground water table due to leakage into adjacent sewers. A change in soil volume under the exterior edge of the footings resulted, causing an outward tilt to the walls.

When the repairs were undertaken, the roof structure was in danger of collapse. The wall movements tended to tear the roof trusses apart.

The renovators could have dismantled the damaged portions of the structure and rebuilt it with new footings. This would have been prohibitively expensive and would have taken the entire building out of service for a long period of time. It was decided that the addition of new pilasters or buttresses on new footings would adequately stabilize the exterior walls.

The roof trusses were repaired by reinforcing all joints with steel plates.

It was originally intended to clad the new buttresses with stone to match the existing masonry. However, a shortage of funds necessitated leaving the concrete exposed. Meanwhile, ivy has grown over the concrete, softening the visual impact of the different materials.

The repairs mentioned added significantly to the useful life of the church. Encouraged, the parish has recently undertaken renovations to conserve energy. One change was an efficient re-zoning of the heating system. When activities are held in the parish hall (in the basement), the main part of the church does not have to be maintained at a similar temperature. Also, the roof has been insulated and double windows have been added.

Photo 5.2.1 St. Brigid Church-Front View

Photo 5.2.2 Ivy Covered Butress

Photo 5.2.3 Butress Detail

Project Information

Original Construction
Built:	1889
Architect:	G.R. Bowes
Owner:	Catholic Archdiocese of Ottawa
Architectural Style:	Russo - Byzantine

Redevelopment
Owner:	Catholic Archdiocese of Ottawa
Architect:	J.S. LeFort
Structural Engineer:	K.M. Design Consultants Ltd.
Contractor:	Doran Construction Ltd.
Repairs Started:	1968
Duration	Four months
Cost of Repairs:	$70,000 (1968 dollars) including new footings, concrete buttresses and roof truss repairs
Conservation Techniques Used:	Masonry Repair, Heavy Timber Repair

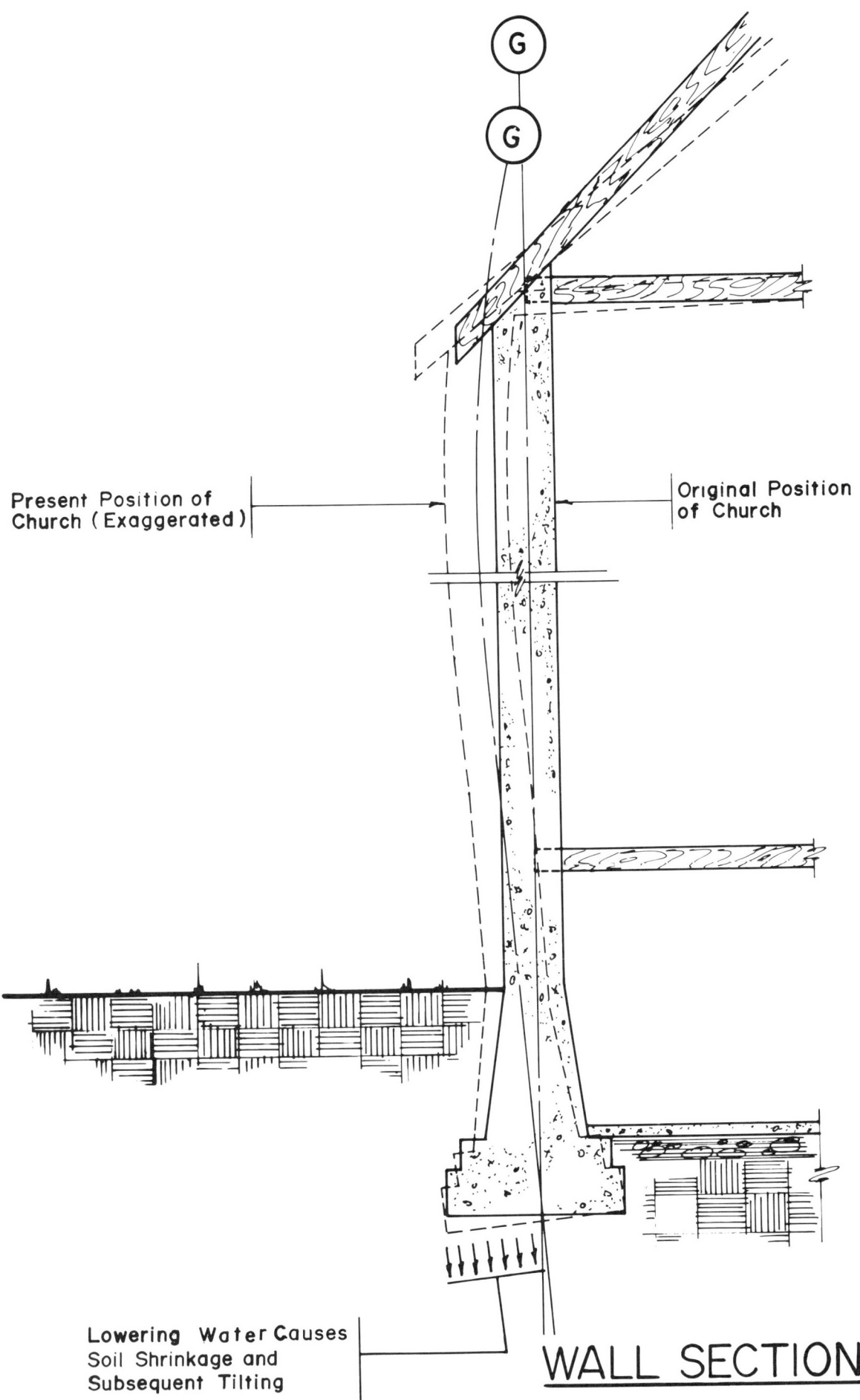

Figure 5.2.1 - Wall and Truss Details

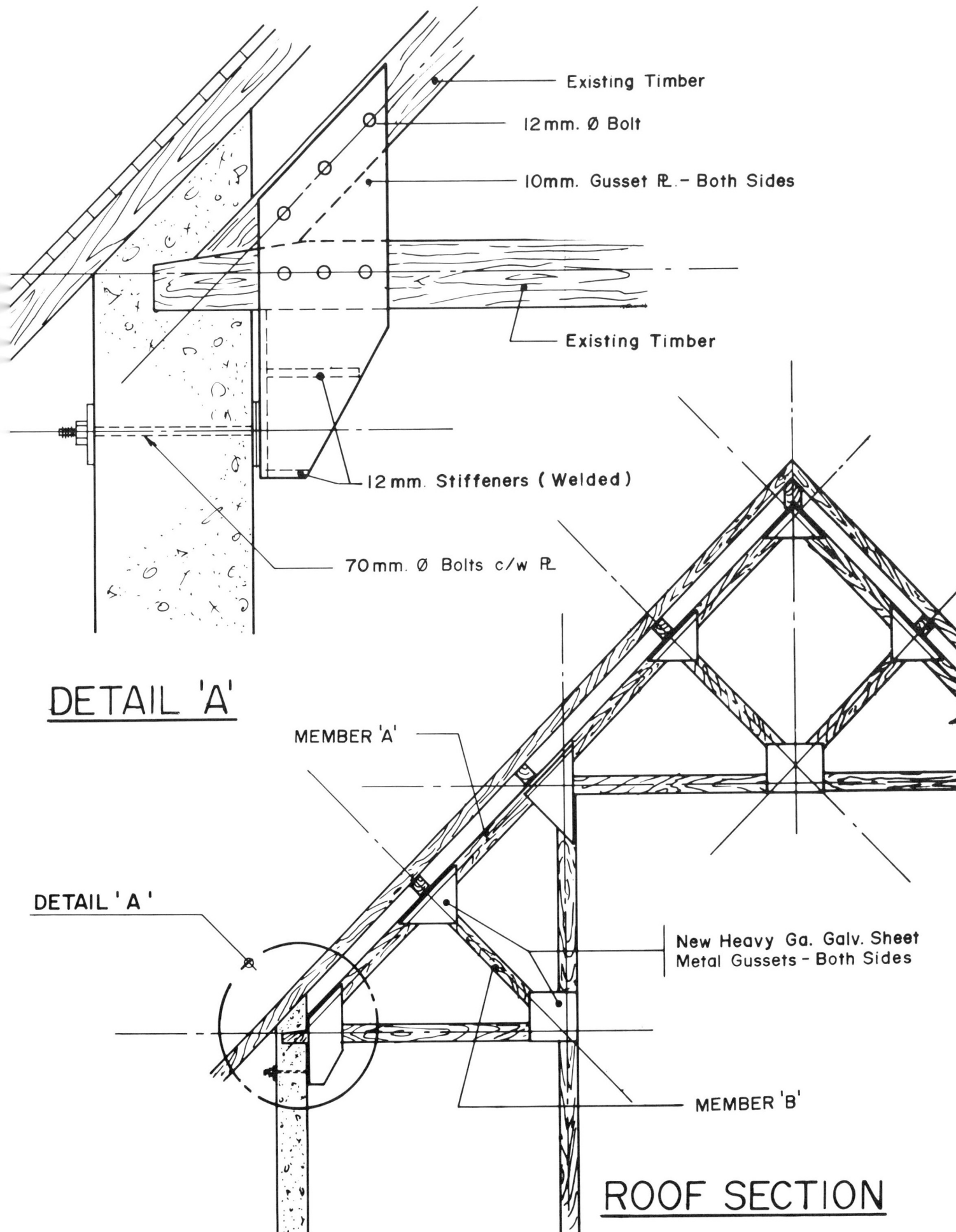

Figure 5.2.1

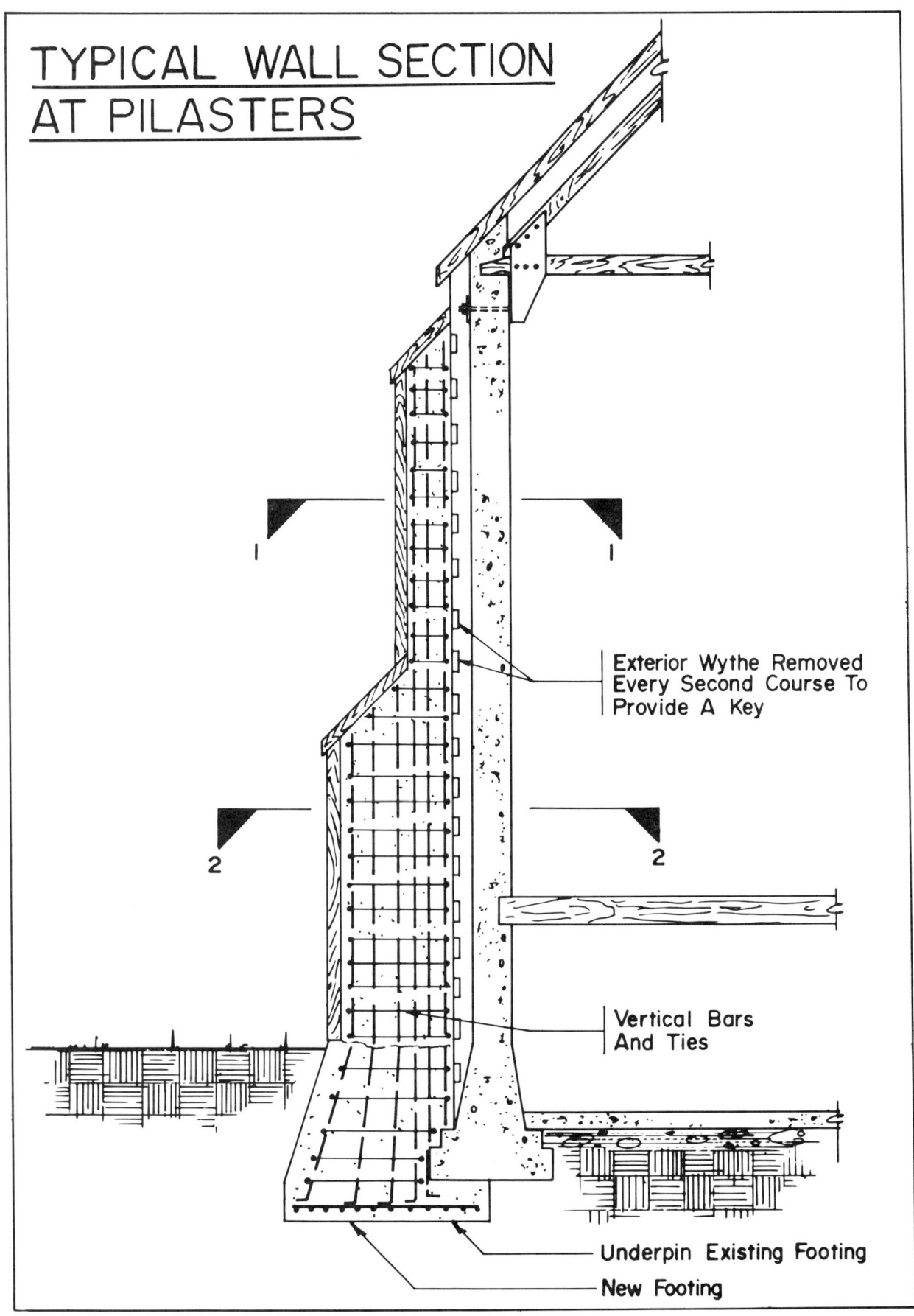

Figure 5.2.2

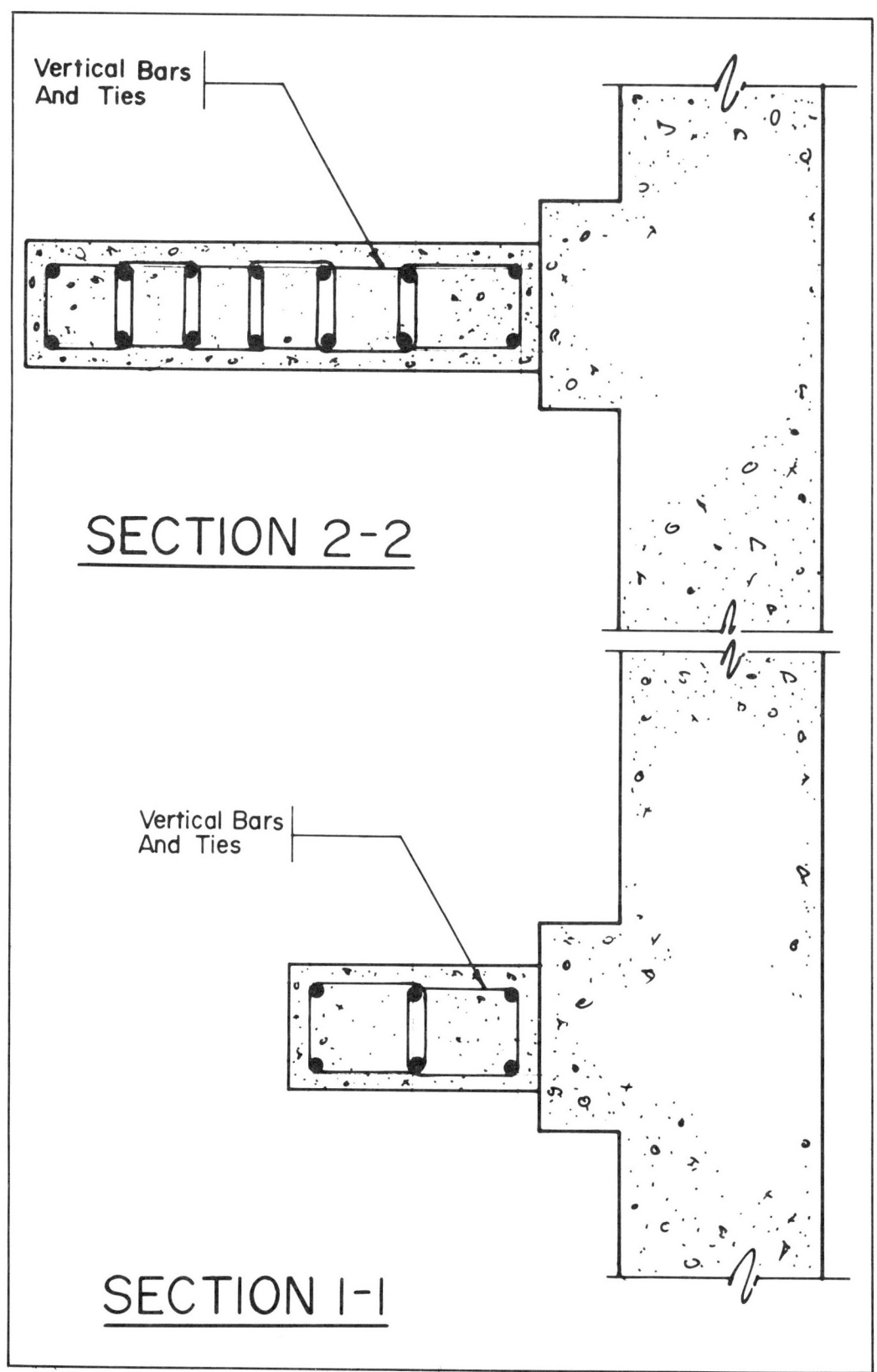

Figure 5.2.2 - Wall Reinforcing

3. ROTHESAY APARTMENTS, EDMONTON

In 1979 the City of Edmonton acquired the Rothesay Apartments as part of the Canada Place land assembly.

Design studies showed that the structure as a whole could not be incorporated into the new proposed Canada Place. Edmonton city-planners wished to retain only the original elements of the apartment's facade. These could later be reincorporated in the Canada Place development, or moved to the East Jasper block.

The original intent was to number and dismantle, brick by brick, the portions of the facade to be retained but, it was felt that dismantling a brick structure and storing it could result in lost portions of the stored material. Also, there was concern that this approach was not totally honest to the concept of heritage conservation.

A feasibility study was undertaken to determine how the facade might be panelized into larger sections. It was recommended that the upper two storeys and parapet be panelized into individual pieces by applying a reinforced shotcrete backup. These panels would then be lifted off and transported to a secure site until they could be incorporated in the new project.

The lower storey consists of sandstone columns and details with masonry infill. The recent addition will be discarded, and the sandstone numbered and crated for storage with the larger panels.

Project Information

Original Construction
Completed:	1914
Owner:	McDougall & Secord
Contractor:	George Archibald
Achitect:	Magoon & MacDonald
Architectural Style:	Commercial

Heritage Conservation
Owner:	The City of Edmonton
Architect:	The City of Edmonton Architectural Branch
Architectural Consultant:	A.M. Holland, M.R.A.I.C.
Structural Consultant:	Quinn Dressel Jokinen
Contractor:	Noranda Builders
Start of Construction:	May 1983
Cost:	$70,000 (1983 dollars) to panelize, remove and store the East facade and a portion of the North facade
Conservation Techniques Used	Large scale Panelization Dismantling Selective Demolition

Photo 5.3.1 Rothesay Apartments-Before Demolition

Photo 5.3.4 Transport

Photo 5.3.3. Dismantling

Photo 5.3.2 Design Model

Photo 5.3.4 Storage

4. CARNEGIE LIBRARY, VANCOUVER

The rehabilitation of the Carnegie Library structure involved many conservation techniques such as: shotcreting; seismic upgrading; reinforcing of wooden floors; and extensive repairs to the exterior sandstone.

Lateral resistance as a protective measure against earthquakes was required. To achieve this, a reinforced shotcrete wall was mechanically connected to the exterior brick and stone masonry. The shotcrete was applied continuously from the foundation to the top. Existing masonry pilasters were found to be inadequate, and were reinforced with either shotcrete or new concrete columns.

The wood frame floors, also found to be insufficient for transfer of earthquake loads, were reinforced. New steel beams were added below and a reinforced concrete topping applied over them to act as a seismic diaphragm.

The domed rotunda, by its sheer mass, created a considerable problem for earthquake resistance. A new steel space frame was added inside to transmit seismic loads to other elements of the structure.

The Carnegie Library has had a varied life. It served as a library, a museum, then was left vacant for a considerable time, and later became a movie set. It has now been restored to function as a library and community centre, serving as a focus for the Chinatown district of Vancouver.

Project Information

Original Construction
Completed:	1905
Architect:	G. Grant
Owner:	City of Vancouver

Redevelopment
Owner/Developer:	City of Vancouver
Architect:	Downs & Archambault
Structural Engineers:	Bush, Bohlman & Associates
Contractor:	Byers Construction
Completed:	1978
Duration:	One year
Cost:	$1.7 million (1978 dollars) including: all structural, mechanical, electrical and architectural renovations
Conservation Techniques Used:	Seismic Upgrading, Shotcreting, Masonry Repair, Structural Upgrading, Adaptive Re-use

Vancouver Public Library

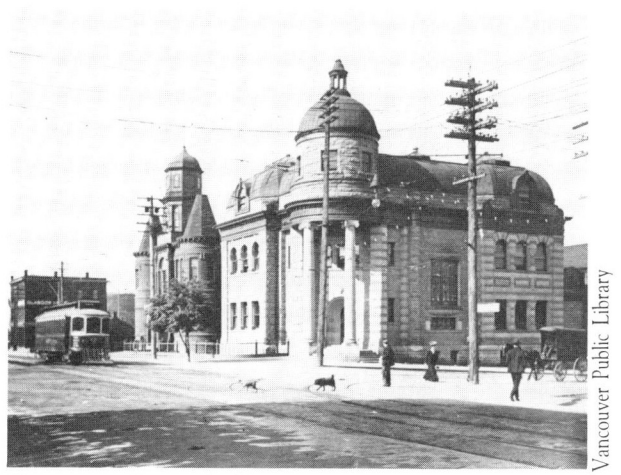

Photo 5.4.1 Carnegie Library ca. 1904

Hardy Associates

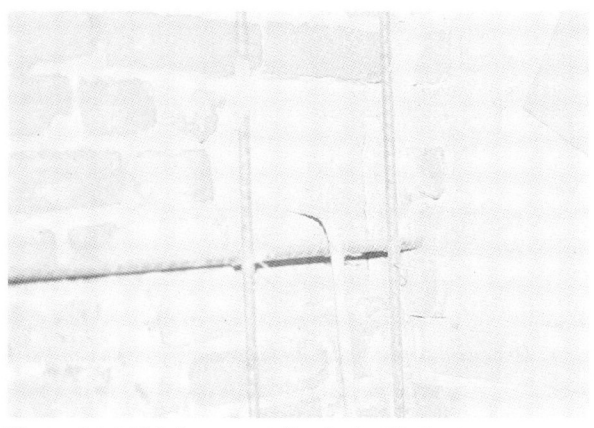

Photo 5.4.2 Reinforcement Ready for Shotcrete

Vancouver Public Library

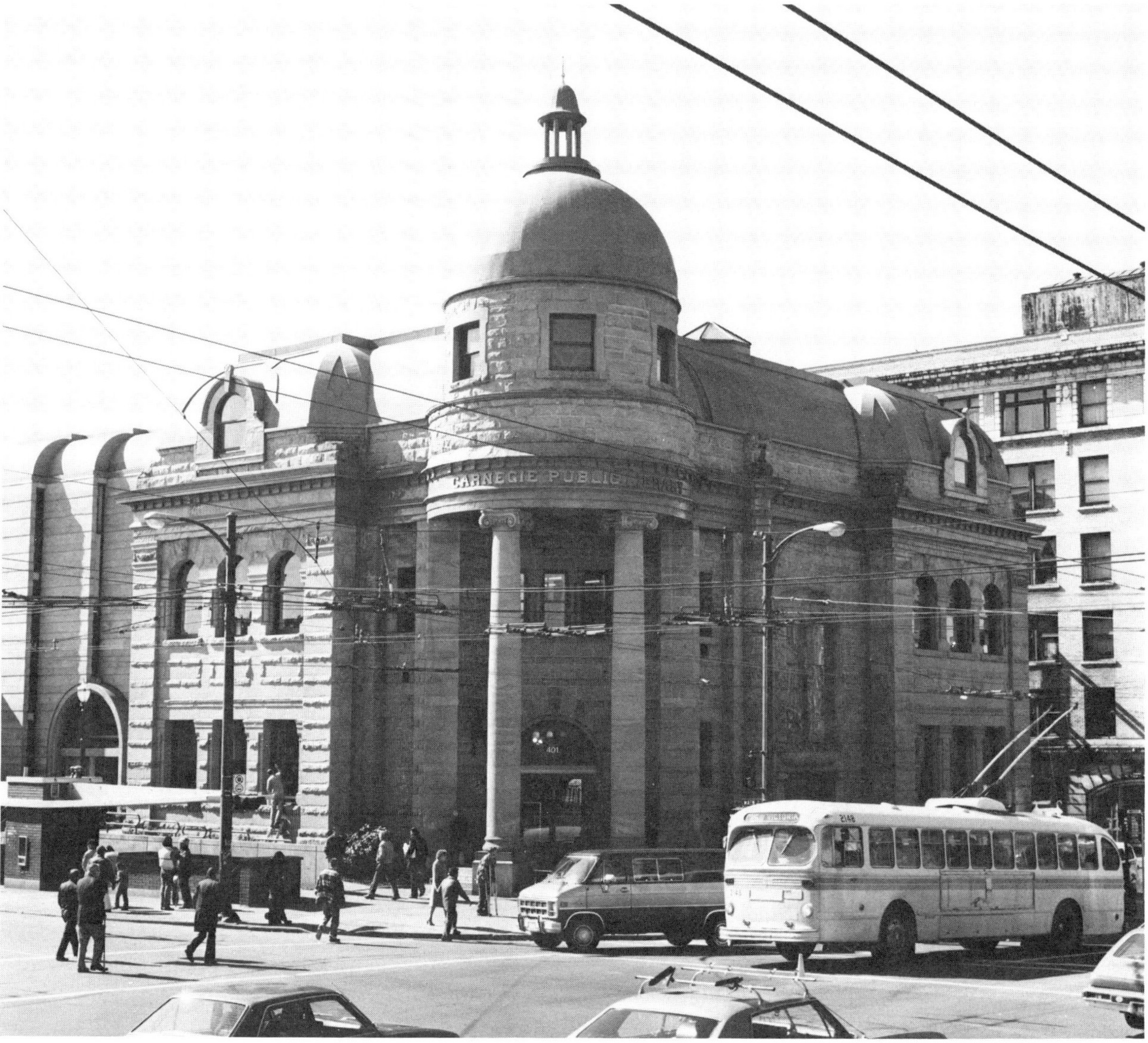

Photo 5.4.4 After Renovation

Photo 5.4.3 Steel Bracing to Entrance Dome

5. HOLLINSWORTH BUILDING, CALGARY

The Hollinsworth Building project involved the redevelopment of an entire city block in downtown Calgary. The most important street frontage of the project is on the 8th Avenue Pedestrian Mall.

Planners determined that the Hollinsworth Building in its entirety, and the facade of Willsons Stationers, were of significant historical value. These structures were to be incorporated into the new project.

The Hollingsworth Building was totally renovated with considerable structural upgrading. A new service core including stairs, elevators and mechanical shafts was necessary. Selective demolition was used, and new structures were tied in with the old utilizing epoxy adhesives and drilled inserts.

A new mezzanine floor was added to accomodate the banking services to be incorporated in the building.

In addition, extensive upgrading of the original structural elements was required. Investigations found that a number of unauthorized structural renovations had taken place during the life of the building, which rendered it structurally unsafe. The most serious of these was the replacement of the original load-bearing arches at the main floor with more modern storefronts. This appears to have occured when Hollinsworth took over the building from the Canada Life Insurance Company in the 1920's.

Several footings were underpinned to upgrade their strength, and to allow better use of the basement space by lowering certain footings.

The facades on the Pedestrian Mall and 2nd Street S.W. frontages will be restored to their original appearance. All work has been completed with the exception of the terra-cotta veneer, which is a long delivery item. There is a limited number of suppliers in North America doing this type of work, and a strong demand exists for this material. The construction of the exterior wall, from a building sciences point of view will be maintained as it existed at the start of renovations. It was felt that any change in vapour barriers and insulation could result in serious deterioration of the wall in the future.

The Willson Stationery facade will be numbered, dismantled, and reassembled adjacent to the Hollinsworth. In this location it will not conflict with the connection between the new atrium on the site and the Galleria, which is to be provided over the Pedestrian Mall by the developer.

Project Information

Original Construction

Owner:	Canada Life Insurance Company
Architect:	Brown and Vallance
Completed:	1913

Redevelopment

Owner/Developer:	Trizec Corporation
Architect:	ARCOP Associates/Cohos Evamy & Partners
Structural Engineer:	Jablonsky & Associates
Contractor:	P.C.L. Construction Ltd.
Developed Area: Building only	3,500 square metres Hollinsworth
Cost:	$5 million (1982 dollars) including total renovation of the Hollinsworth Building. Of this amount, $500,000 is for restoration of the terra-cotta exterior
Conservation Techniques Used:	Underpinning Structural Upgrading Minor Additions Selective Demolition Terra-cotta Reconstruction Dismantling and Reassembly

Photo 5.5.1 Hollinsworth Building ca. 1919

Photo 5.5.2 ca. 1930

Photo 5.5.5 - 1983 Awaiting Restoration of Terra-Cotta

Photo 5.5.4 Willson Stationery Facade

Photo 5.5.3 Entrance Detail

Photo 5.6.4 Preserved facade

6. 527 SUSSEX DRIVE, OTTAWA

This project is in the By Ward Market area of Ottawa, two blocks from the Parliament Buildings. It is an excellent example of the "facade retention" technique.

The original structure was timber frame of a quality not worth upgrading. Therefore, it was decided to save only the facade and construct a new reinforced concrete frame building behind it.

Considerable shoring and underpinning of rubble foundations was required under the preserved facade and adjacent partywalls. The partywalls were porous and had to be protected extensively during the construction period.

Structural steel bracing towers were erected on temporary footings in the sidewalk, the facade was tied back to the towers, and the balance of the structure was demolished.

Sometime during the life of the building, a fourth storey in a totally different style was added to the block. This storey was removed and the facade restored to its original appearance.

Project Information

Original Construction
Completed: 1875
Owners: Riel-McDougall-Bedard
Use: Commercial and Warehouse

Redevelopment
Owner/Developer: National Capital Commission
Architect/Structural Engineer: National Capital Commission
Contractor: W.S. Burnside Ltd.
Completed: May, 1983
Duration: Ten months

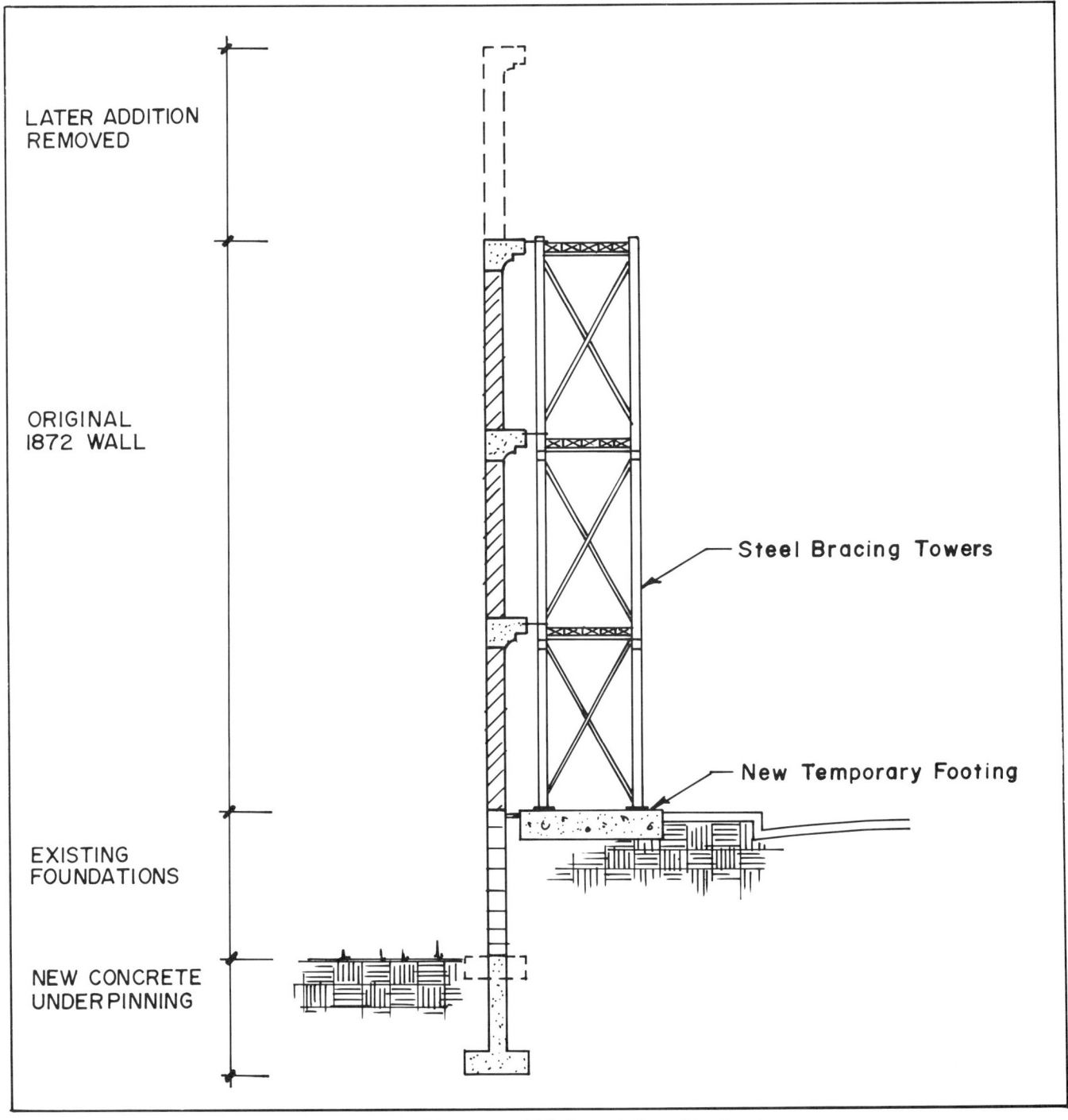

Figure 5.6.1 - Temporary Wall Support From The Exterior

New Use: Office Building
Cost: $2.0 million (1982 dollars) including $180,000 for selective demolition, temporary facade bracing and protection of adjacent properties

Conservation Techniques Used: Selective Demolition
Facade Retention
Underpinning
Foundation Shoring

7. BUREAU DE POSTES, VILLE DE QUEBEC

In 1983, the Federal Government undertook to restore its old post office in Quebec City. No major changes were required to the exterior of the building. The interior was another matter. Basic structural elements required upgrading.

The steel columns supporting the clock tower had deteriorated severely due to corrosion. This corrosion was due to rain penetration at the junction of the clock tower and main roof. In order to minimize disruption to the structure, the columns were repaired one at a time. First, the stone cladding of one corner of the tower was removed, exposing the corroded column. Timber shoring was installed and the column removed. The new steel column was then threaded into place through the roof. The original stone pieces were then reinstalled.

A 50 mm thick structural concrete topping was bonded to the floors throughout the building to increase their live load capacity. This required the removal of the existing hardwood floors finish. The stairs were also completely rebuilt to meet current fire code requirements.

The renovated building is now occupied by federal government agencies including Parks Canada, custodians of our national historic sites.

Photo 5.7.2 Tower Reinforcement

Project Information

Original Construction
Completed: 1860
Owner: Government of Canada

Redevelopment
Owner: Government of Canada
Architect: Begin et Rodrique
Structural Engineers: Bergeron, Cote et Assoc.
Contractor: Les Construction Roger Blouin Inc.
Completed: 1983
Duration: Eighteen months
Cost: $3.6 million including all architectural, mechanical, structural and electrical
Conservation Techniques Used: Replacement of deteriorated members
Structural bonded topping
Fire code upgrading

Photo 5.7.1 Bureau de Postes, Quebec

Photo 5.7.3 *After renovations*

8. 330 BAY STREET, TORONTO

The redevelopment of the 330-336 Bay Street block in Toronto included the relocation of a very pleasing facade in the office structure's atrium. The facade was part of the Savarin Tavern. The new project became a typical infill development, landlocked on three sides by other buildings.

For redevelopment it was necessary to dismantle the three-storey stone facade to provide construction access to the site. The facade was reassembled on new footings in the interior atrium which now functions as a restaurant.

It is interesting to note the "braided" arches which were also seen on the Berkeley Hotel (Maison ALCAN Project Study).

The facade could have been reassembled at its original location after the new construction was complete. The owners, however, decided that their requirement for modern open banking frontage was not compatible with the rather ornate stonework of the original facade.

Project Information

Original Construction
Completed: 1929
Owner: Savarin Tavern
Architect: N. Armstrong
Use: Restaurant / Tavern

Redevelopment
Owner/Developer: Imbrook Properties
Architect: Webb Zerafa Menkes Housden

Structural Engineer:	Quinn Dressel Associates
Contractor:	UMA Spantec
Completed:	1982
Duration:	Eighteen months
Costs:	$30 million (1980 dollars) including renovation of 330 Bay, a new in-fill office tower at 336 Bay and dismantling and reassembly of the facade ($300,000)
Conservation Techniques Used:	Dismantling and Reassembly

Photo 5.8.2 Dismantling

WZMH Group/Lenscape

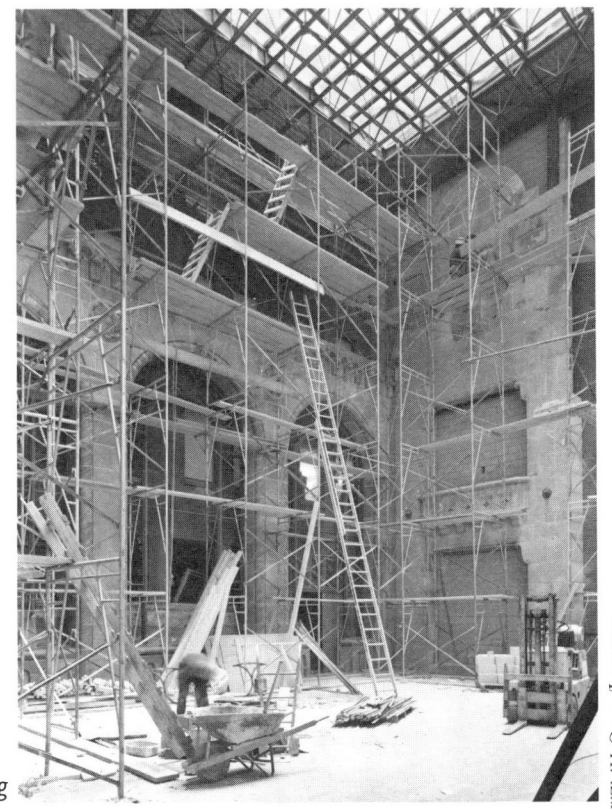

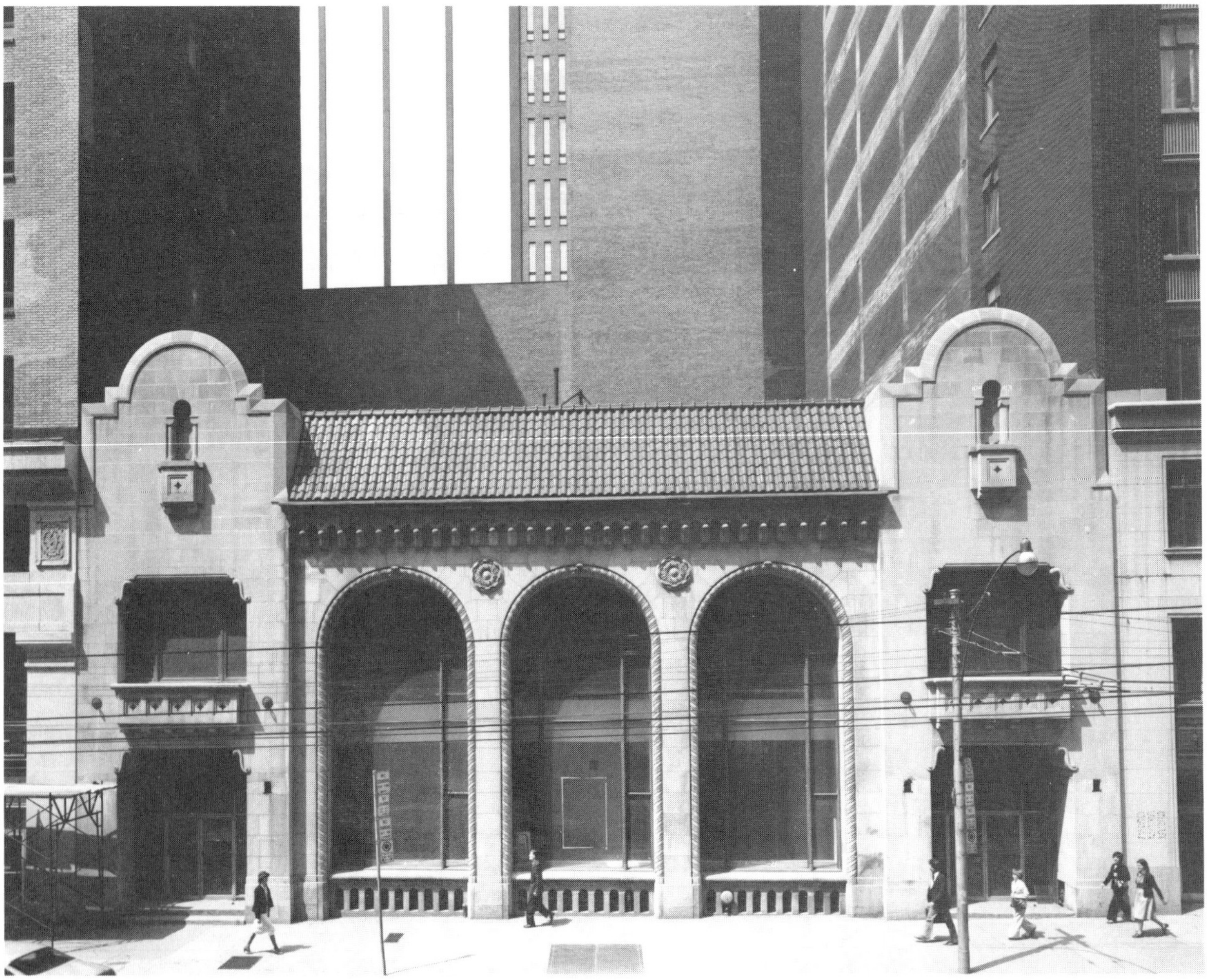

Photo 5.8.1 330 Bay ca. 1980

WZMH Group/Lenscape

Photo 5.8.3 Completed atrium

Photo 5.8.4 Completed atrium

Photo 5.8.5 Complexed exterior

9. BARRINGTON PLACE, HALIFAX

The previous project studies have given excellent examples of facade retention techniques. These included large scale panelization, shoring externally, and shotcrete reinforcing. The Barrington Place development is a fine example of another technique-the dismantling, storage and re-assembly of an historic facade.

This project is located two blocks from the Historic Properties area on the Halifax waterfront. All the buildings in the neighbourhood date back to the 1860's. The original structures at these locations were destroyed in the Great Fire of 1859.

A redevelopment of the entire block was undertaken in 1978 and completed in autumn 1979. An historic evaluation revealed that only the facades on Granville Street were worth saving. They consisted of mansard roofs supported on three-storey high stone facades. These, in turn, were supported on a one-storey base structure. This base structure caused considerable difficulty. It was made up of cast iron columns and beams resting on granite block bases. The structures behind this facade were composed of wood framed floors with masonry partywalls.

The original intent of the development team was to brace the retained walls externally while carrying out selective demolition of the remaining structure. Unfortunately, as demolition progressed it became apparent that this was not feasible. The various elements of the base structure were interconnected solely by friction. No anchor bolts were provided between granite bases and columns. Beams rested on column capitals without the benefit of bolts, rivets or welding (which of course had not been invented in 1860). In retrospect it is a wonder the structure survived the Great Explosion of 1917.

The inherent instability of the beam and column base required a reassessment of the retention scheme. A bracing scheme might work, but at the risk of totally losing the facade if this "house of cards" folded. A decision was made to number and dismantle the pieces. They were stored on site while a new concrete structure was erected. The cast iron elements were restored, cleaned, painted and re-used. The stone elements were re-erected on top of the cast iron frame. A new mansard roof using modern materials was constructed on top.

The rebuilt facade now acts as a veneer, tied back laterally to the new building frame. It is non-load bearing except for it's self-weight.

This project highlights once again the element of

Photo 5.9.1: Barrington Place - Cast Iron Beam - Column Junction

surprise to be found in heritage conservation projects. The developer had originally budgeted $400,000 for bracing and restoration of the retained facades. The need to dismantle and reassemble added $1,000,000 to the final cost of this component.

The Granville Street facades are now protected by the Nova Scotia Heritage Property Act. It is interesting to contemplate the incongruity of designating parts of a building which during most of 1979 were merely a pile of numbered stones sitting on the curb at Granville Street.

The finished project is a full block of mixed use development. Tenants include restaurants, forty retail outlets and a two hundred and three unit hotel. The site is in the shadow of the historic Citadel, which is undergoing an extensive restoration. The project offers the closest hotel accomodation to the home of the Bluenose II, a fine example of Canadian maritime heritage.

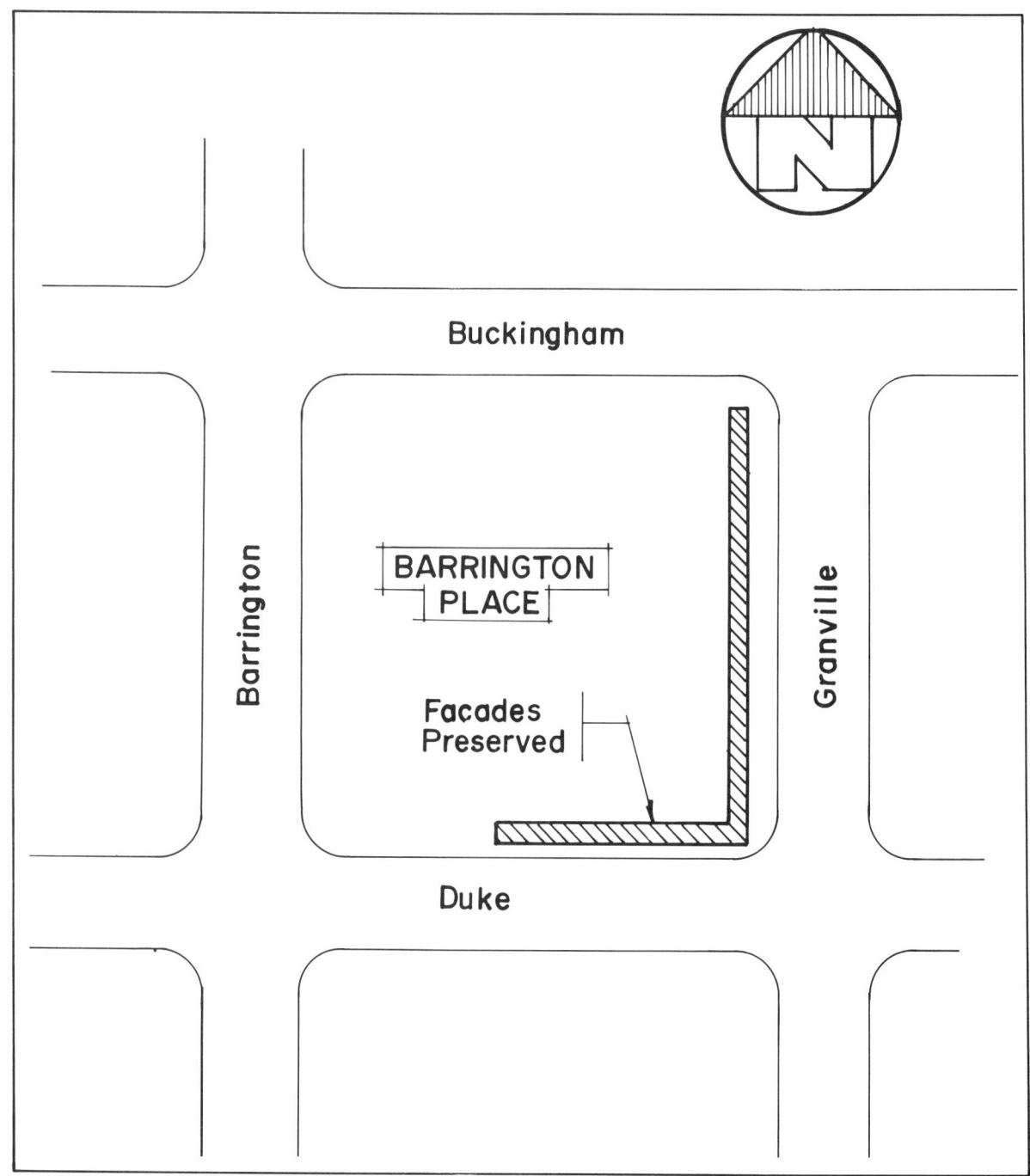

Figure 5.9.1 Location Plan

Project Information

Original Construction
Completed: ca. 1860
Architect: William Thomas & Sons, Toronto

Redevelopment
Owner: Durham Leaseholds (Halifax Developments & Oxford Developments)
Architect: Page & Steele, Toronto
Contractor: PCL Construction
Completed: 1979
Cost: $1,400,000 (1979 dollars) for dismantling, restoration and reassembly of the historic facades only.

Conservation Techniques Used: Selective demolition
Dismantling and Reassembly

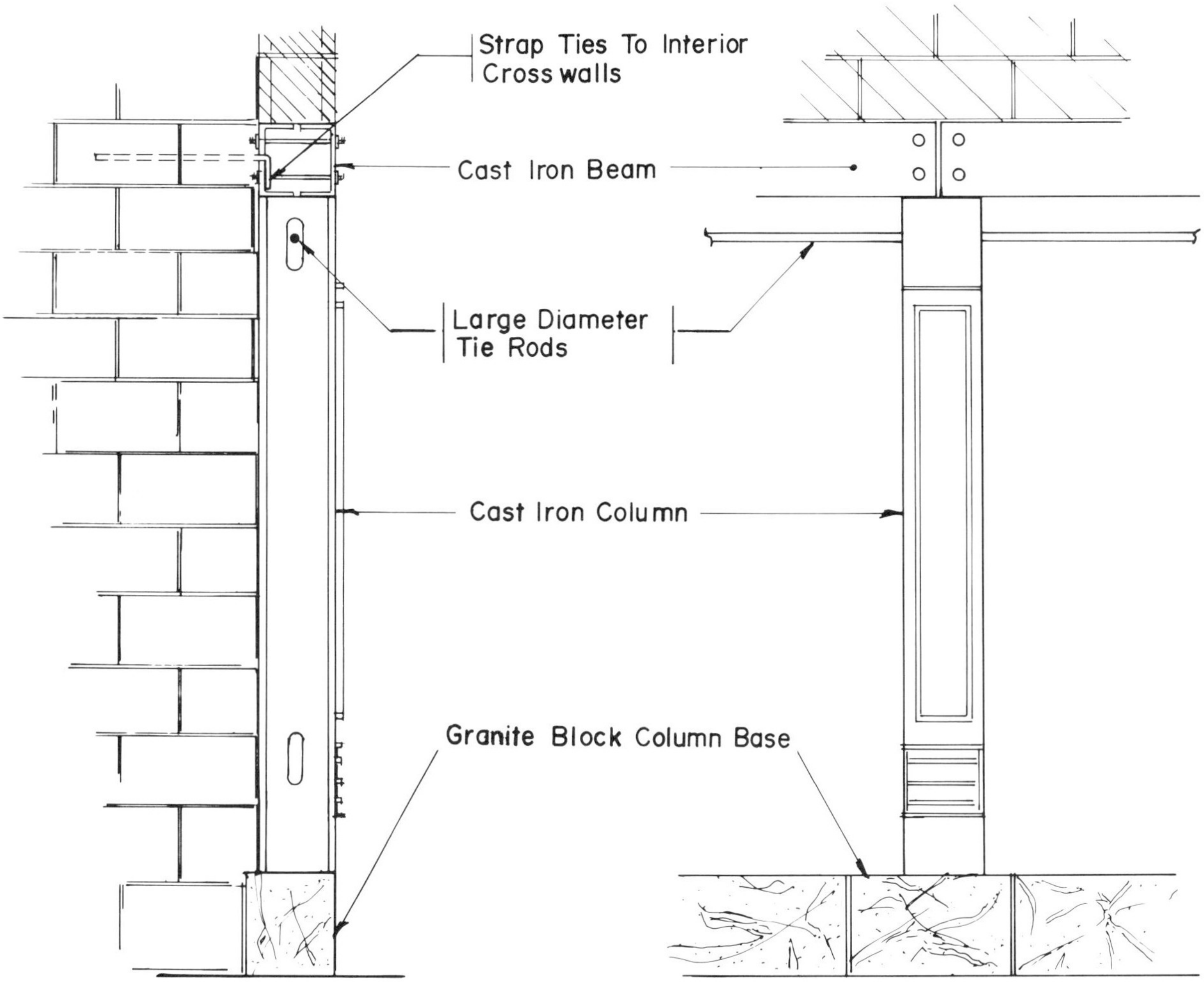

Figure 5.9.2 - Cast iron beam - column detail

Halifax Development Corp.

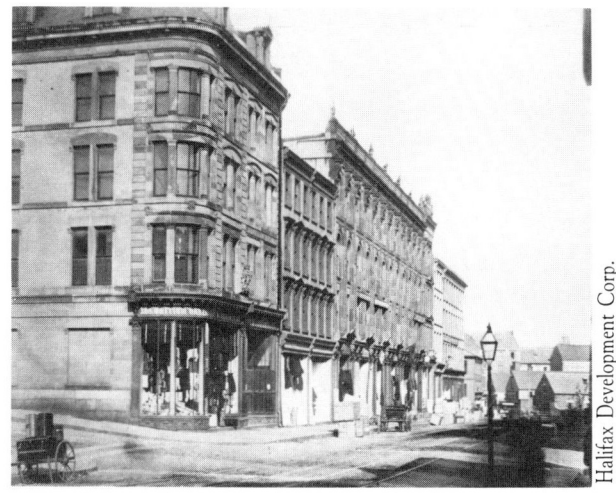

Photo 5.9.2 Original Facade ca. 1880

Halifax Development Corp.

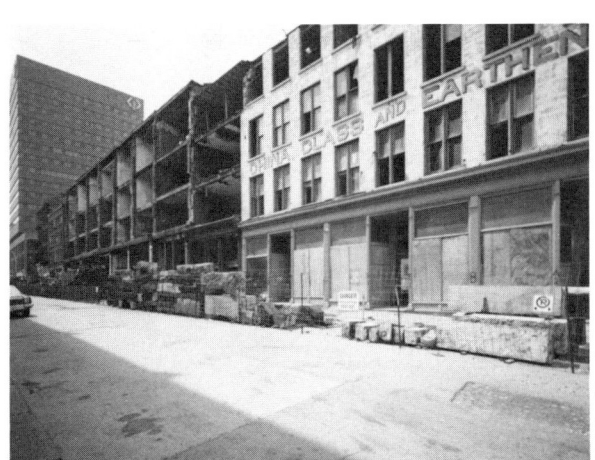

Photo 5.9.3: Numbered Pieces in Storage

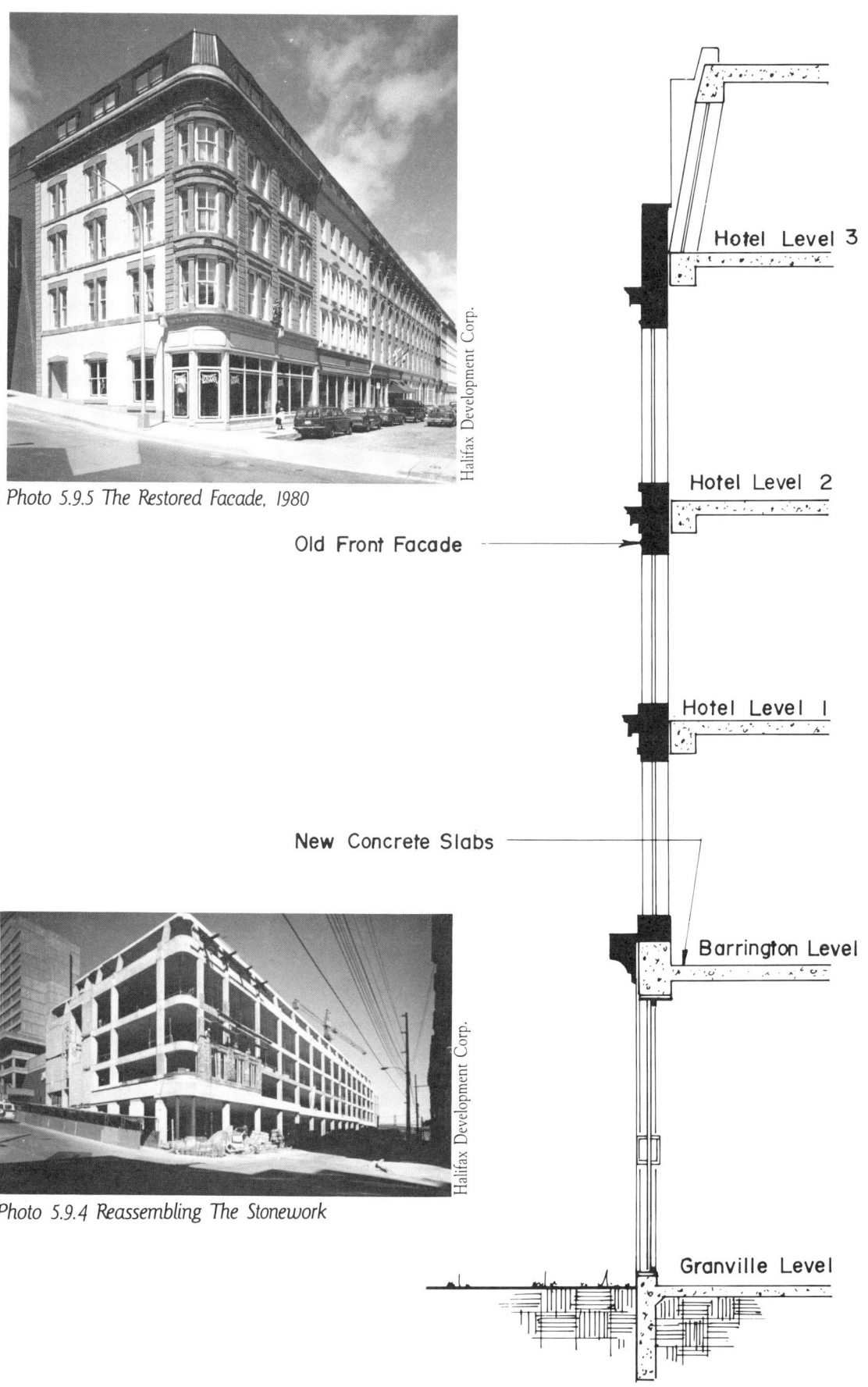

Photo 5.9.5 The Restored Facade, 1980

Photo 5.9.4 Reassembling The Stonework

Figure 5.9.3 - Retained facade cross section

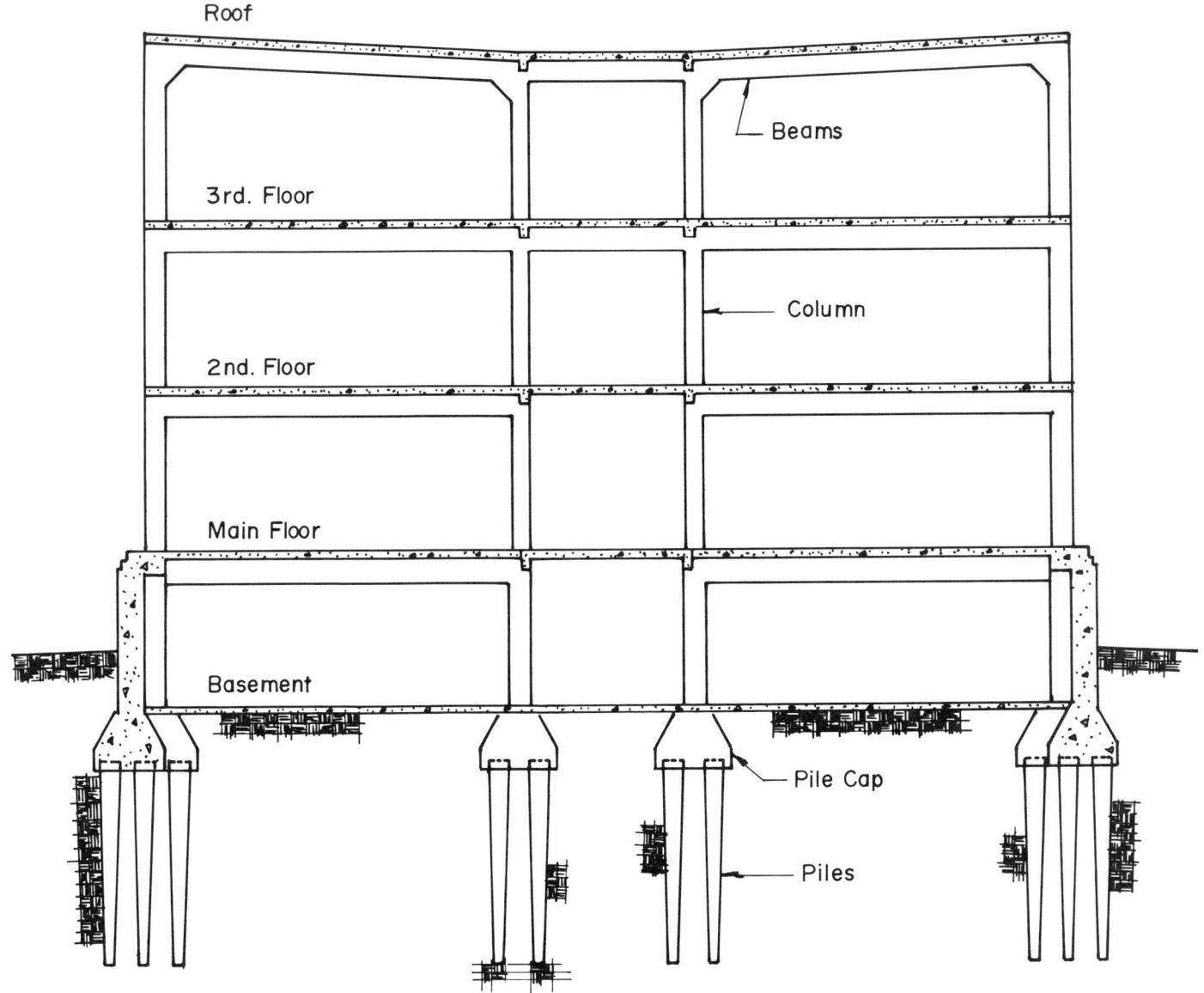

Figure 5.10.1 Building Cross Section

10. PROVINCIAL LEGISLATIVE BUILDING, REGINA

The Saskatchewan Legislative Building is a four-storey reinforced concrete structure, faced with granite and Tyndal stone. The building is situated on the Wascana Lake bank and founded upon rather short piles embedded in the Regina clay.

The building served well until the mechanical system of the West wing was renovated in 1968. Renovation activities included the installation of air ducts in the crawl space under the main floor. Unfortunately, air leaks caused drying of the sensitive clay, and a characteristic reduction in their volume. The result was an overall settlement of some 100mm and a differential settlement of 50 mm between the interior columns and the exterior walls. The reinforced concrete frame was ductile enough to withstand this differential settlement. The interior partitions suffered extensive cracking, and doors did not fit in their frames.

To prevent further settlement of the damaged pile support system, a new foundation was constructed. Jacked pipe piles of 220 mm diameter were installed beneath the existing pile caps. During this underpinning operation, the movements of the building were accurately monitored using photogrammetric techniques. Following the pile installation, a bank of seventy-two hydraulic jacks, each with a capacity of 45 tonnes, was used to return the wing to a near level condition. Portions of the exterior walls were lifted as much as

25 mm while some interior columns were raised 65 mm.

Project Information

Original Construction
Completed: October 1912
Owner: Province of Saskatchewan
Architect: E & W.S. Maxwell, Montreal

Rehabilitation
Structural Engineers: Donovan Engineering Ltd.
Contractor: W & R Foundation Specialists Ltd., Edmonton
Completed: April, 1983
Duration: Three months
Cost: $2.8 million including underpinning and mechanical system renovation
Conservation Techniques Used: Underpinning Photogrammetric Monitoring

Photo 5.10.1 Saskatchewan Legislature-West Wing

Photo 5.10.2 Pipe Piles

Photo 5.10.3 Broken Original Piles

11. MANITOBA TEACHER'S COLLEGE, WINNIPEG

The project studies in this chapter are either in construction or are completed with this exception. The proposed conversion and rehabilitation of the Manitoba Teacher's College is outstanding for a number of reasons. The sheer magnitude of the undertaking is impressive. As well, several social and economic considerations associated with the conservation are noteworthy.

The pre-conversion building is typical of early Western Canadian institutional buildings. The exterior is indigenous Manitoba Tyndal stone bearing walls, supporting wood frame floors and roof. The three storeys are typically high, giving ceiling heights approaching 3.6 m. The lowest floor is several feet below exterior grade.

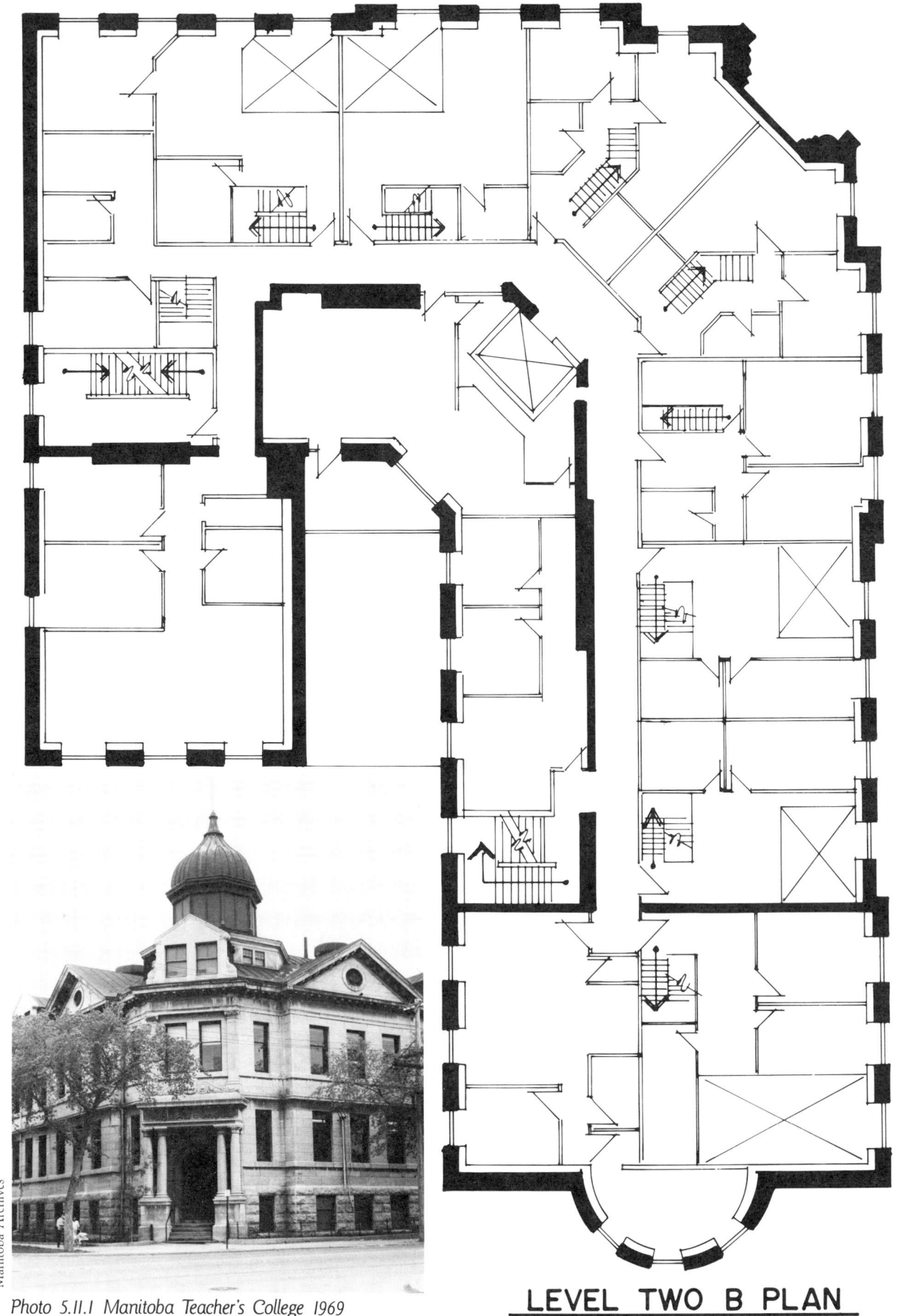

Photo 5.11.1 Manitoba Teacher's College 1969

LEVEL TWO B PLAN

Figure 5.11.1 Proposed New Floor Plan

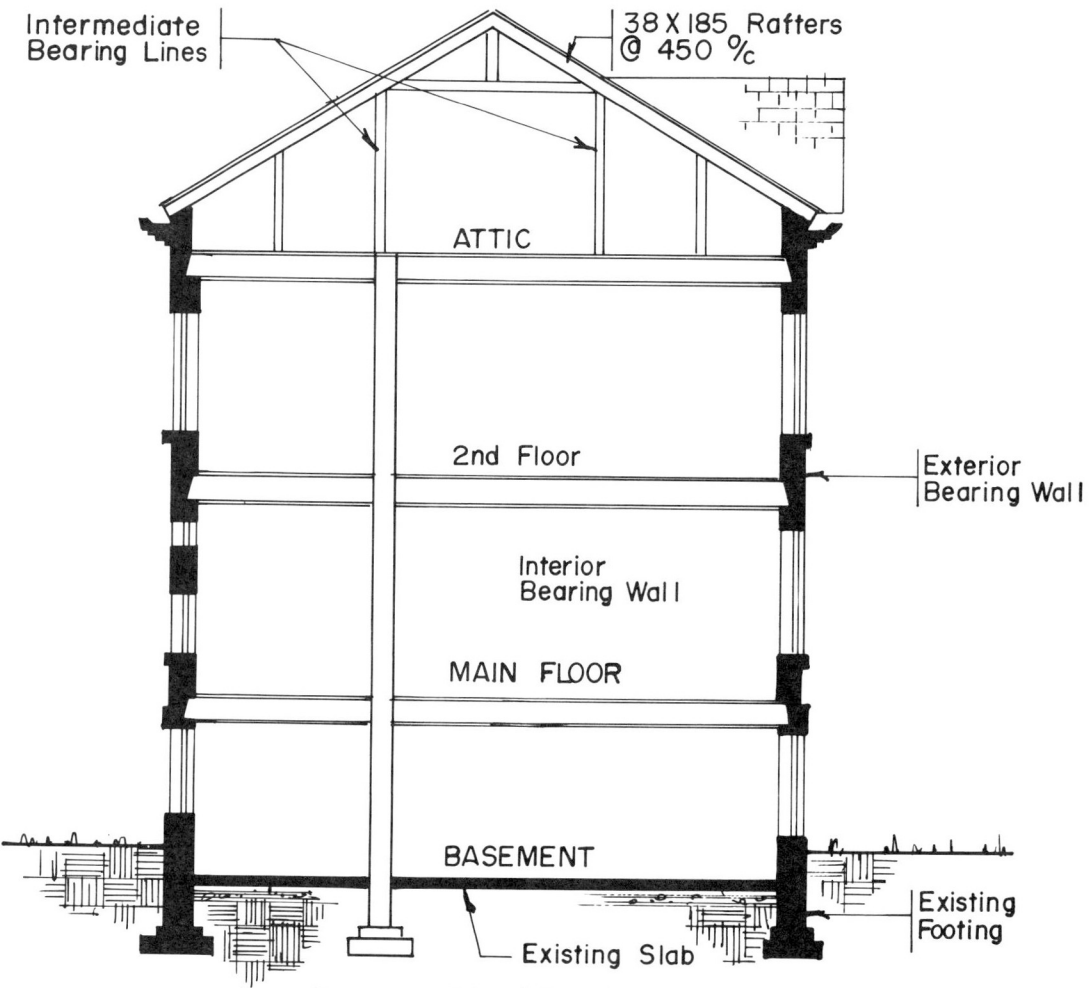

Figure 5.II.2 Original Cross Section

The decision to gut the building's interior was a natural one because the existing floor structure was dangerously combustible. As well, the large volume defined by the exterior shell offered the architects irresistible potentials. Five different proposals were prepared on how the space might be used. The final scheme envisions the creation of five useable floors, rather than the original three. In the process the structural elements, and the other building systems, will be upgraded to meet current fire code requirements.

The exterior walls are sound with one exception. There is a bulge in one area which has been restrained in the usual manner. Tie bolts were attached to the structure and extended to the exterior through holes drilled in the stone joints. An anchor plate was then attached to the exterior face. The structural engineer for this project has theorized that cross wall openings caused a rotation in the cross wall. This could have caused undue stress in the exterior wall. The tie plate and rod repair is typical of "band-aid" repairs applied to buildings of this vintage.

One of the most common causes of similar bulging is the shrinkage or deterioration of wood joists let into the exterior walls at each level. The infiltration of water initiates rot in the joists. They start to crush, causing movement in the wall. This in turn opens cracks that allow even more moisture to reach the joist. The entire process then accelerates in a cyclical pattern.

The project's intent is to provide family housing in an older neighbourhood of Winnipeg. The Winnipeg Housing Rehabilitation Corporation is seeking funding under the National Housing Act. Loans under this act require that the cost of housing in converted buildings must not exceed eighty per cent of the cost of equivalent new construction. Current costing for the project indicates that forty units can be provided at seventy six per cent of the cost of comparable new units. As stated in Chapter 1, many social benefits can

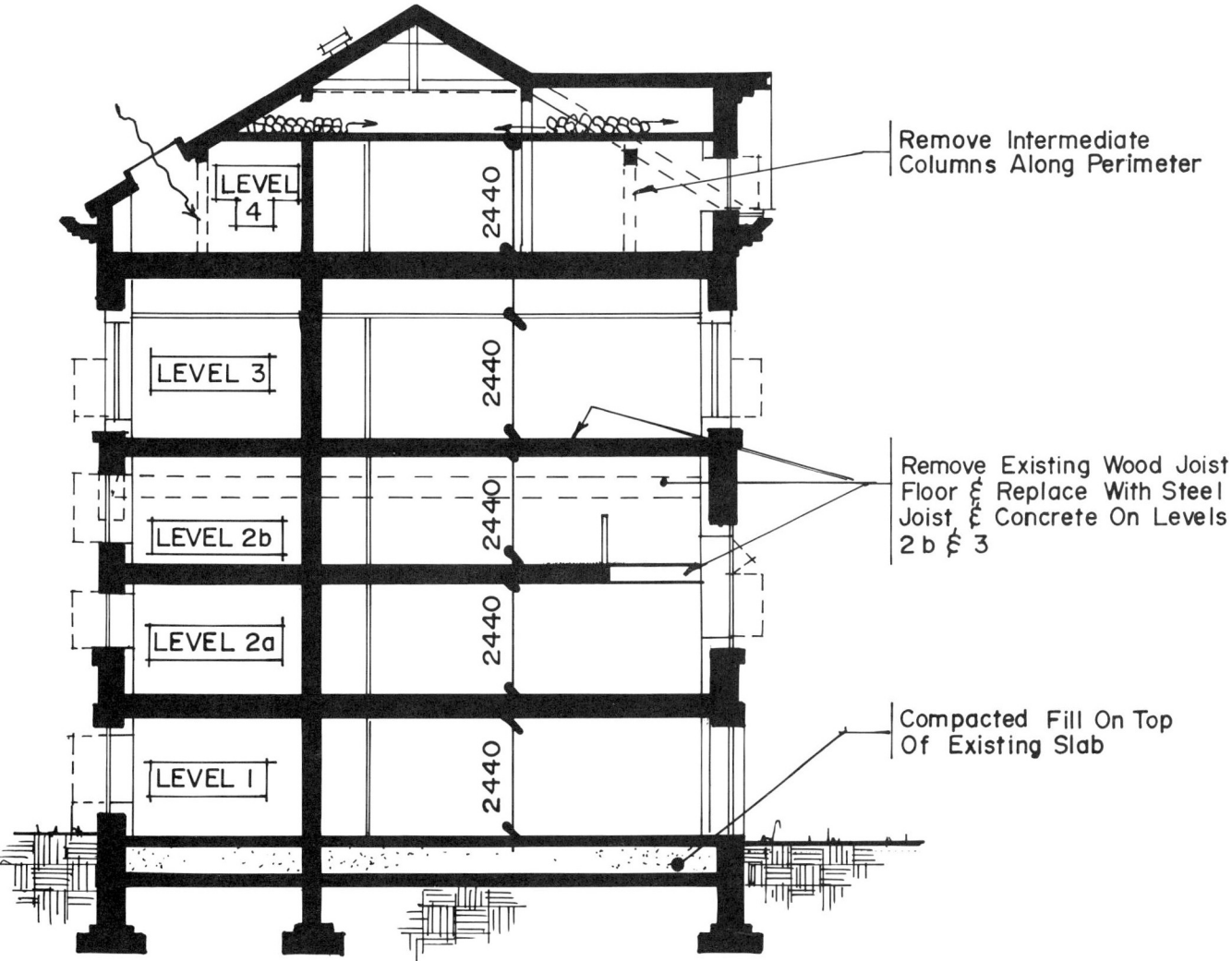

Figure 5.11.3 Proposed New Cross Section

derive from a restoration project. In this case economical family housing will be provided in an inner city location.

Although construction details are not yet available, the planned layout of exterior walls will allow the interior to be gutted with a minimum of external bracing. It may be possible to leave the walls free standing.

Project Information

Original Construction
Owner: Government of Manitoba
Architect: Samuel Hooper
Contracter: W. M. Rourke
Cost: $10,000 (1906 dollars)
Completed: ca. 1907

Proposed Renovation
Owner: Winnipeg Housing Rehabilitation Corporation
Architect: The Prairie Partnership
Structural Engineer: Wm. Hanuschak & Assoc. Ltd.
Construction: 1985 proposed
Cost: $1,640,074 ($41,000 per unit or $41.64 per square foot) in 1984 dollars for construction costs. Development soft costs are not included
Conservation Techniques To Be Used: Facade retention
Replace internal structure
Upgrade fire rating
Redefine internal volumes

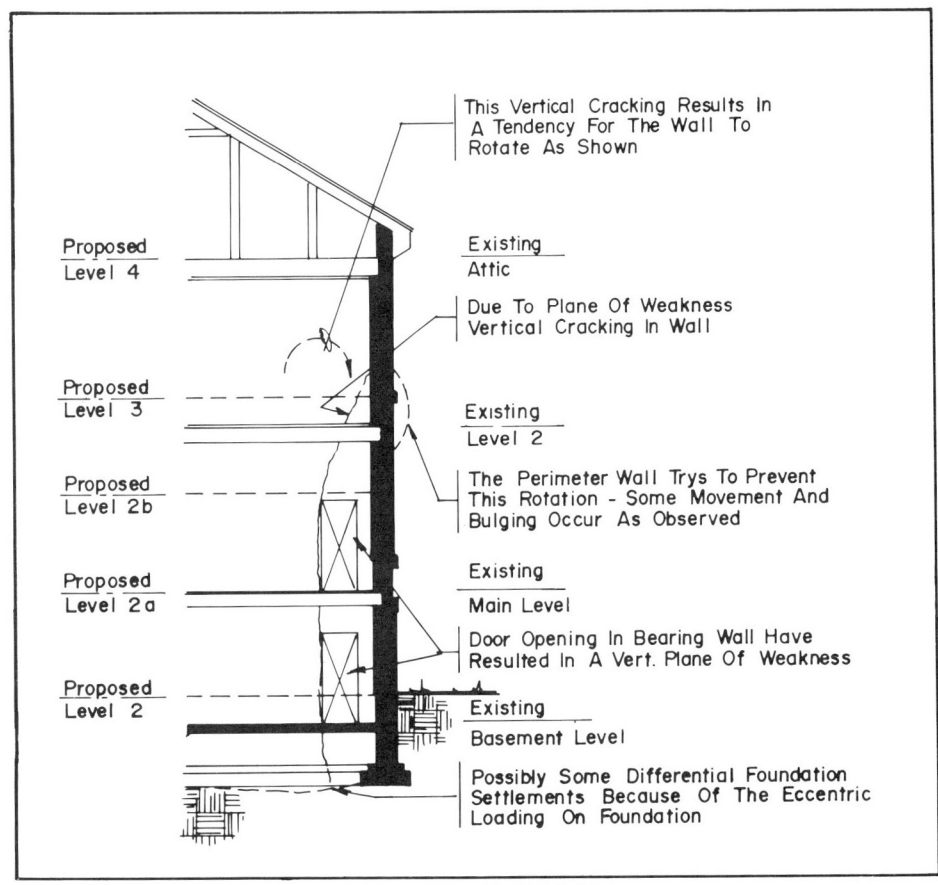

Figure 5.11.4 Section At Wall Distress

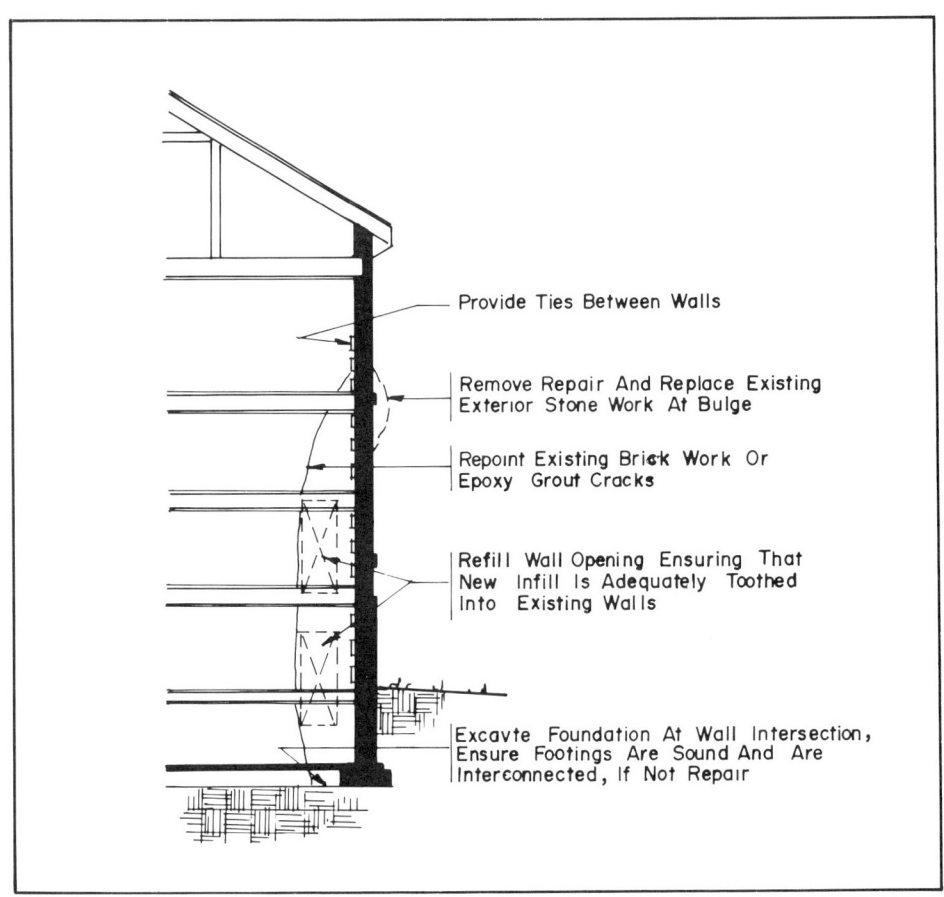

Figure 5.11.5 Proposed Wall Repair

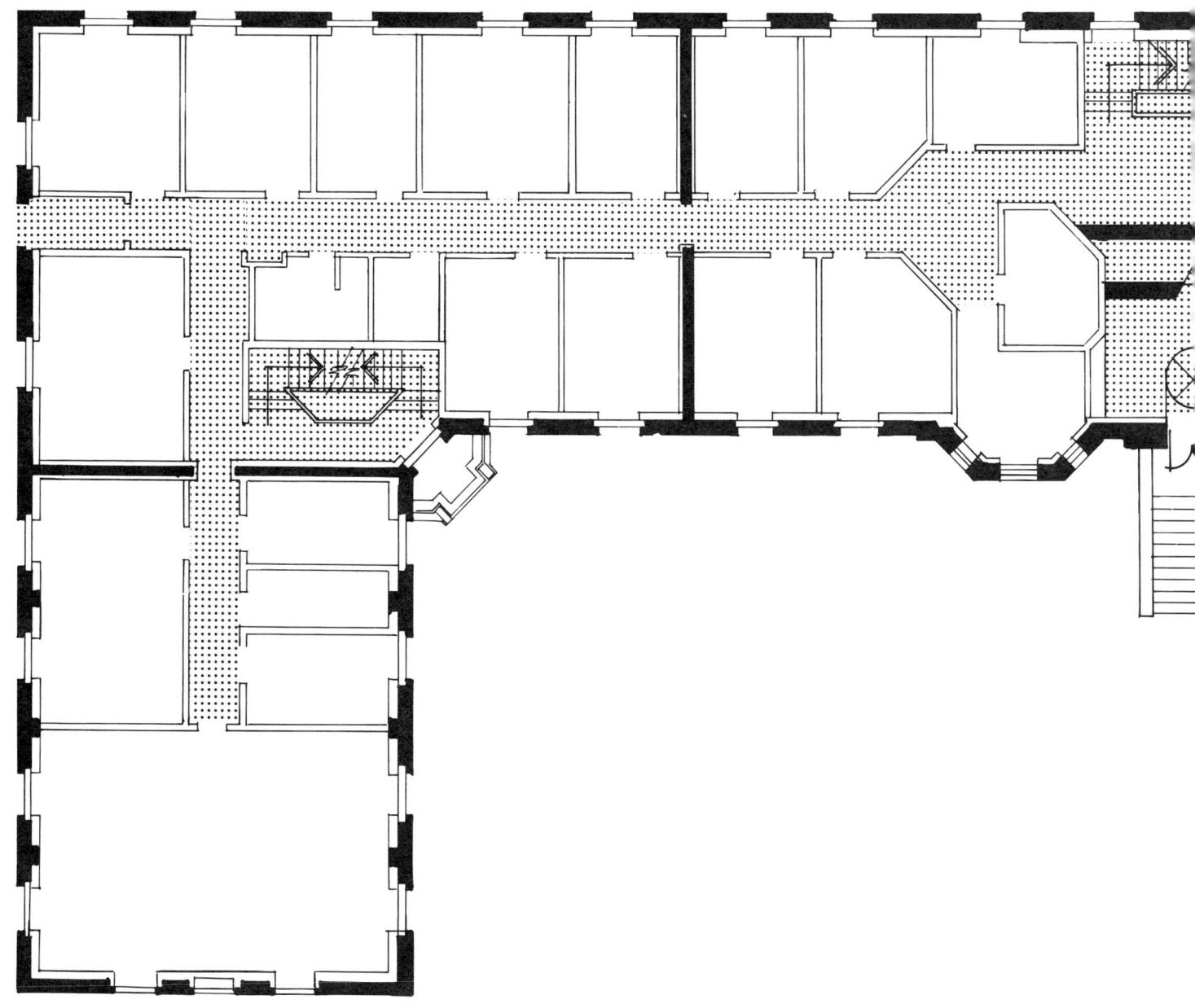

12. UNIVERSITY OF ALBERTA, EDMONTON

The following project studies cover the renovation of three of the original buildings on the University of Alberta campus. They were sited adjacent to each other and were renovated consecutively between 1975 and 1982.

Each project was carried out in a different manner. The specific conditions of the buildings differed as did the preferences of the contractor for each project.

The Pembina Hall renovation does not include any structural techniques relevent to this study. It is included as it is an integral part of this renovation series, and the costing information provided will be of interest.

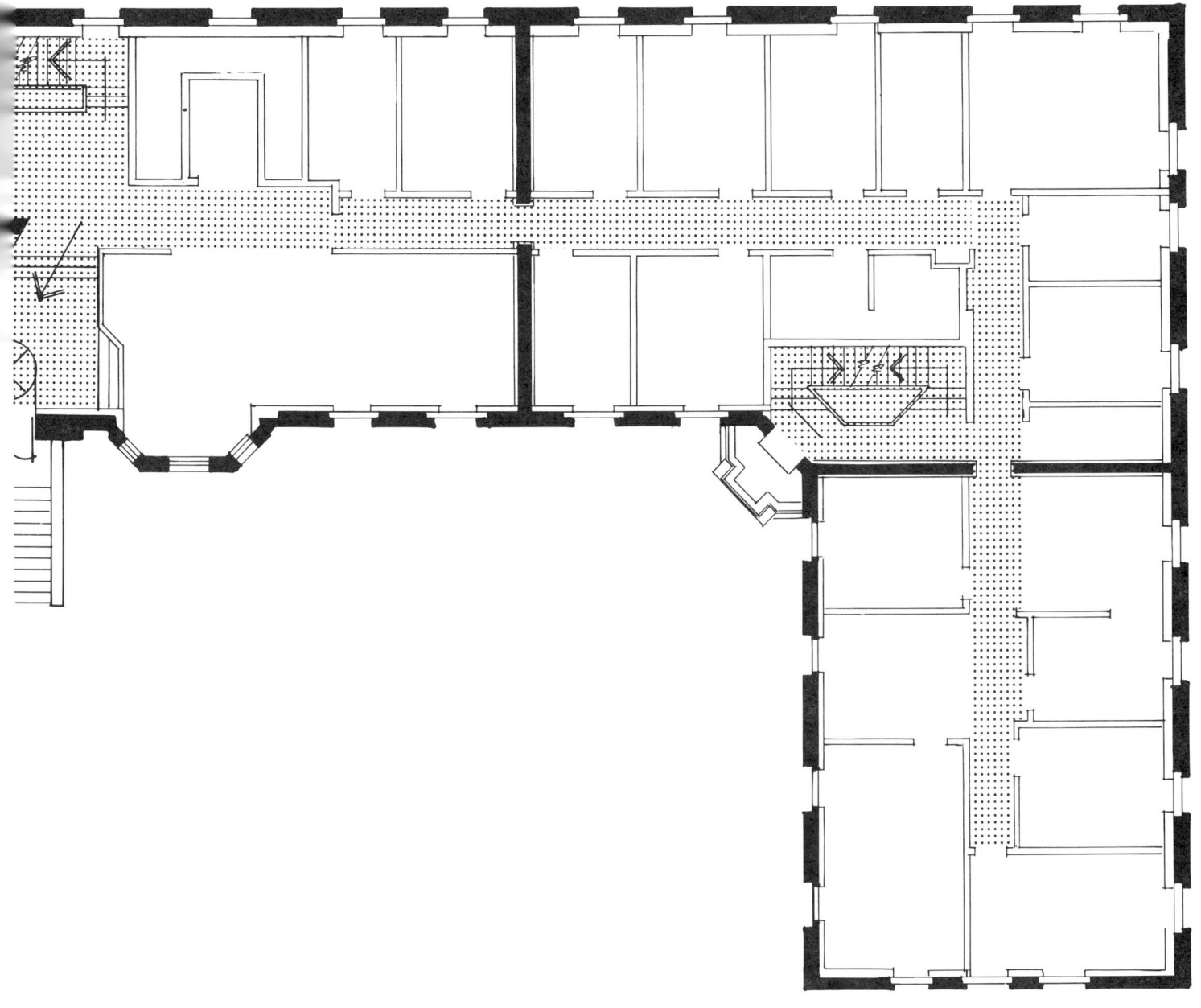

Figure 5.12.1 Typical Floor Plan

a) Pembina Hall

The third oldest of the University of Alberta buildings, Pembina Hall was closed in 1974 because of serious fire code deficiencies.

After lengthy debate and a close threat of demolition, it was decided to renovate. The original structure was reinforced concrete slabs on gypsum block bearing walls.

As the structure was still sound, it was necessary only to upgrade fire separations and exiting, and to install new mechanical and electrical systems. The renovation was carried out at less than one-half the cost of equivalent new space at the time.

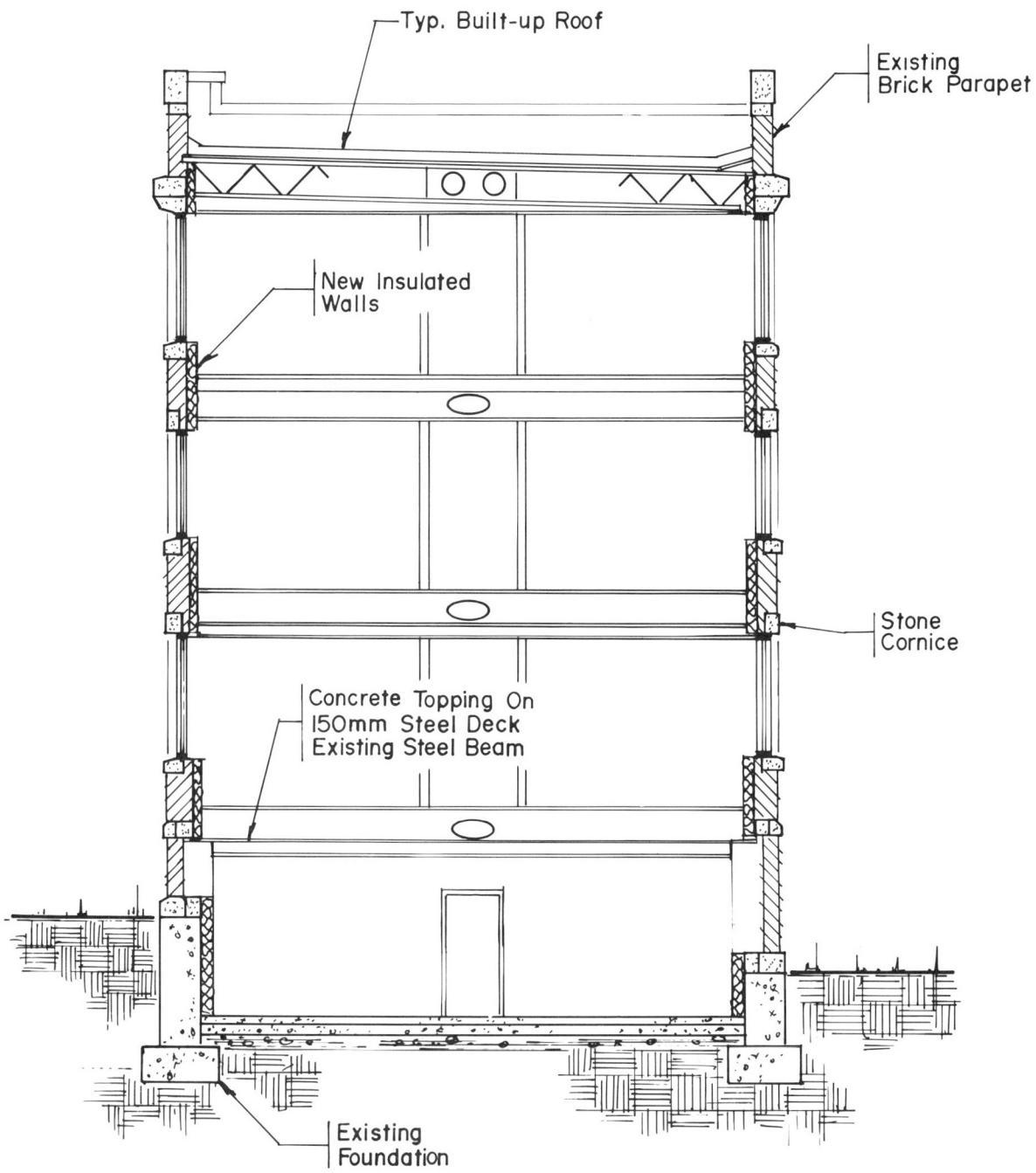

Figure 5.12.2 Typical Cross Section — Athabasca Hall

Project Information

Original Construction
Owner: University of Alberta
Architect: C. Burgess
Completed: 1914

Renovations
Owner/Developer: University of Alberta
Architect: Bittorf Holland Christiansen
Structural Engineer: J.A. Illmayer

Photo 5.12.1: University of Alberta - Aerial View ca. 1919

Photo 5.12.2 Pembina Hall After Renovation

Photo 5.12.3 Athabasca Hall ca. 1912

Contractor:	A.V. Carlson Construction Ltd.
Completed:	1975
Duration:	1 year
Cost:	$810,000 (1975 dollars) which equals $200.00 per square metre including restoration of millwork, new exits, completely new mechanical and electrical systems
Conservation Technique Used:	Adaptive reuse Fire code upgrading

b) Athabasca Hall

This was the first building on the University campus. The structure was framed in wood with load-bearing exterior walls.

In 1974, it was determined that fire code and structural deficiencies necessitated either demolition or extensive renovation. A "design-build" proposal was requested from three contractors for a fee of $4000 each.

The winning bid was submitted by Poole Construction (PCL). PCL braced the exterior walls externally, erected a tower crane on a concrete footing outside the building and proceeded to gut the interior. The existing floor and roof structures were removed, and new clearspan open-web steel joist floors were added. Parts of the original millwork were stored, refinished, and reincorporated in the new building. After dismantling the crane, the base was left in place and incorporated in the landscaping.

The cost of renovations were equivalent to the replacement costs of a new building at the time.

Project Information

Original Construction

Owner:	University of Alberta
Architect:	A.M. Jeffers / Nobbs & Hyde
Completed:	1911

Renovation

Owner:	University of Alberta
Architect:	Bittorf Holland Christiansen
Structural Engineer:	Illmayer/Sivam Consultants Ltd.

Photo 5.12.5 Selective Demolition, Athabasca Hall

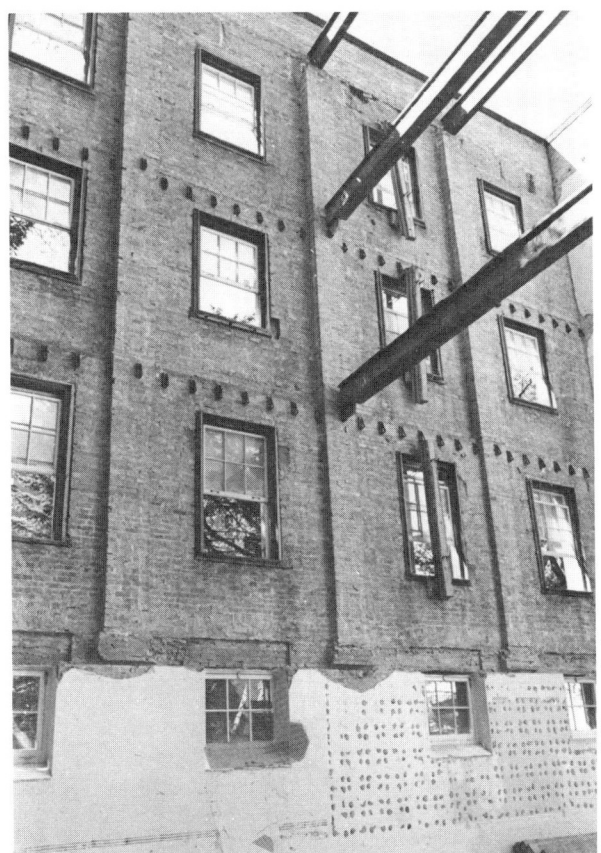

Photo 5.12.4 Selective Demolition, Athabasca Hall

Photo 5.12.6 Athabasca Hall After Renovation

Photo 5.12.7 Tower Crane at Athabasca Hall

Contractor:	Poole Construction Ltd.
Completed:	1977
Duration:	Sixteen months
Developed Area:	4,600 square metres
Costs:	$1,855,000 (1978 dollars) including new floor and roof structures, interior finishes and new mechanical and electrical systems
Conservation Techniques Used:	Selective Demolition Structural Replacement Facade Retention Fire Code Upgrading Adaptive Reuse

c) Assiniboia Hall

Assiniboia Hall was the second of the three halls to be completed originally, and was the last to be renovated.

Based on the experience of the previous two projects, it was decided to tender this contract on a full

Photo 5.12.8 Assiniboia Hall- New Floor Construction

Photo 5.12.9 Assiniboia Hall - New Roof Construction

set of drawings. The contractor was left latitude only in the method of temporary support of walls and sequence of demolition.

The original and new structural systems are identical to that of Athabasca Hall. However, the contractor opted for the use of mobile cranes rather than a tower crane. He also carried out an in-depth study of the wide U-shape of the building. He found that no wall bracing was required if the floors were removed and replaced in sections rather than gutting it all at one time.

Considerable work was required on sandstone detailing in the exterior walls. Elements which had to be removed were replaced with matching precast concrete.

Project Information

Original Construction
Owner: University of Alberta
Architect: C. Burgess
Completed: 1912

Renovation
Owner: University of Alberta
Architect: Bittorf Holland Christiansen
Structural Engineer: Illmayer/Sivam Consultants Ltd.
Contractor: P & M Construction Ltd.
Completed: 1982
Duration: One year
Developed Area: 4,600 square metres

Photo 5.12.10 Assiniboia Hall After Renovation

Costs: $2,983,000 (1981 dollars) including new finishes, exterior wall repairs, new structural, mechanical and electrical systems

Structural Costs:
 Demolition: $182,000.
 Excavation: $ 63,000.
 Rebar & concrete: $270,000.
 Structural steel & deck: $340,000.
 Masonry & precast: $132,000.

Conservation Techniques Used:
 Selective Demolition
 Structural Replacement
 Fire Code Upgrading
 Facade Retention
 Adaptive Reuse

13. UNIVERSITY OF QUEBEC, MONTREAL

The construction of the University of Quebec, Montreal campus is an example of a major institutional redevelopment of an historic site. The project included the total redevelopment of two city blocks in the Latin Quarter of Montreal. One church structure was retained intact to act as a chapel for the University. The clock tower and south transept wall of the other major church on the site were retained and integrated into the new University structures.

The main construction techniques used in redevelopment on this site were facade retention, selective demolition, and reinforcing for seismic loading. It is interesting to note that in facade retention the transept wall and clock tower were left free-standing during the construction period. These elements were selected because they had sufficient lateral resistance to remain unbraced during construction. As well, they had great architectural significance.

The transept wall is connected by a structural steel truss roof to the balance of the structure. The base of the clock tower is buttressed with new reinforced concrete members. Both elements are securely tied into the earthquake resisting system and the new buildings. Considerable shoring and underpinning of the existing structures was also carried out.

Major portions of the development are below grade. There are under-street connections between the north and south blocks of the campus, as well as a direct tie-in to the major hub station of the Montreal subway system.

Project Information

Original Construction
Owner: Catholic Archdiocese of Montreal

Redevelopment
Owner: Province of Quebec
Architect: Dimakoupoulos Associates/Jodoin LeMarre Pratte
Structural Engineers: Nicollet Carrier Dressel Mercille
Contractor: Louis Donolo & Sons
Completed: 1979
Duration: Two and one-half years
Conservation Techniques Used: Shoring and underpinning
Facade retention
Seismic upgrading
Selective Demolition

Photo 5.13.1 St. Jacques Church ca. 1975

Photo 5.13.2: UQAM Clock Tower

Photo 5.13.3 South Transept Wall

Photo 5.13.6 Interior of Transept Wall

Photo 5.13.4 Tower and Wall Freestanding

Photo 5.13.5 Clock Tower Buttresses

14. BANK OF COMMERCE, EDMONTON

The bank building at 100th Street and Jasper Avenue in Edmonton may not be considered a heritage structure. Recent construction at the site, however, is a good example of the use of a transfer system and jacked pipe pile underpinning.

When the City of Edmonton finalized its plans for a rapid transit system to be operational for their hosting of the 1978 Commonwealth Games, the alignment chosen ran beneath five buildings northeast of the Central Station on Jasper Avenue. This seven-storey bank was one of these buildings. Its spread footings were only 3.6 metres above the lining of the transit tubes. As these tubes were to be installed using a tunnelling mole, it was not feasible to support the foundation loads on the tunnel lining. The decision was made to pick the loads up on a series of transfer beams. These would span over the tunnel right of way and rest on pipe piles jacked into the ground.

To maintain the buildings banking operations, including the secure use of the vault in the basement, the entire operation was accessed from an adjacent shaft and tunnels beneath the structure. The restricted access and working depth available made the selection of post-tensioned concrete beams a logical choice. The entire underpinning system was pre-loaded to reduce potentional settlement.

Project Information

Original Construction
Opened: 1952
Owner: Bank of Commerce
Architect: Rule, Wynn & Rule/ AJ Everat
Structural Engineers: Margison & Babcock
Contractor: WC Wells Construction Ltd.

Rehabilitation
Developer: City of Edmonton
Structural Engineers: BW Brooker Engineering Ltd.
Contractor: Mergentine
Completed: 1976
Conservation Techniques Used: Underpinning

Photo 5.14.1: CIBC - Access Tunnel

Photo 5.14.4 Underpinning Pile Group

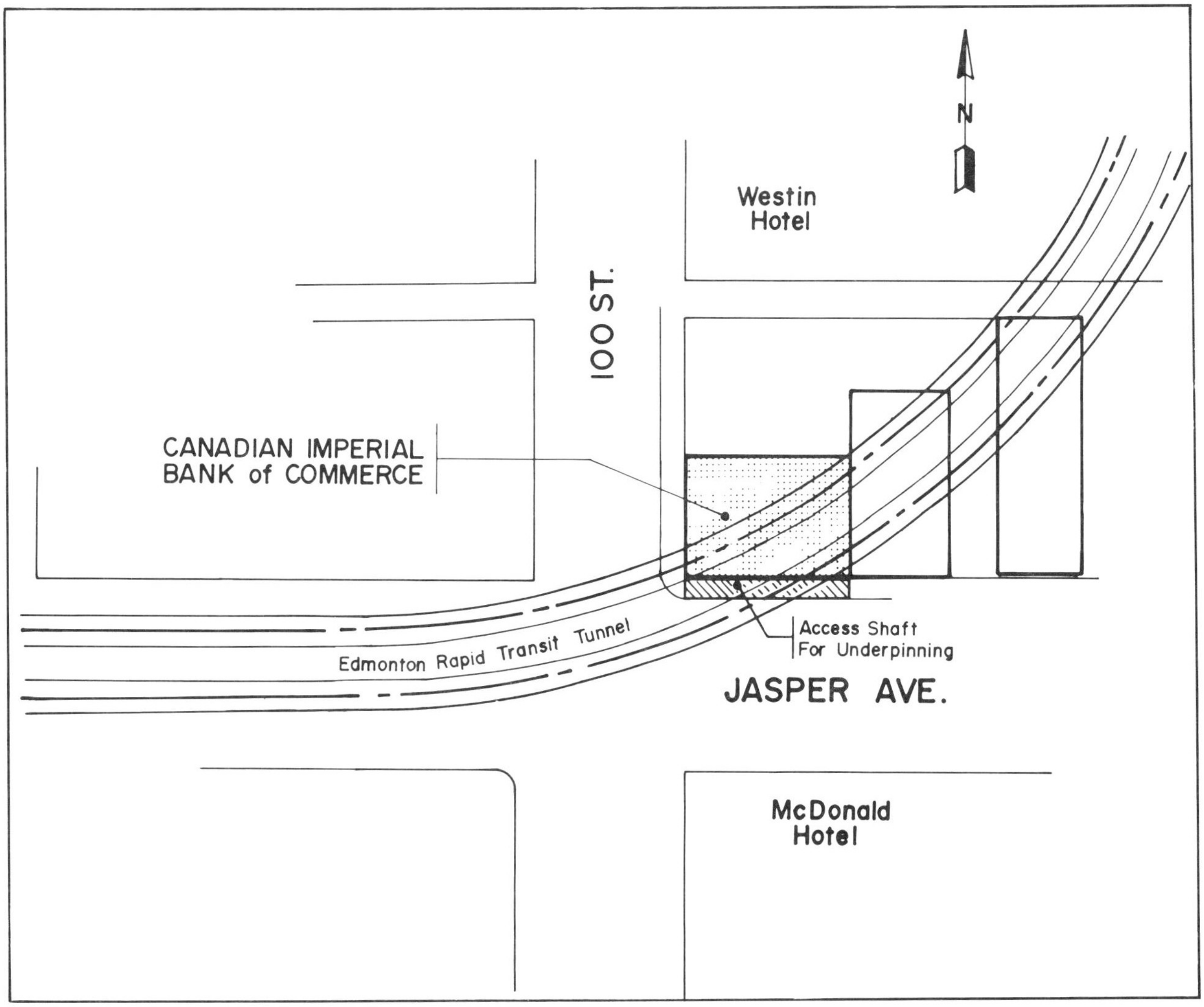

Figure 5.14.1 Location Plan

B.W. Brooker Engineering

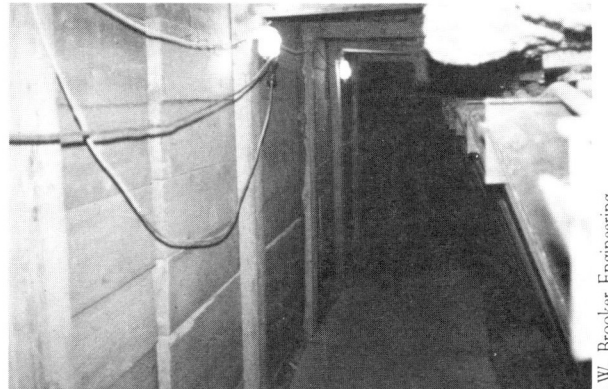

Photo 5.14.2 Tunnel Shoring

B.W. Brooker Engineering

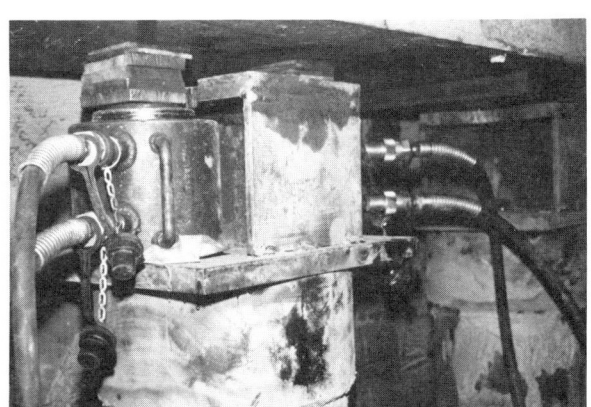

Photo 5.14.3 Preloading a Pile

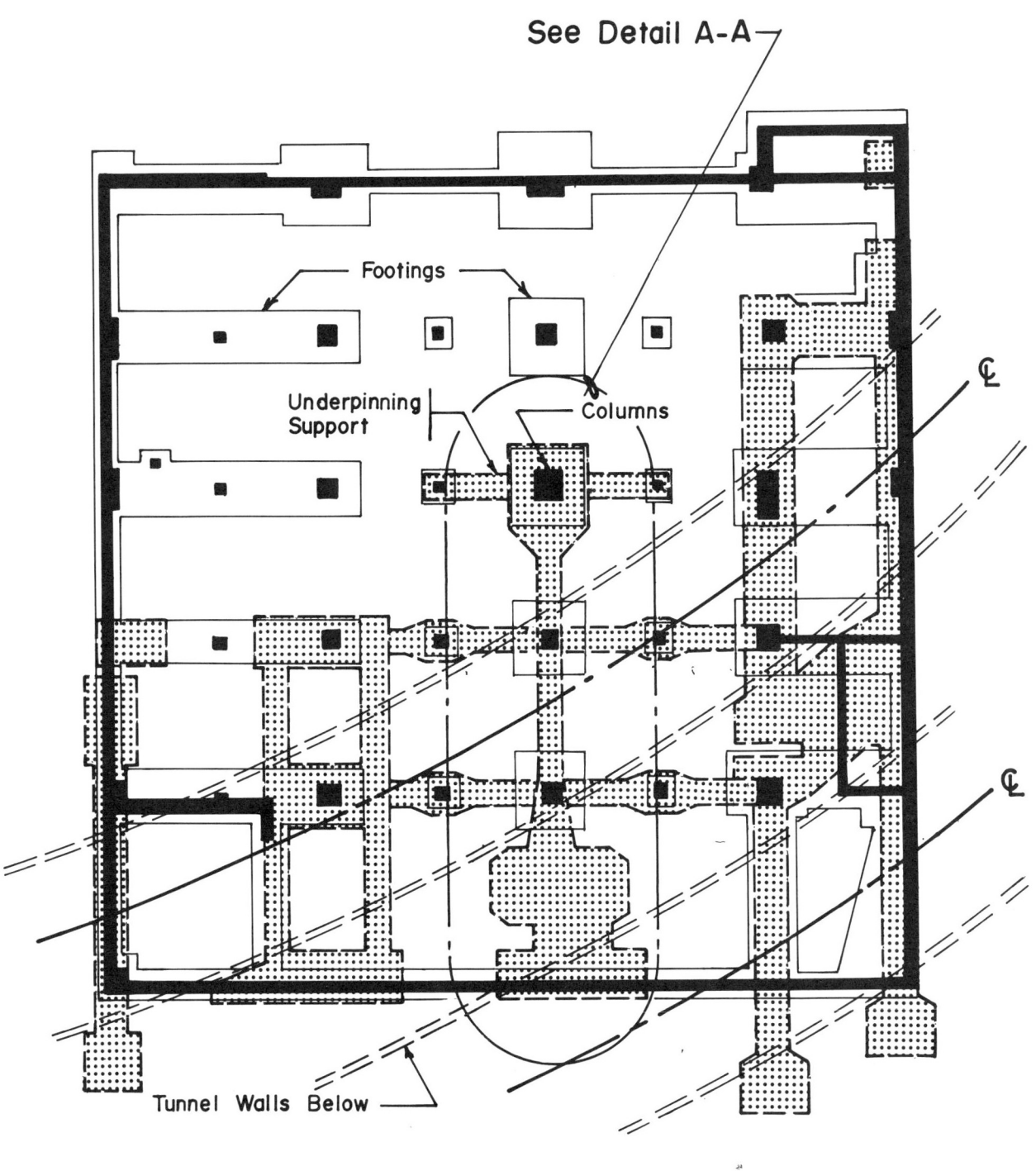

Figure 5.14.2 Tunnel and Beam Plan

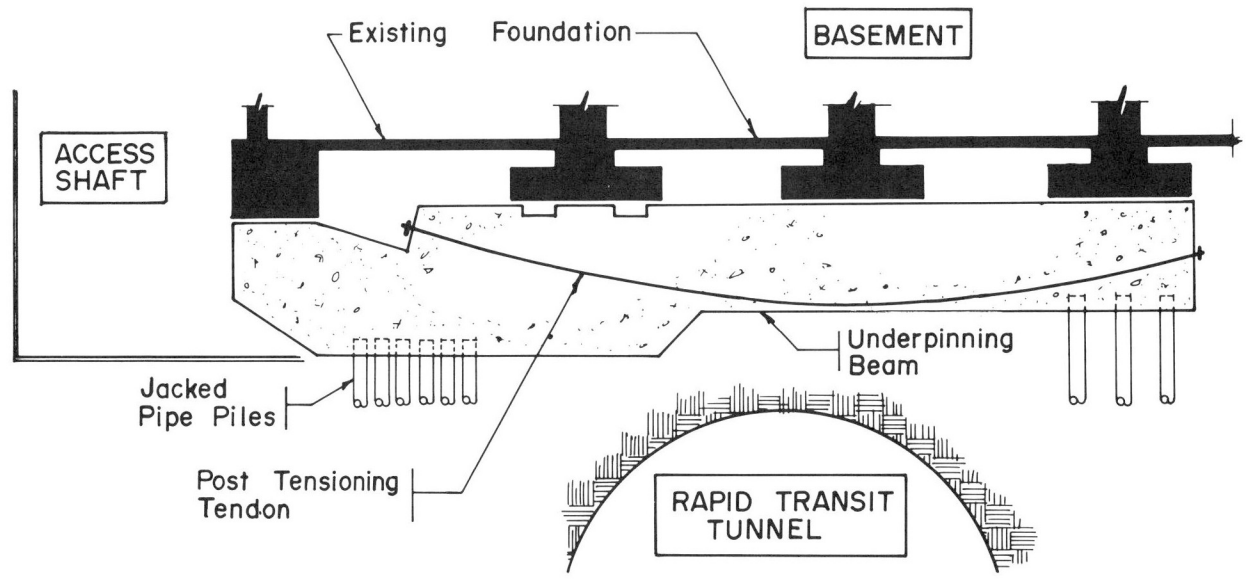

SECTION B-B

Figure 5.14.3 Beam Cross Section

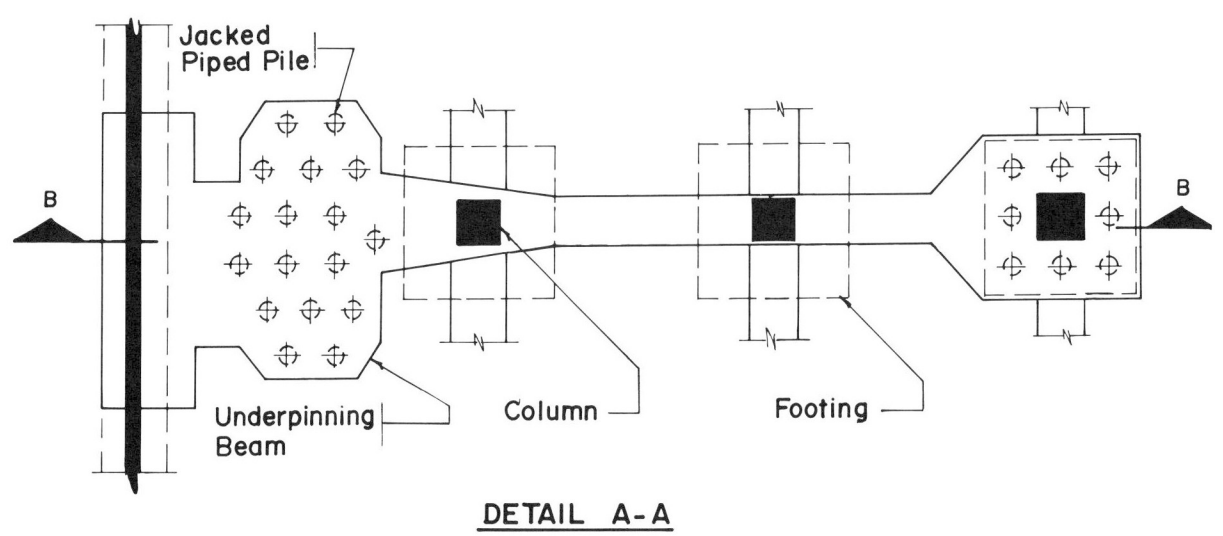

DETAIL A-A

Figure 5.14.4 Beam Plan Detail

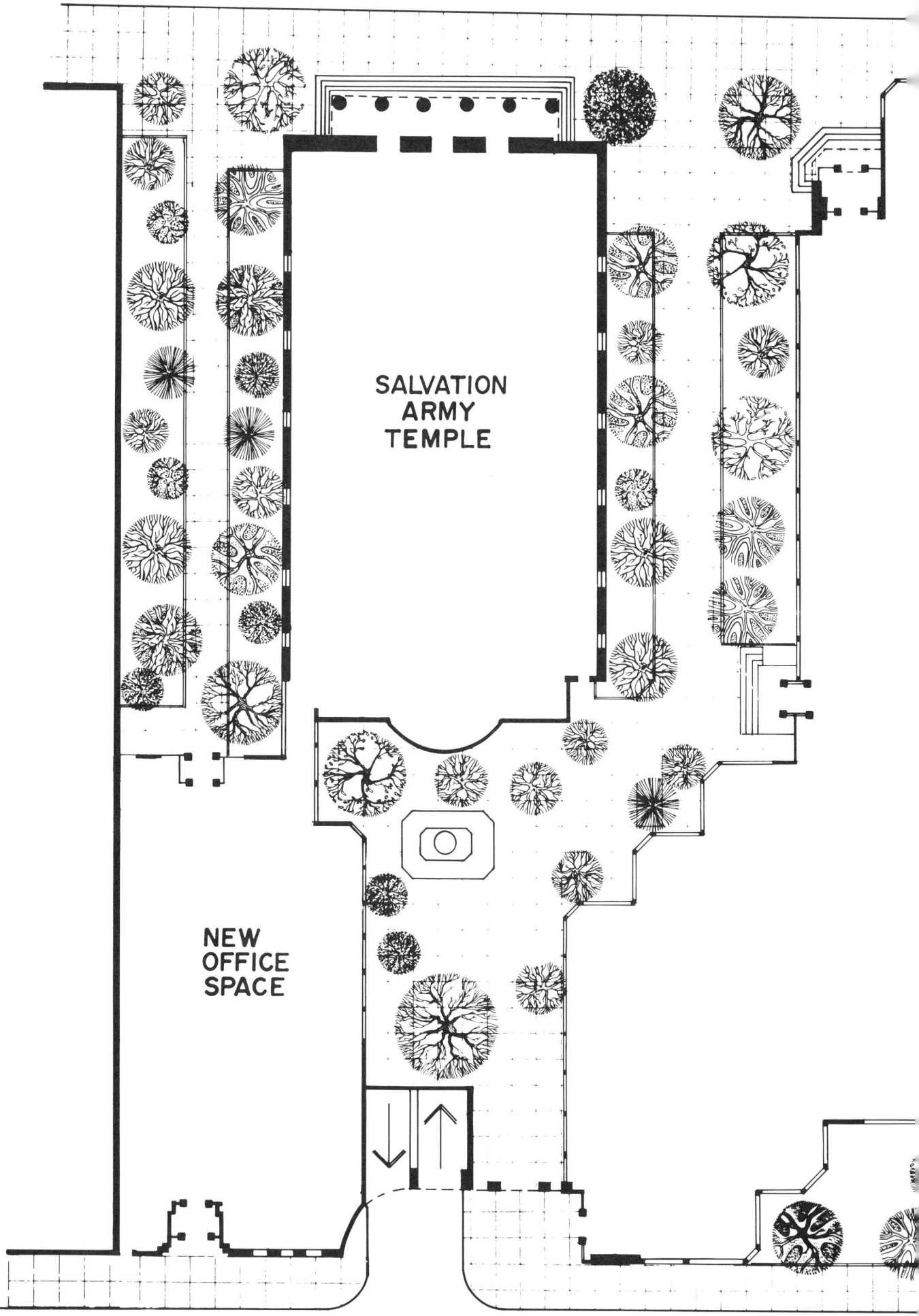

Figure 5.15.1 Key Plan—Maison Alcan

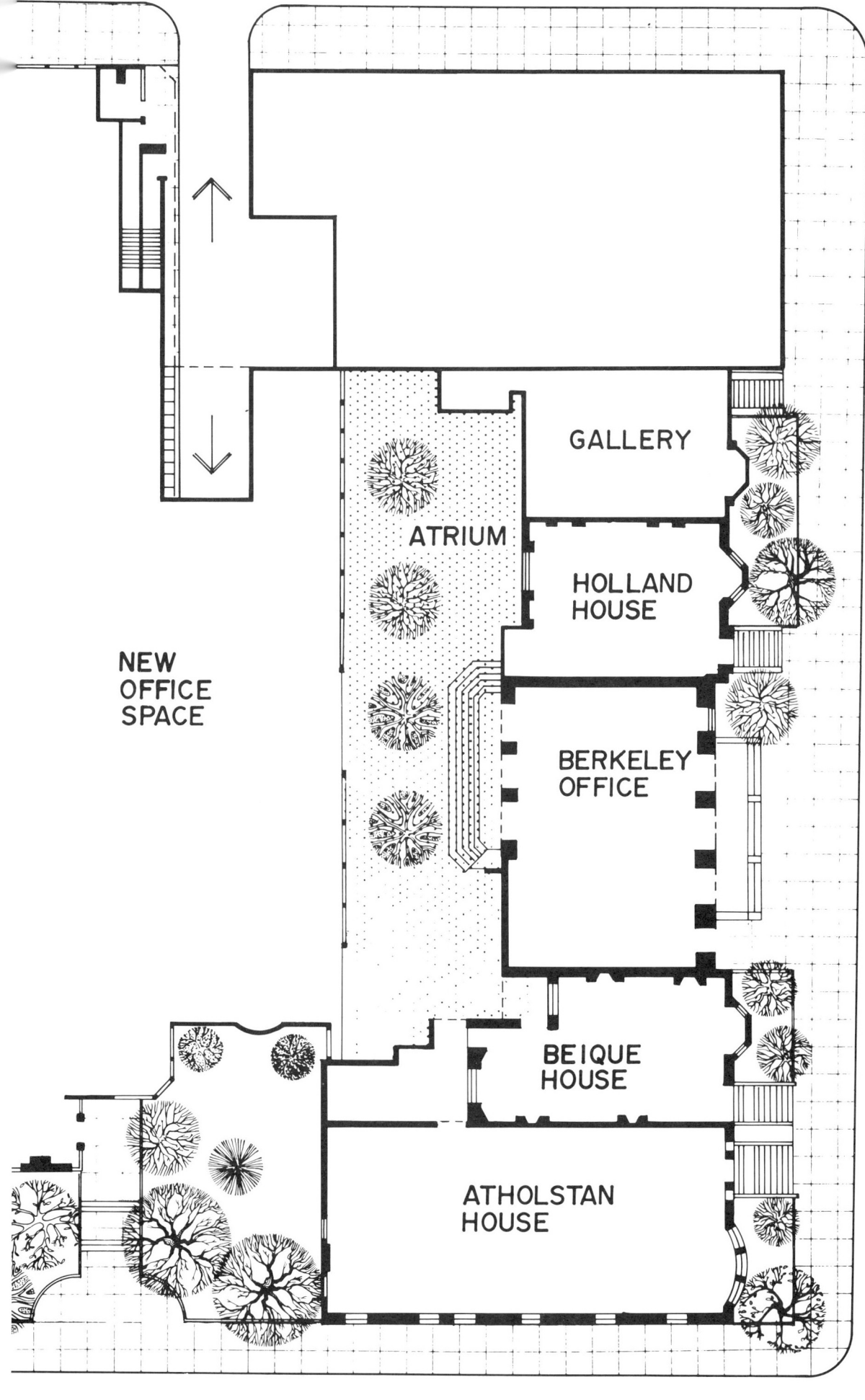

15. MAISON ALCAN, MONTREAL

This outstanding project involves the redevelopment of most of a city block in downtown Montreal. The principal heritage elements retained are several of the grand old private dwellings for which Sherbrooke Street is well known, the Berkeley Hotel, and the Salvation Army Citadel.

The Salvation Army Citadel was left untouched and is free-standing in a garden courtyard. More recent construction on the South portion of the site was demolished to make way for redevelopment. This included a major horizontal addition, connected by an atrium to the South side of the retained houses and hotel on Sherbrooke Street. The new office construction is of a height that does not overpower the mansions on Sherbrooke Street. In fact, it is barely noticeable from most viewpoints along this major thoroughfare.

The restored Salvation Army Citadel will continue to be used as a church by this organization. The Berkeley Hotel and the private residences on Sherbrooke Street have been converted for use as office space for ALCAN's head office functions.

As well as being a corporate showcase for a multi-national corporation, this project is a showcase of construction techniques which can be used in redeveloping heritage sites.

Some of the techniques used here were:
- shoring and underpinning of sensitive structures
- controlled, monitored blasting for rock excavation
- long span support beams spanning over the existing roofs to support the new atrium
- replacement of deteriorated wood framed floors
- removal of main floor columns in a concrete frame to open up circulation at the main entrance

Externally, the existing structures were restored as closely as was practical to their original condition. Internally, the preservation policy was to restore public areas and adapt private rooms from residential to office use, while preserving the elegant Victorian style. The interior configuration of the Berkeley Hotel could not be adapted for office use and was demolished and rebuilt to meet the requirements of a modern office structure. However, through architectural elements, decorative elements and the use of warm, rich colours ALCAN attempted to re-create an ambiance of the 1920's.

The importance of the Sherbrooke Street location required the restoration of the exterior facades facing it. This required selective demolition of recent additions on the Berkeley Hotel, revealing three "braided" arches which serve as the main entrance to the complex. As well, a bay window in the Holland House, and front stairs for the Beique House were restored.

In addition to the ALCAN building, ALCAN constructed a six-storey office building on the site for the Salvation Army. This was in exchange for exterior architectural control and certain land exchanges, an exemplary case of co-operative development. A consolidated lease on the upper storeys of the Klinkoff Galerie was negotiated, allowing ALCAN additional integrated office space. Klinkhoff continues to operate in three floors of commercial space. This property was renovated by ALCAN and the Klinkoff Galerie. The gallery was temporarily relocated, at ALCAN's expense, in the adjacent Holland House while renovations were carried out.

ALCAN has stated that the overall project cost is competitive with that of other first-class office towers in the Montreal area.

A major stumbling block in the design process was the strict adherence to building code provisions which the City of Montreal officials required. As several of the heritage structures had wood frame floors, a fire separation was required between adjacent units (provided by existing masonry partywalls) and, between the combustible structures and the atrium (provided by existing masonry walls and rolling steel shutters on all openings linked to the smoke detection system).

Project Information

Original Construction
Atholstan House
Completed: 1895
Architect: A.F. Dunlop
Owner: Hugh Graham (Lord Atholstan)

Beique House
Completed: 1894

Berkeley Hotel (formerly Hermitage Apartments)
Completed: 1928
Architect: Lawson & Little

Holland House
Completed: 1872
Architect: W.T. Thomas
Owner: Holland family

Salvation Army Citadel (formerly Emmanuel Congregational Church)
Completed: 1907

Architect:	Saxe & Archibald		including renovations of existing properties, 30,000 square metres of new office space, atrium and "mini-park", and three levels of underground parking
Architectural Style:	Green Revival		

Redevelopment

Owner/Developer:	ALCAN Aluminum Ltd.		
Architect:	ARCOP Associates		
Structural Engineers:	Quinn Dressel Associates and Shector Barbacki Shemie	Conservation Techniques Used:	Selective Demolition Fire Code Upgrading Controlled Blasting Shoring and Underpinning Column Removal
Contractor:	Concordia Management Ltd.		
Completed:	May 1983		
Duration:	Two years		
Costs:	$43 million (1981 dollars)		

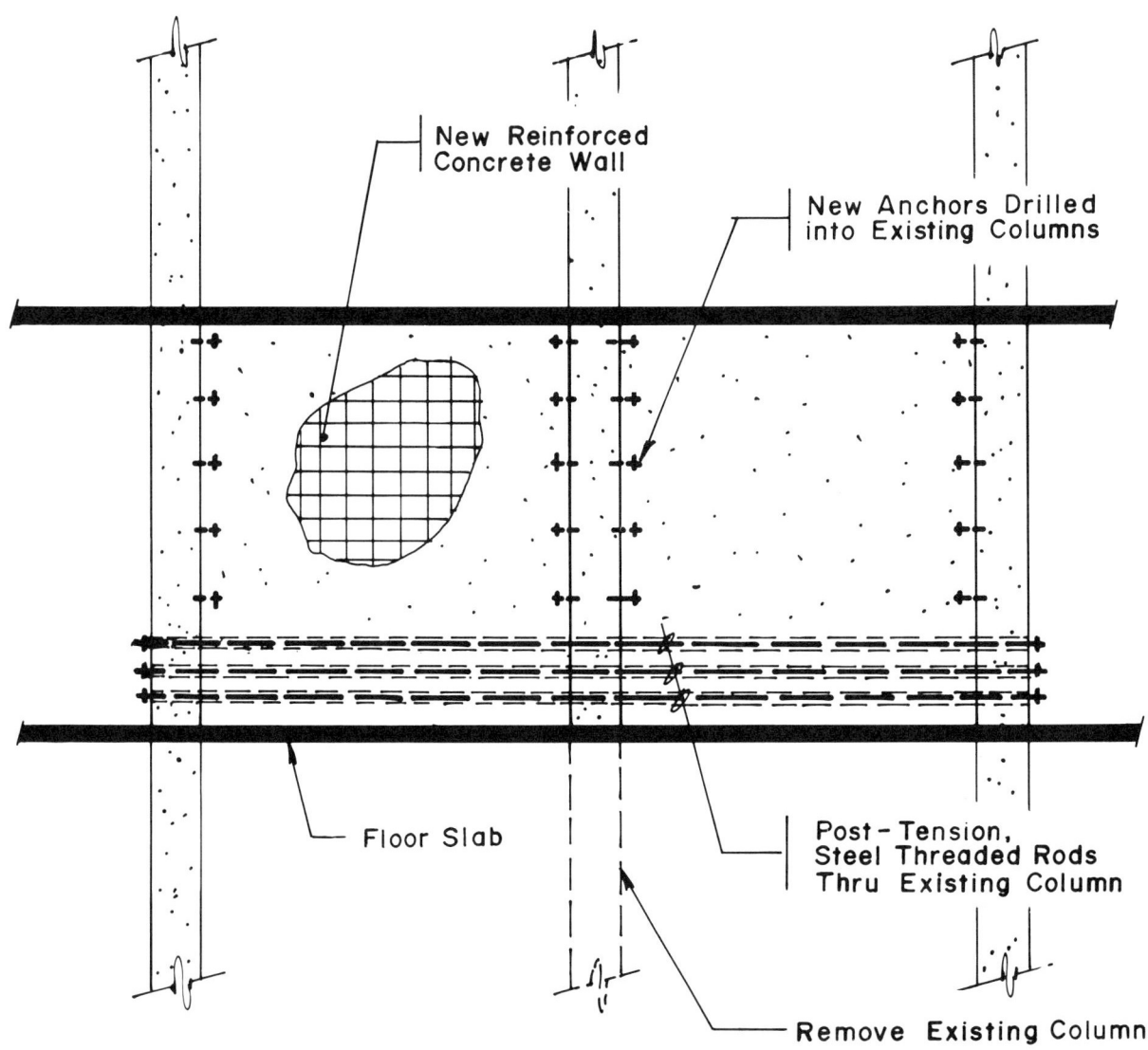

Figure 5.15.2 Permanent Support for Removed Column

Photo 5.15.1: ALCAN - Sherbrooke Street View

Photo 5.15.2 Sherbrooke Street View

Photo 5.15.3 Atrium

Photo 5.15.4 Atrium Roof

Photo 5.16.2 Model of Redevelopment

Photo 5.16.1: 53 State Street - Prior to Redevelopment

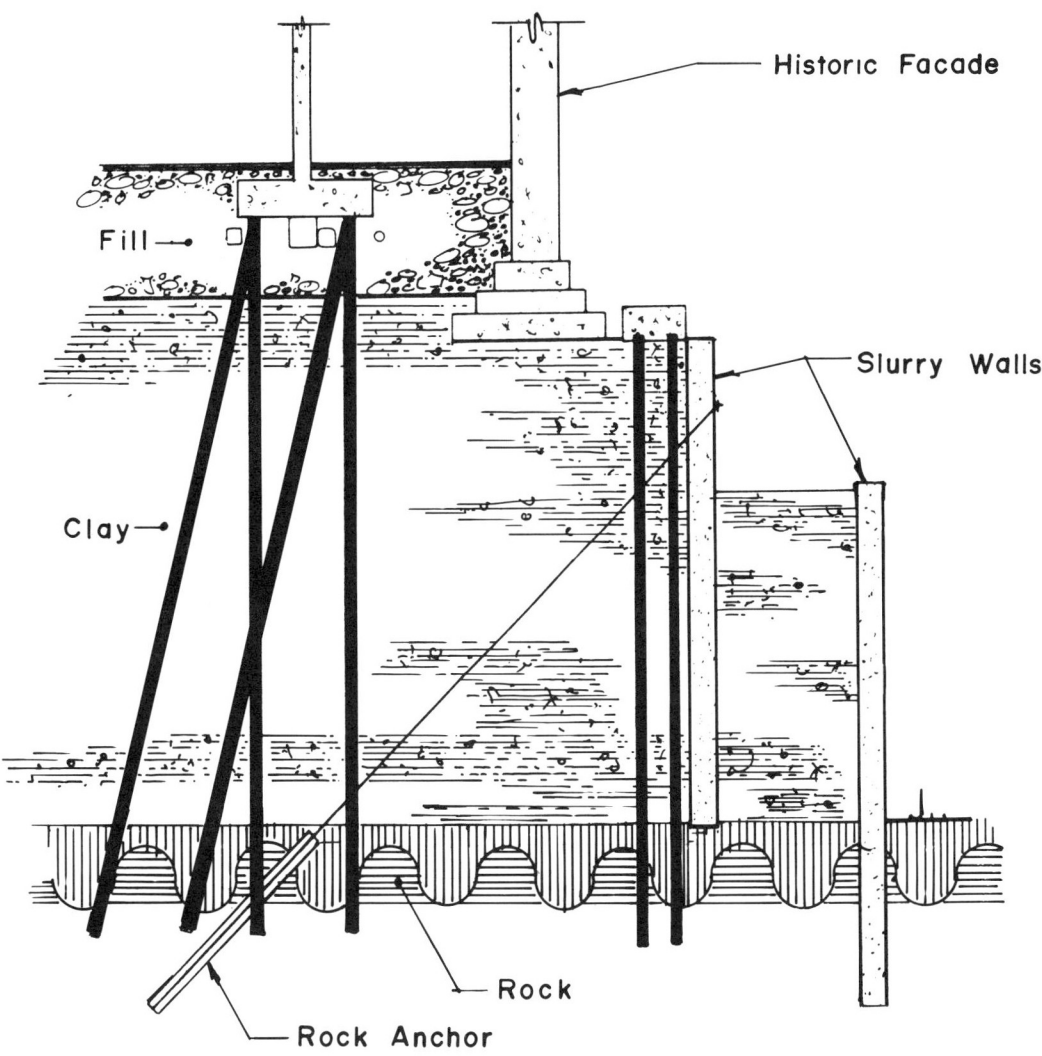

Figure 5.16.1 Shoring Detail

16. 53 STATE STREET, BOSTON

This project is an example of the facade retention technique on a grand scale. The original structure was twelve-storeys, concrete and steel framed with a stone exterior. This building covered the entire block. To develop the property to its highest potential, a portion of the structure was demolished to accommodate a new high-rise tower.

Because the building's facade on State Street was a significant element of the streetscape, it was retained. As the design developed, it was found that the Kilby Street facade could also be retained. This had considerable benefit for it provided a braced corner for both facades after selective demolition had taken place.

The techniques used on this site were shoring and underpinning, facade retention, and selective demolition.

This major structure is in an historic area of one of the most heritage-conscious cities in North America. It is interesting to note that its redevelopment has been undertaken by a Canadian developer using a Canadian design team.

Although drawings were available for the original construction, these were found to be very inaccurate. This is typical for projects of this vintage.

The major concern for the structural engineers in marrying the high-rise tower to the facade was the lateral deflection or drift at the twelfth-storey level. In one direction the tower deflected 75 mm under maximum wind load at this level, whereas the facade was very stiff and had essentially no deflection. It was impossible to transmit these loads to the facade without causing serious damage. The designers decided to provide a sliding connection which allows the tower to

Photo 5.16.3: Temporary Bracing

Photo 5.16.4: Temporary Bracing of Facade

move independently in one of the horizontal directions and vertically while providing lateral support to the walls in the other horizontal direction.

When analyzing the cost of this project, it is significant to note that the preservation of the facade cost approximately one per cent of the total project cost. This was more than compensated for by development concessions.

Project Information

Original Construction
Architect: Peabody & Stearns
Completed: 1891

Redevelopment
Owner/Developer: Olympia & York Developments Ltd.
Architect: W Z M H Habib
Structural Engineers: Quinn Dressel Associates
Completion: May 1984
Duration: Three and one-half years
Developed Area: 110,000 square metres in a forty storey tower
Cost: $100 million U.S. (1981 dollars) These costs include: $1 million for retaining the facade and $7 million for foundation work

Conservation
Techniques Used: Underpinning and Shoring
Facade Retention
Selective Demolition

17. QUEEN'S QUAY TERMINAL, TORONTO

The previous projects studied have involved temporary bracing, horizontal additions and shoring techniques. This project is noteworthy, rather, as an adaptive re-use of a sound structure.

The terminal is located on the Toronto waterfront and is founded on timber piles. The high water-table precludes excavation for elements other than new elevator pits. Even this was a very difficult undertaking.

Whatever the project may lack in below grade interest, it more than makes up for in the superstructure. The project is a veritable showcase of structural renovation techniques.

The wind bracing system was totally revamped. Interior shearwalls were added at architecturally acceptable locations. This allowed the exterior window openings to be greatly enlarged. A parking ramp was installed by threading it through the first two storeys to reach a new third-floor parking area. This parking facility has been completely waterproofed to protect the retail space below.

Large areas of floor have been removed to create a full-height atrium space. Some columns were retained to define the space, and support facilities higher up in the building. The bracing of these columns is shown in Figure 5.17.2.

Several large spaces have been opened up in the interior with transfer trusses provided over them to carry new construction above. The best example of these is the roof over the dance theatre, which supports an outdoor garden for the residential and office components above.

The other major structural technique used is the transfer grid system installed in the roof of the building to support four floors of condominiums. The condominium structure uses a totally different structural grid than the original building. It is set back to highlight the original building, particularly the North facade and tower.

The entire redevelopment of the site took one year, the same time it took to build the original warehouse. The project started as a design competition initiated by the property's owners, the Harbourfront Corporation, which is responsible for redevelopment of Toronto's waterfront. The successful team was headed by Olympia & York, who are redeveloping the entire site at a cost of $50 million dollars. The project is a true mixed-use development encompassing retail, commercial, office space, residential, theatre, parking and a private club.

The key to this renovation's success was the soundness of the original construction. It was designed for very heavy floor loading as its original use was warehousing. By changing this use to commercial and office space, condsiderable excess live load capacity became available to redistribute the loads. This in turn allowed the removal of certain columns and the vertical addition of four new floors.

Project Information

Original Construction
Completed: 1926
Architect: Thomas H. Moore
Owner: Terminal Warehouse Corp.
Use: Warehousing

Redevelopment
Owner: Government of Canada
Developer: Olympia & York Developments Ltd.
Architect: Ziedler Roberts Partnership
Structural Engineer: M.S. Yolles and Partners
Contractor: Olympia & York Developments Ltd.
Completed: Spring 1983
Duration: One year
Cost: $50 million (1982 dollars)
Accomodations: 80,000 square metres total developed area including: 90,000 square metres commercial and retail (seventy-five outlets)
Four hundred and fifty seat dance theatre
38,000 square metres office accommodation
Seventy-two residential units private club

Conservation
Techniques Used: Structural upgrading
Vertical Addition
Wind load resistance upgraging
Transfer systems
Column removal

Photo 5.17.1: Queen's Quay - Site Overview

Photo 5.17.2: Facade Prior to Redevelopment

Photo 5.17.4: Southwest Corner

Photo 5.17.6 Atrium View

Photo 5.17.5: East Elevation

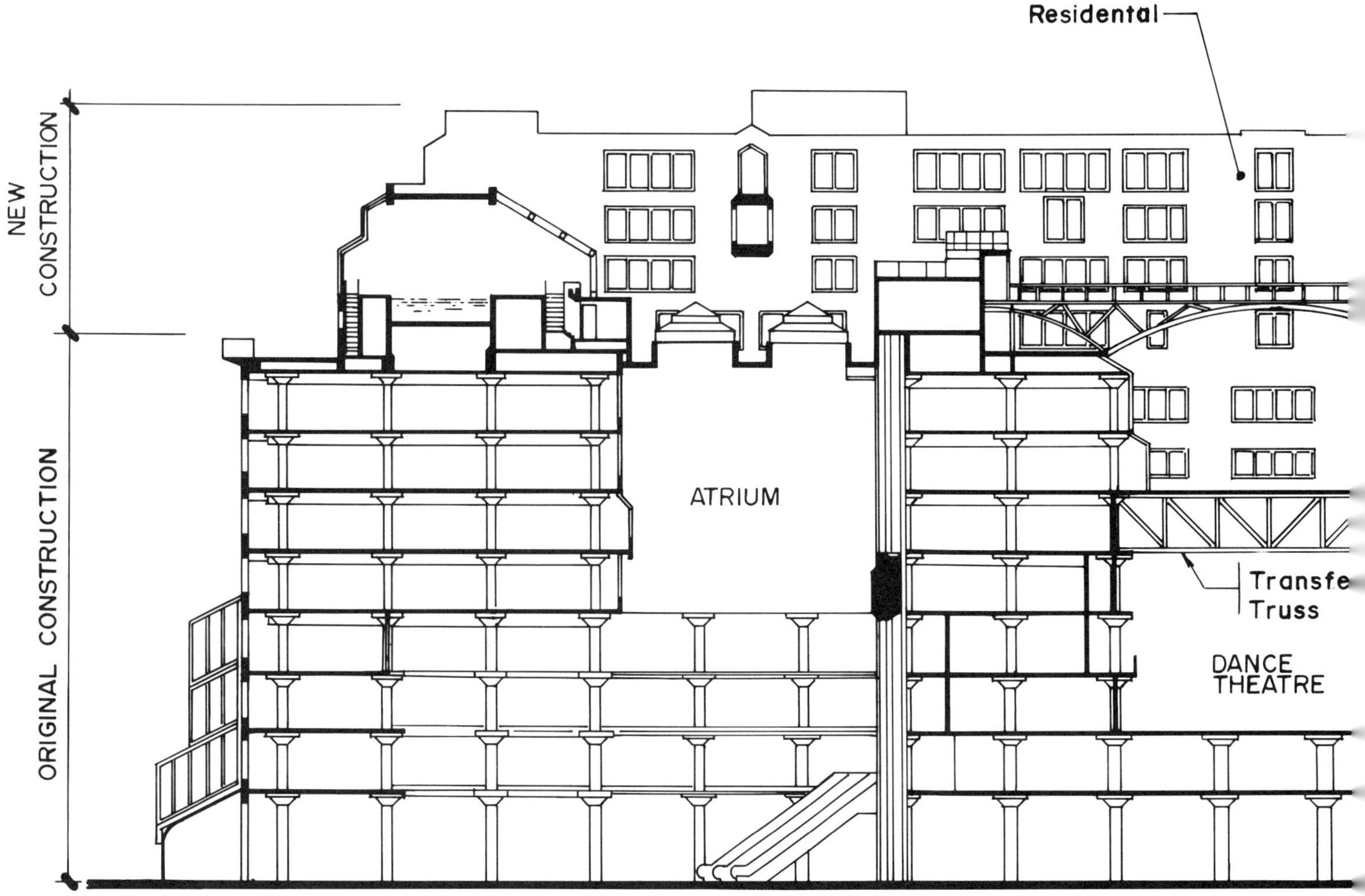

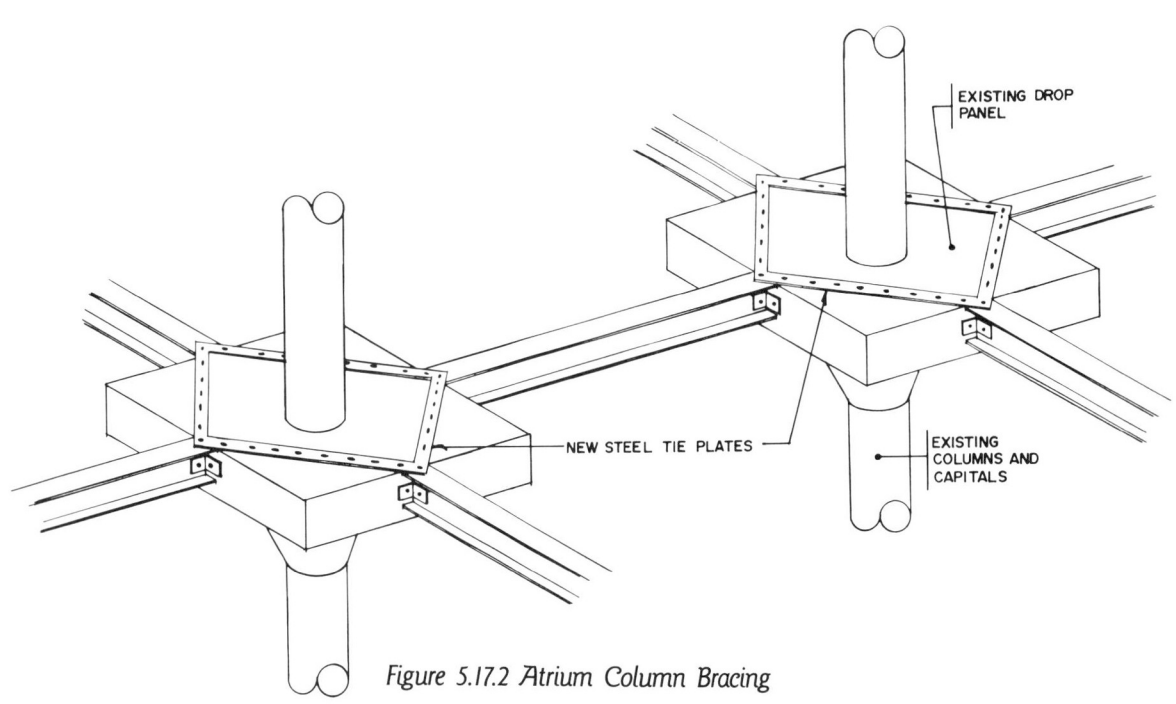

Figure 5.17.1 Building Cross Section

Figure 5.17.2 Atrium Column Bracing

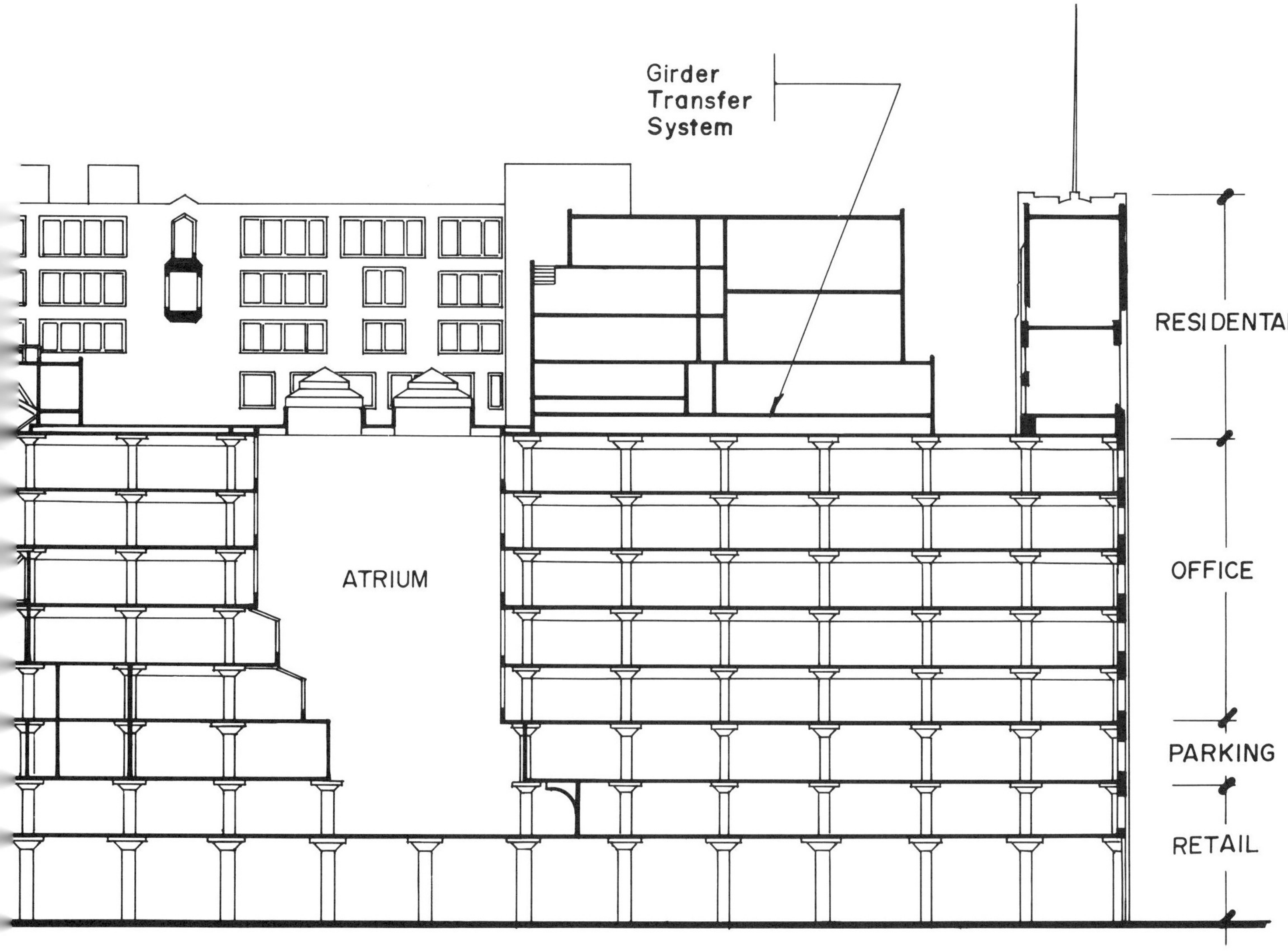

Photo 5.17.6: Atrium View

Chapter 6

APPLICATIONS IN CANADA

EVALUATION OF TECHNIQUES AVAILABLE

When determining the feasibility of a proposed redevelopment of an historic property, the exterior walls and the floor system are the governing factors. Within urban areas, exterior walls are invariably masonry. This includes clay brick, terra-cotta, limestone, granite or sandstone. These walls are either a non-load-bearing veneer, or the main load-carrying elements of the structure for wind and gravity loads. Exterior walls are usually connected to or support beam and column floor systems. The main structural materials in frames are heavy-sawn timber, reinforced concrete, or concrete encased structural steel.

The other type of heritage structures one must consider in Canada are wood frame residential and commercial buildings. These structures have wood-stud exterior bearing-walls with wood siding. Floors and roofs are usually built with light timber framing and decking. Very few of these structures exist in the redevelopment areas of urban centres. Many examples are still in existence in smaller rural municipalities. Because of their combustible nature, they cannot be incorporated in a major redevelopment of a site. The methods explored in Chapter 4 would be suitable for this type of construction.

Analysis of buildings that have masonry exteriors indicates that the entire range of structural techniques found in the case studies of Chapter 5 would be available for similar projects in most parts of Canada. The materials, labour skills, specialty contractors and design skills exist in the major Canadian centres to carry out such projects. The following section includes six hypothetical project studies, showing how typical Canadian heritage buildings might be redeveloped using preservation techniques.

HYPOTHETICAL PROJECT STUDIES

1. Facade Retention

With Major Excavation

This project study involves the retention of a masonry facade in its original location. Redevelopment would require the selective demolition of the balance of the structure. The original building may have had a one-storey basement. The new development would require the provision of underground parking in order to develop the site to its highest and best use. The new development could be residential or for mixed use.

The major difficulty in this type of redevelopment is the retention of the facade during excavation for the new parkade. The concept illustrated here is totally feasible in soil excavation, and a similar system could be used in rock excavation. There would be no real limit to the depth of excavation possible nor to the height of new construction.

The alternatives to this solution would be dismantling of the facade. The original wall could be re-assembled once the new frame is completed or a reproduction could be built using new materials.

The retention of the facade in its original location is the solution closest to the true spirit of heritage conservation. This allows a property owner to economically redevelop an attractive site.

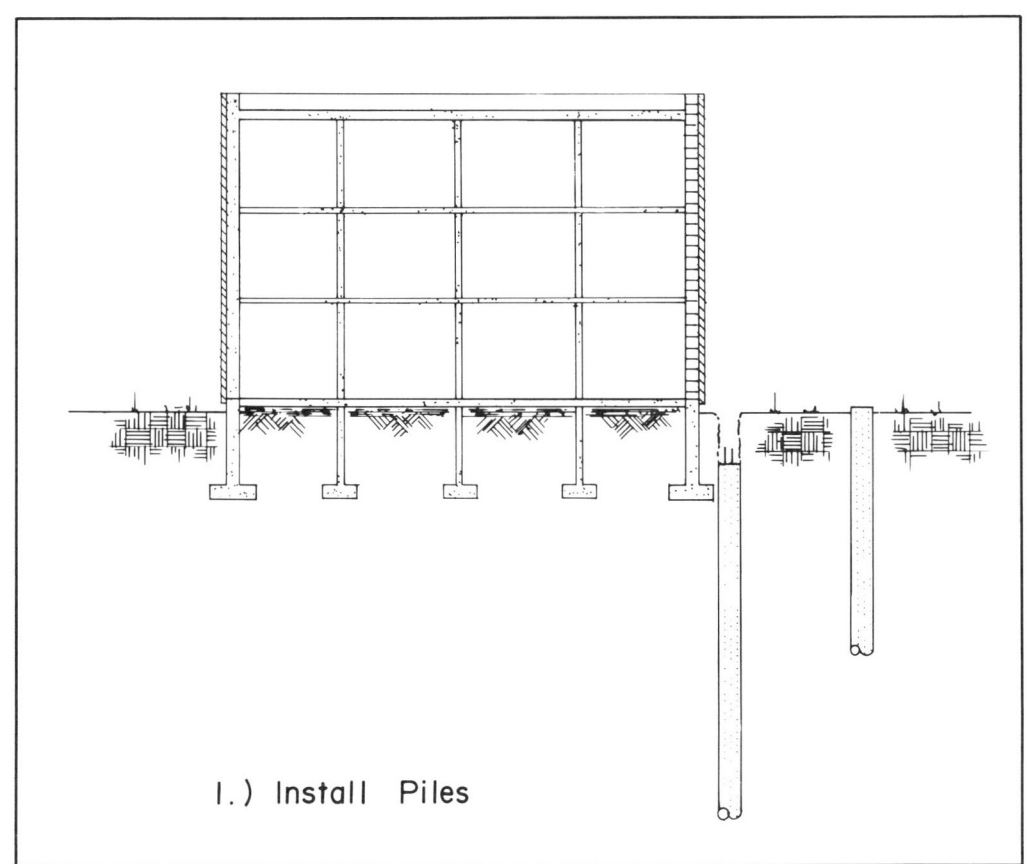

Figure 6.1.1 - Step 1 Piles

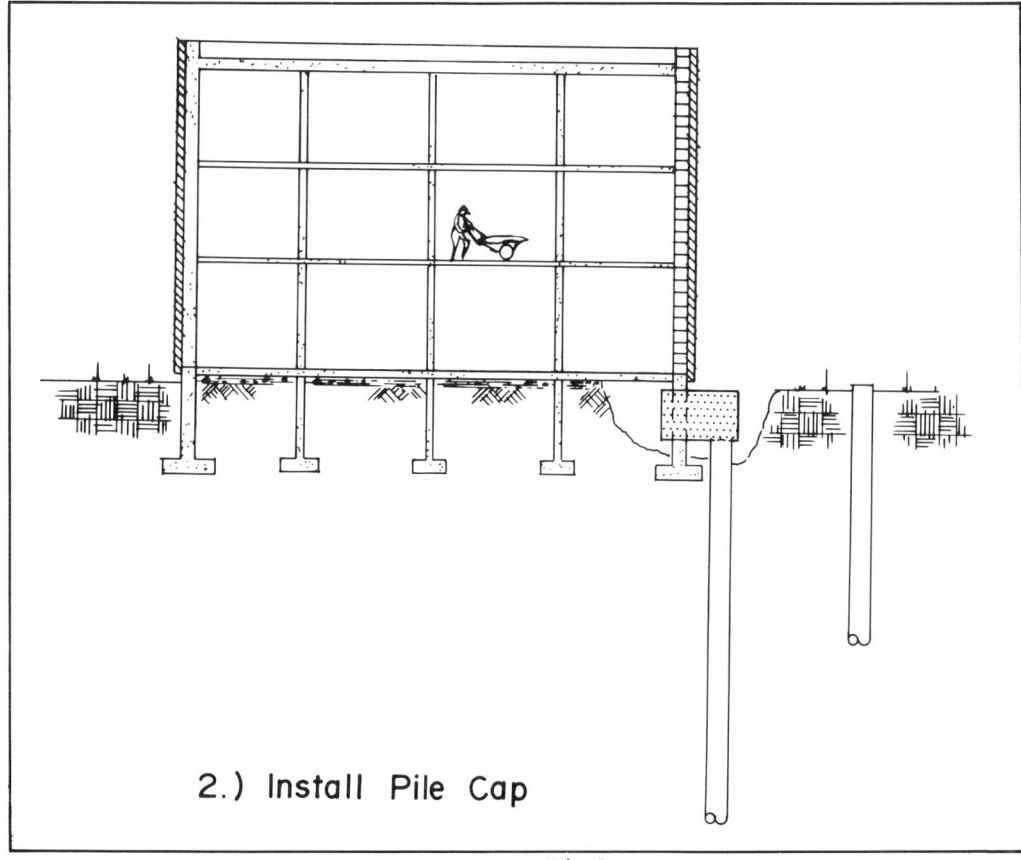

Figure 6.1.2 - Step 2 Pile Caps

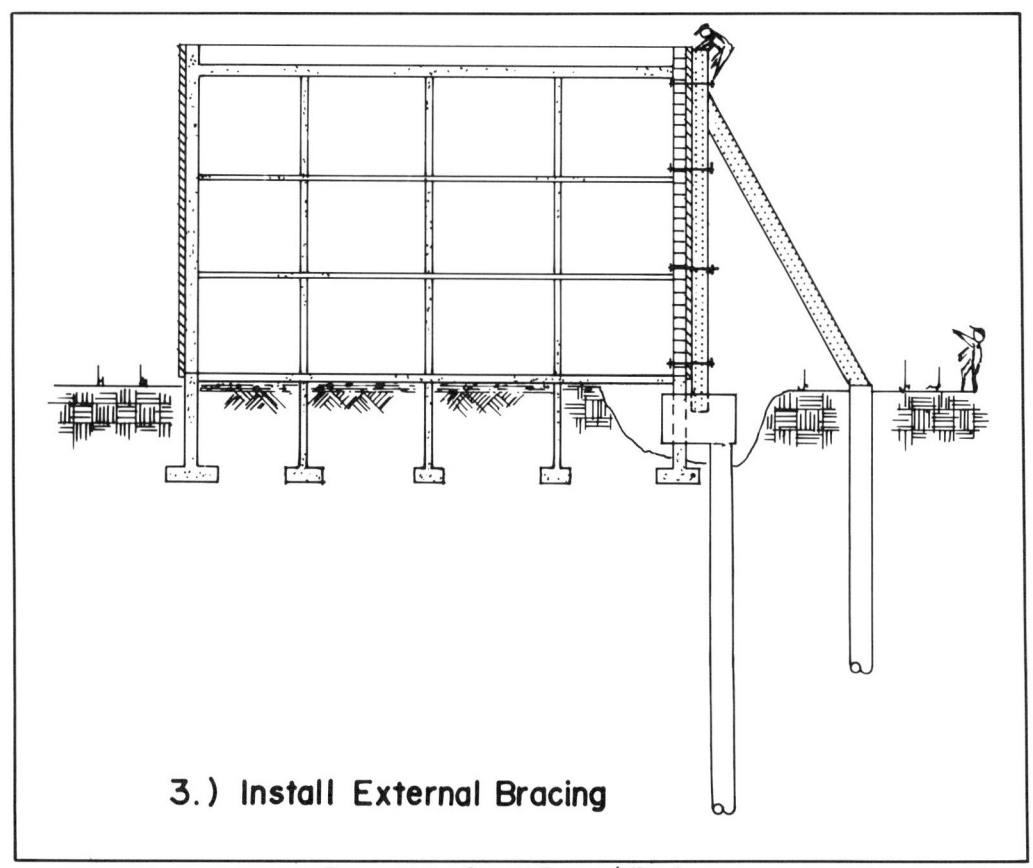

Figure 6.1.3 - Step 3 External Bracing

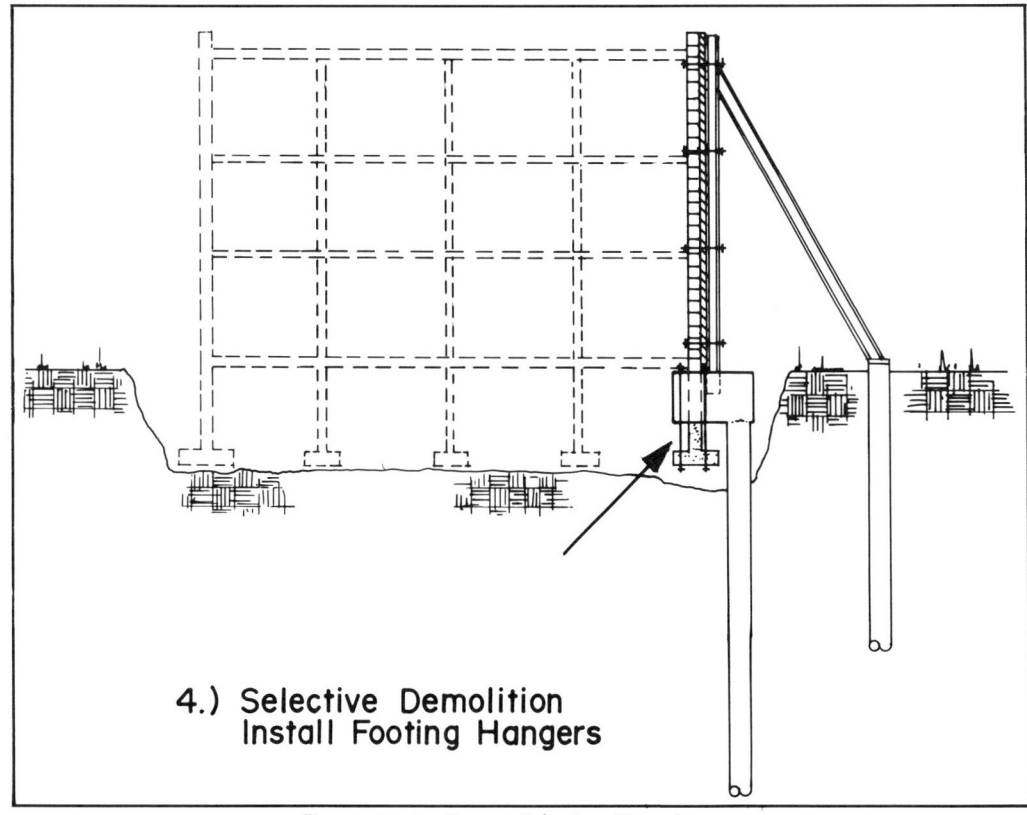

Figure 6.1.4 - Step 4 Selective Demolition

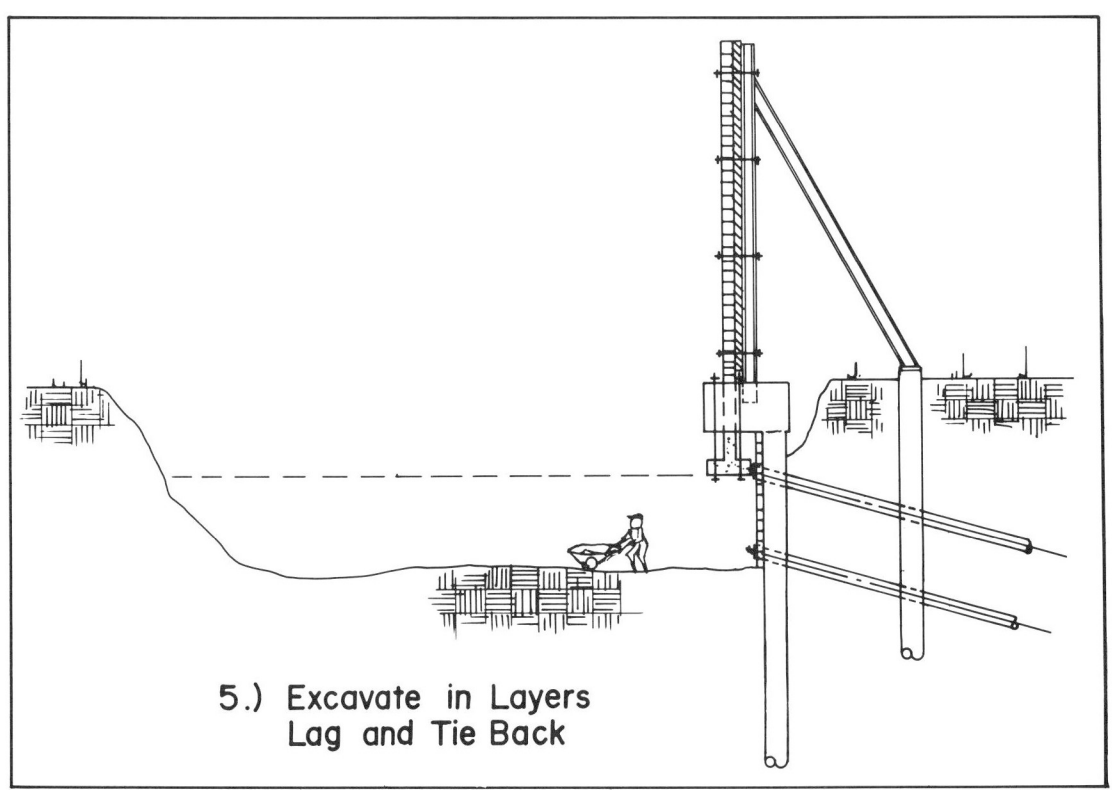

Figure 6.1.5 - Step 5 Excavate

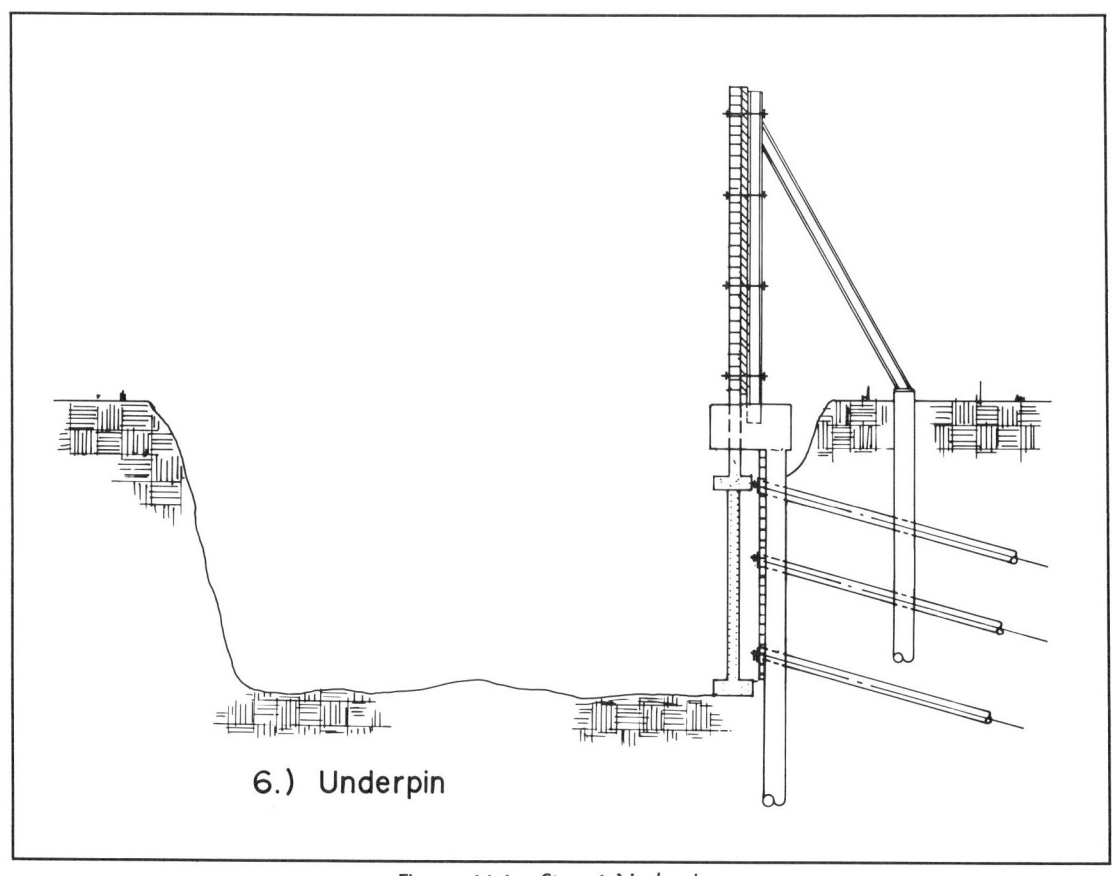

Figure 6.1.6 - Step 6 Underpin

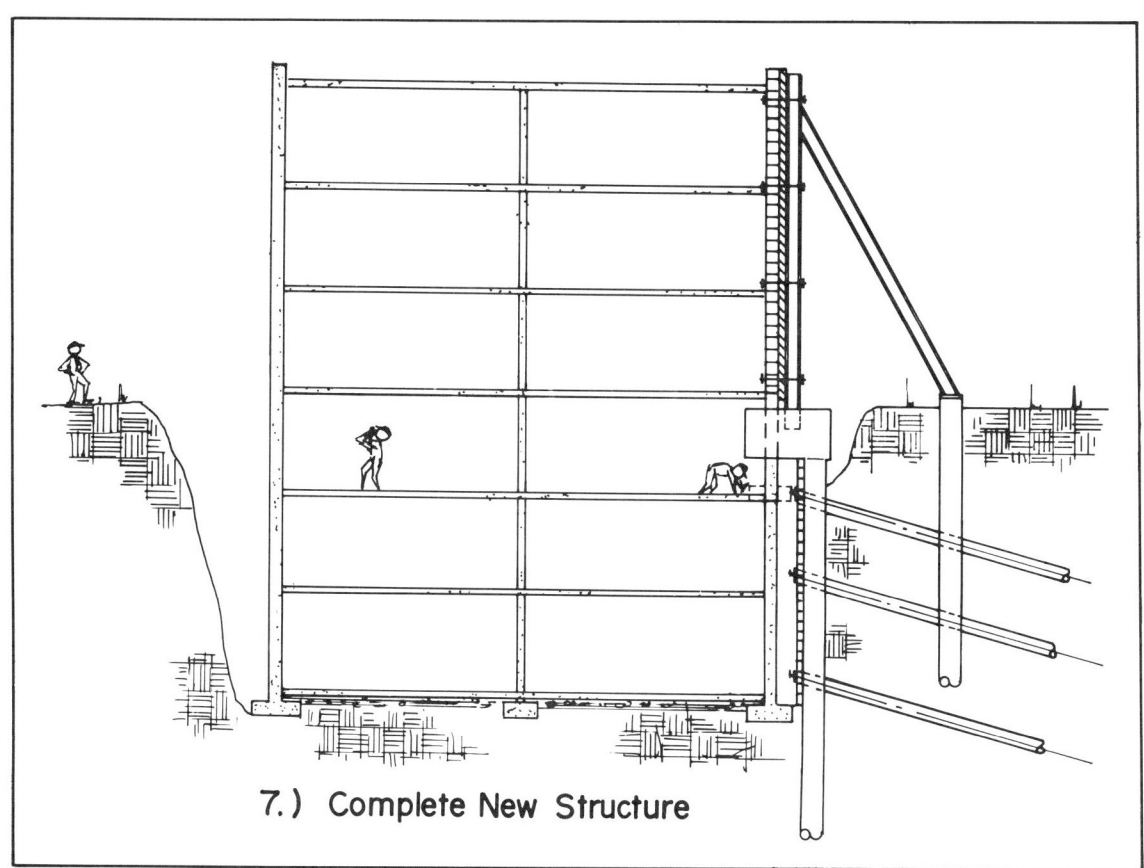

Figure 6.1.7 - Step 7 New Structure

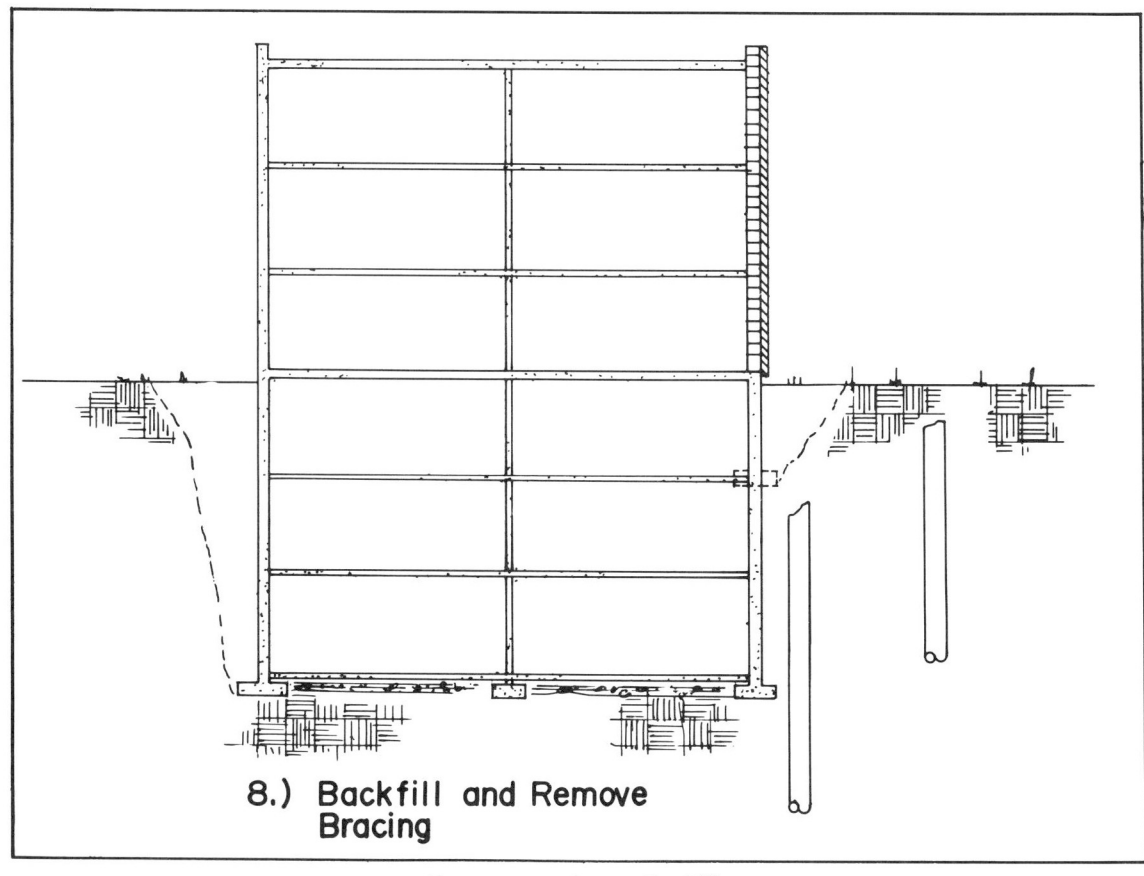

Figure 6.1.8 - Step 8 Backfill

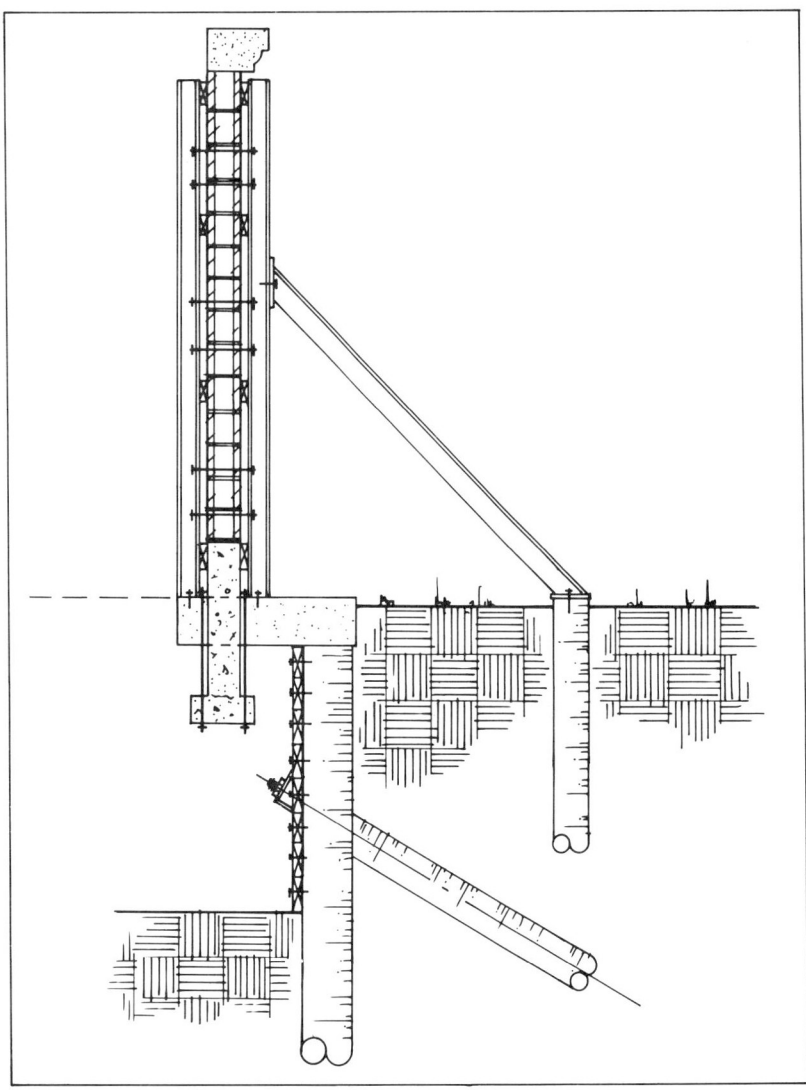

Figure 6.1.9 - Shoring Detail

2. High Rise Facade Retention

The redevelopment of a "skyscraper" built around the turn of the century is a major structural undertaking. Structural frames of that period were generally of non-combustible material in either reinforced concrete or concrete encased structural steel. The exteriors were usually masonry veneers.

The proposed solution assumes that the original structure is in good condition and that original floor to floor heights are adequate for the new use. This solution is most suitable when the new building footprint is considerably larger than the original structure.

The inherent stability of the original structural frame is used to brace the facade. The first structural bay on the exterior is kept in place to act as a bracing tower.

One major technical difficulty arises with this type of redevelopment. Differential settlement between the retained portions of the original structure and the new construction can occur. Normally this problem is solved by providing a hinged "bridge" section between the original and new construction to absorb the differential settlement.

A cost/benefit analysis of this type of redevelopment often indicates that facade-retention costs can be lower than the cost of a new wall at this location. Apart from costs, of course, are the considerable intangible benefits of maintaining a heritage element in a major new development.

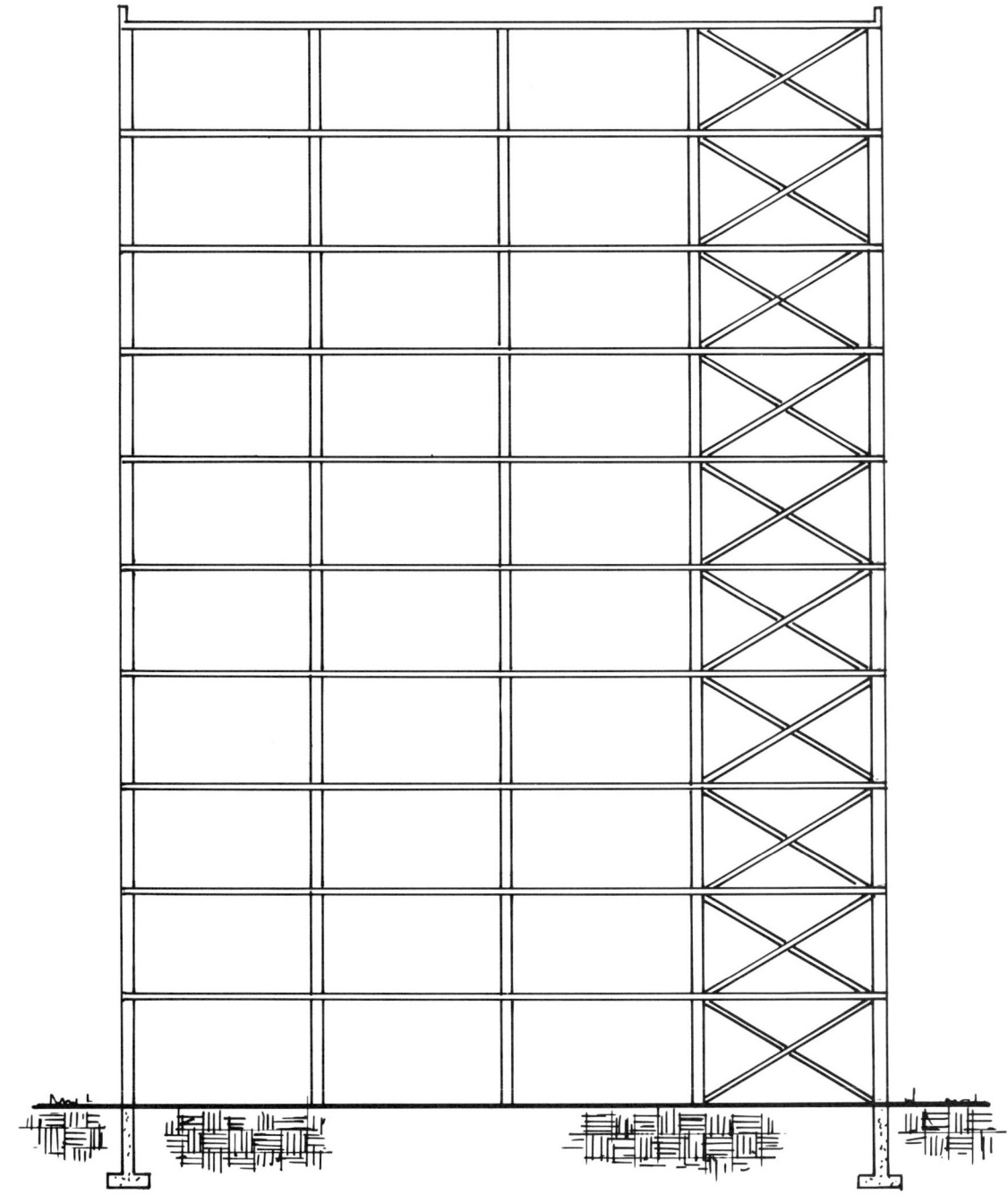

1.) Brace First Exterior Bay

Figure 6.2.1 - Step 1 Brace

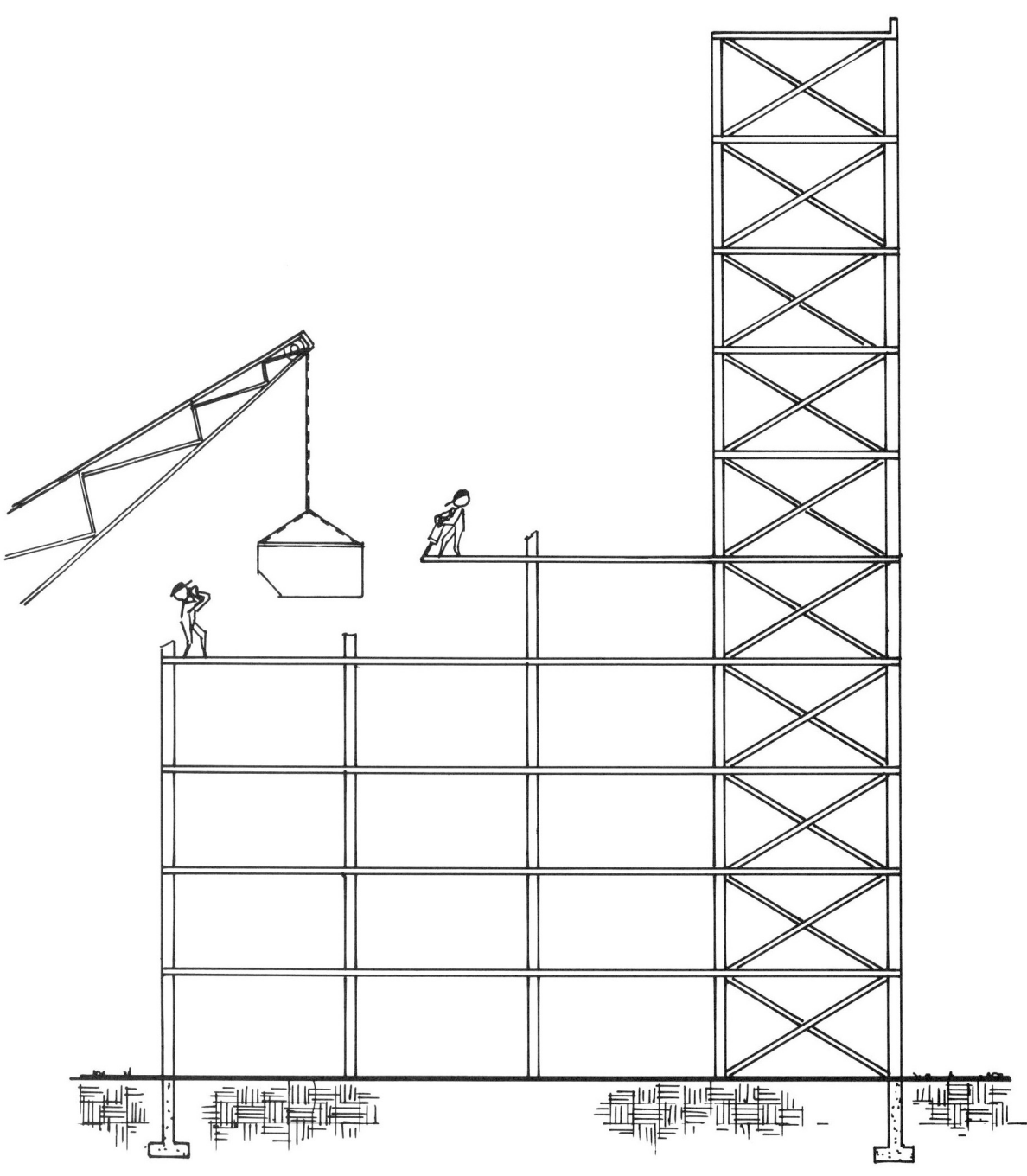

2.) Selective Demolition

Figure 6.2.2 - Step 2 Selective Demolition

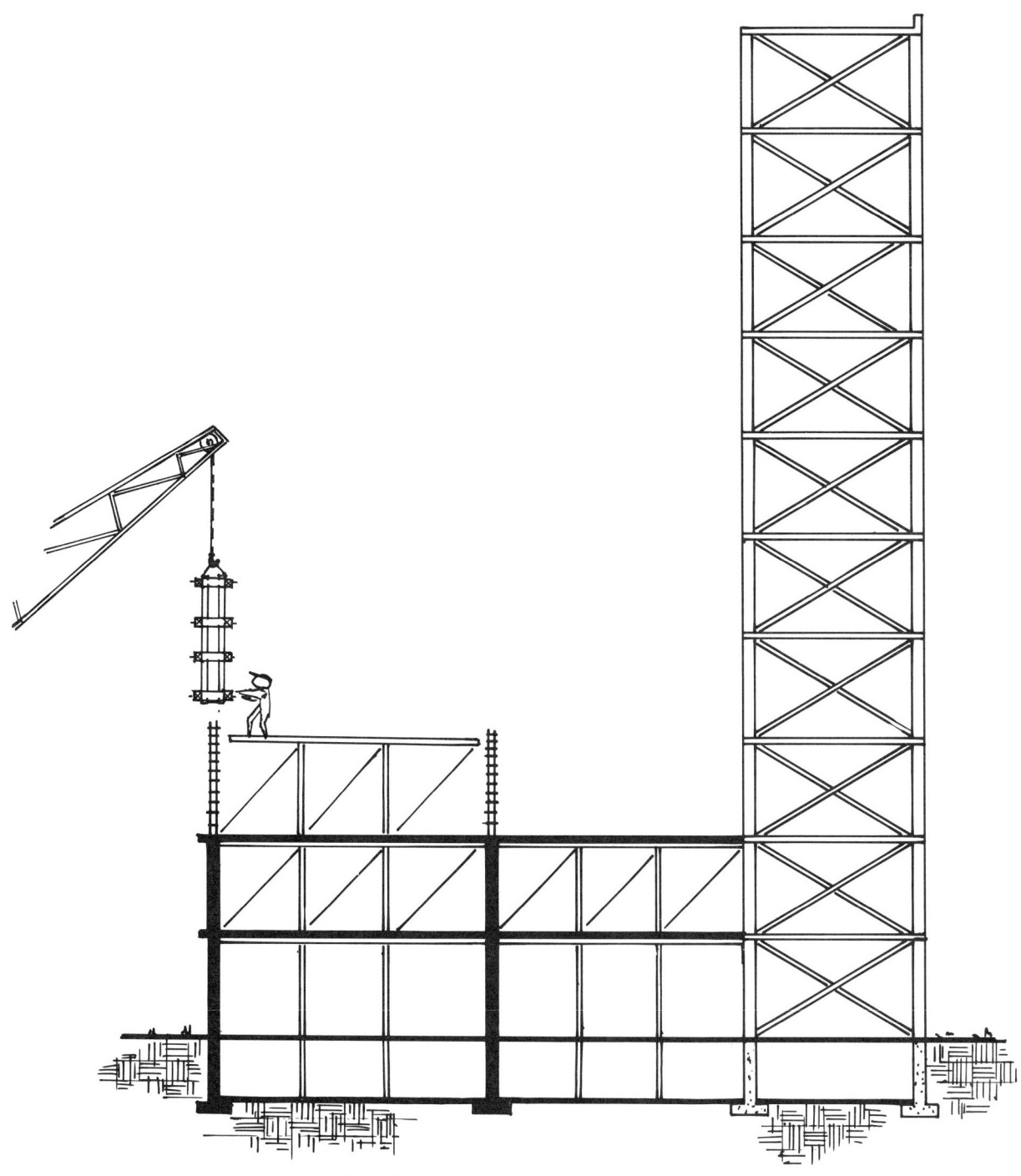

3.) Start New Construction

Figure 6.2.3 - Step 3 New Construction

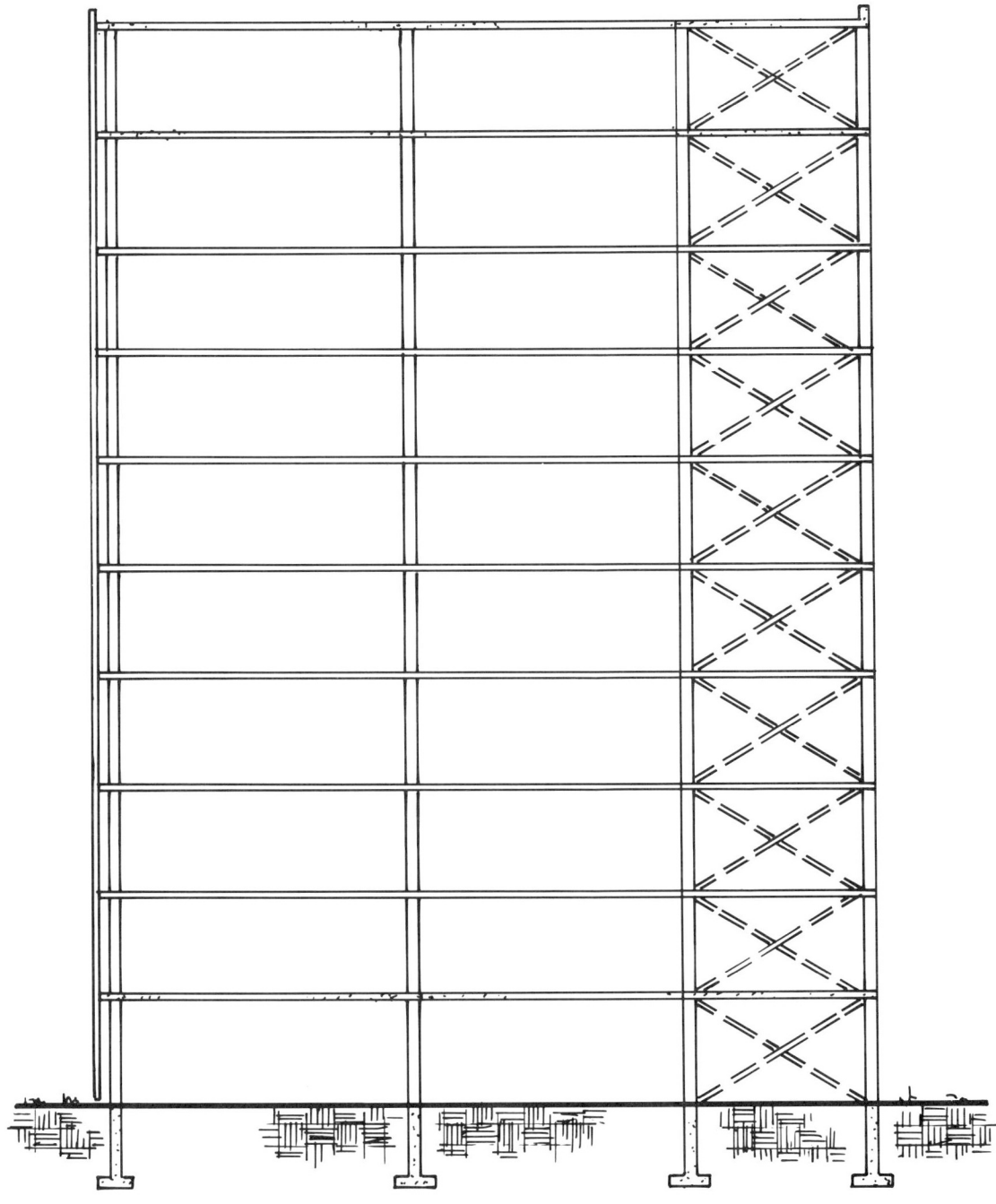

Figure 6.2.4 - Step 4 Remove Bracing

3. Large Scale Panelization

The term facade retention has been used extensively throughout *Canadian Heritage Preservation*. It generally refers to the retention of an historically significant building exterior in its original location. However, this is impossible when the original location does not suit the new development. The facade must then be relocated to a totally new site. A new method has been developed to safely move and store the facade.

The actual process illustrated in this hypothetical case study has been used effectively with a three storey building (Chapter 5, Project 3). Based on the experience of this project, there is no practical limitation to the height of wall that can be panelized. The one limitation for this method is that the masonry be reasonably sound.

Other types of construction such as wood frame, or even metal and glass curtain walls can be panelized. Limitations on panel size are based purely on convenience for handling, total weight for lifting equipment, or the distance the panels must be transported.

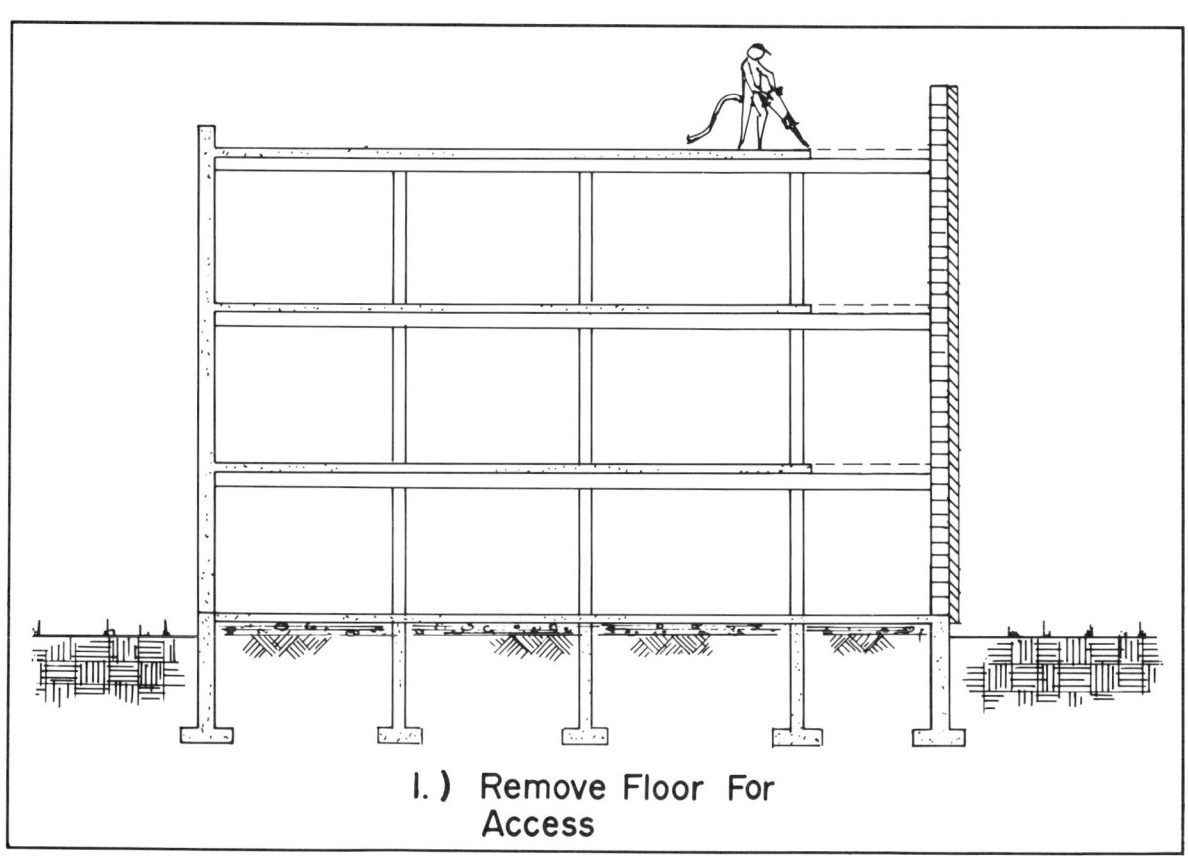

Figure 6.3.1 - Step 1 Remove Floor

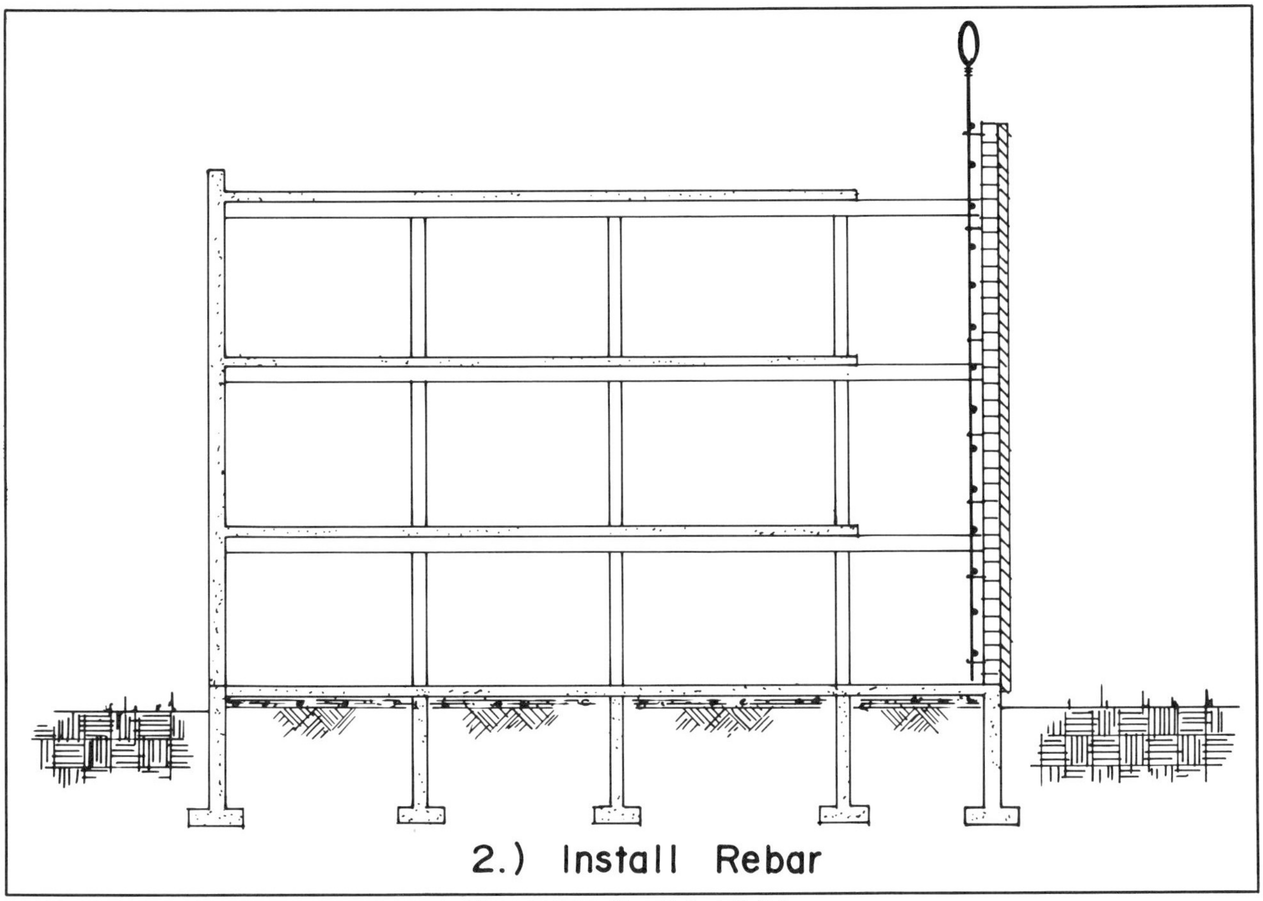

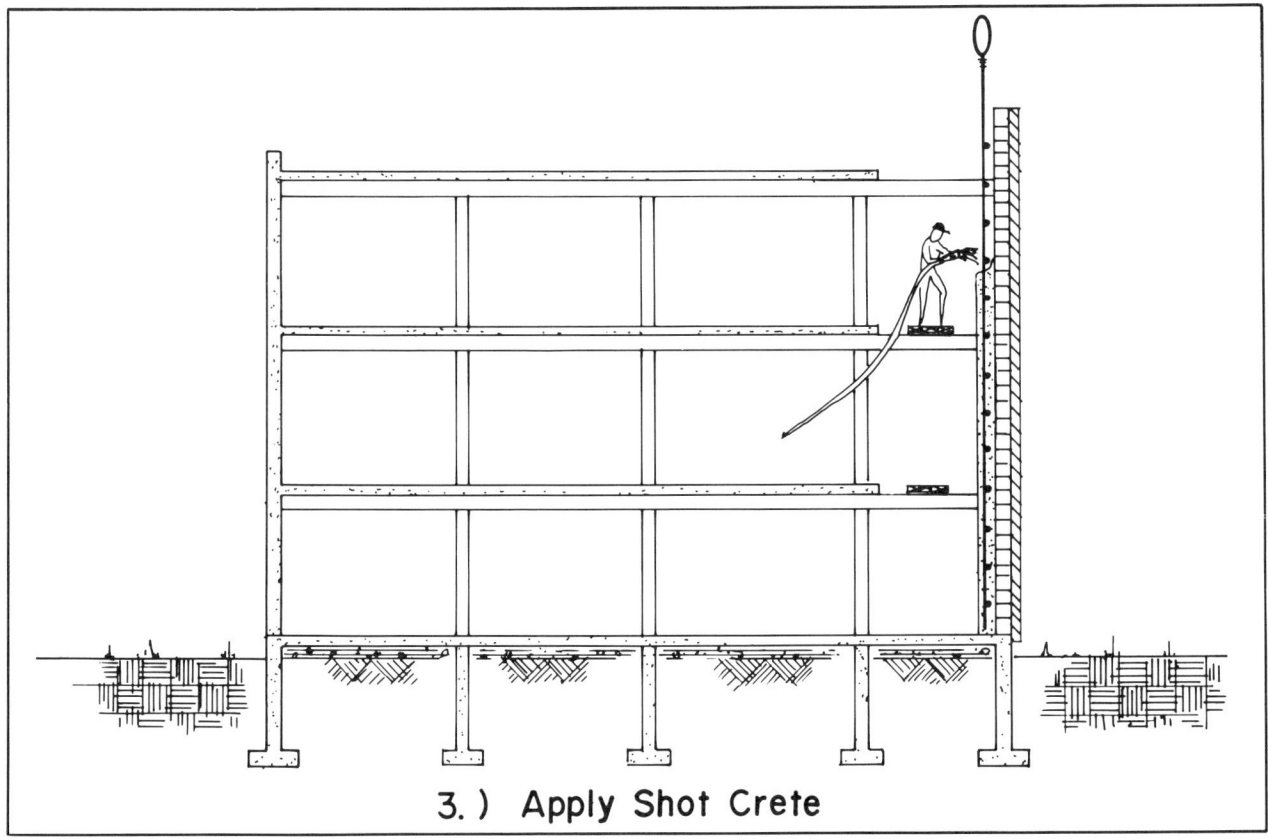

Figure 6.3.2 - Step 2 Install Rebar

Figure 6.3.3 - Step 3 Apply Shotcrete

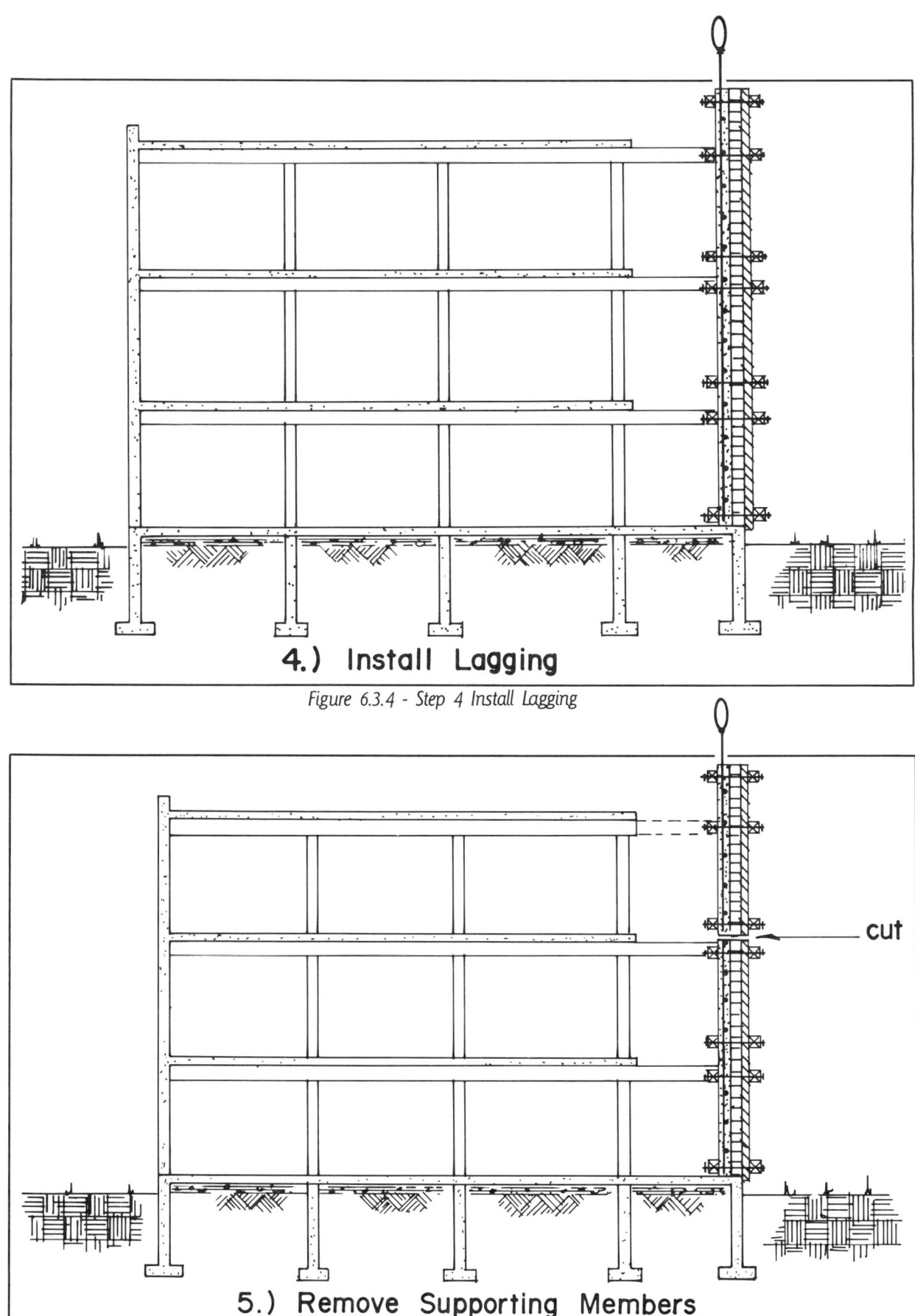

Figure 6.3.4 - Step 4 Install Lagging

Figure 6.3.5 - Step 5 Remove Supporting Members

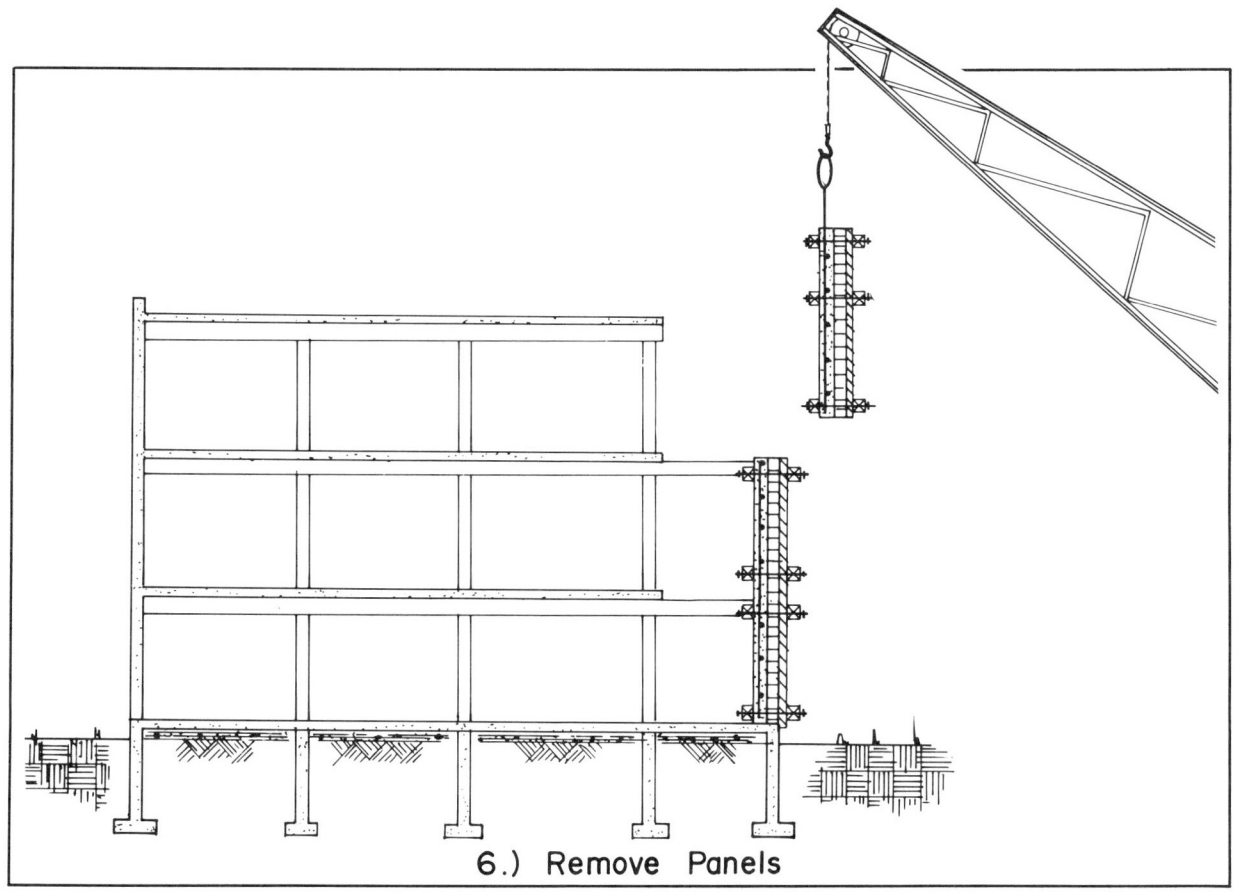
Figure 6.3.6 - Step 6 Remove Panels

4. Cantilever Structure and Underpinning

The hypothetical project illustrated here is a fairly common condition in any urban site. This applies to both heritage structures and contemporary construction. The project involves the excavation of a new basement at a considerably greater depth than the foundations of an adjacent structure. The adjacent structure may be on the same property or belong to a different owner.

A major technique illustrated here is the sequential construction of different elements of the new building. This is required to accommodate the scheduling of work related to the property. The use of earth anchor tiebacks and underpinning would be necessary to protect the existing building's foundations.

Many alternate solutions could be found for this problem. The illustrated solution is probably the most

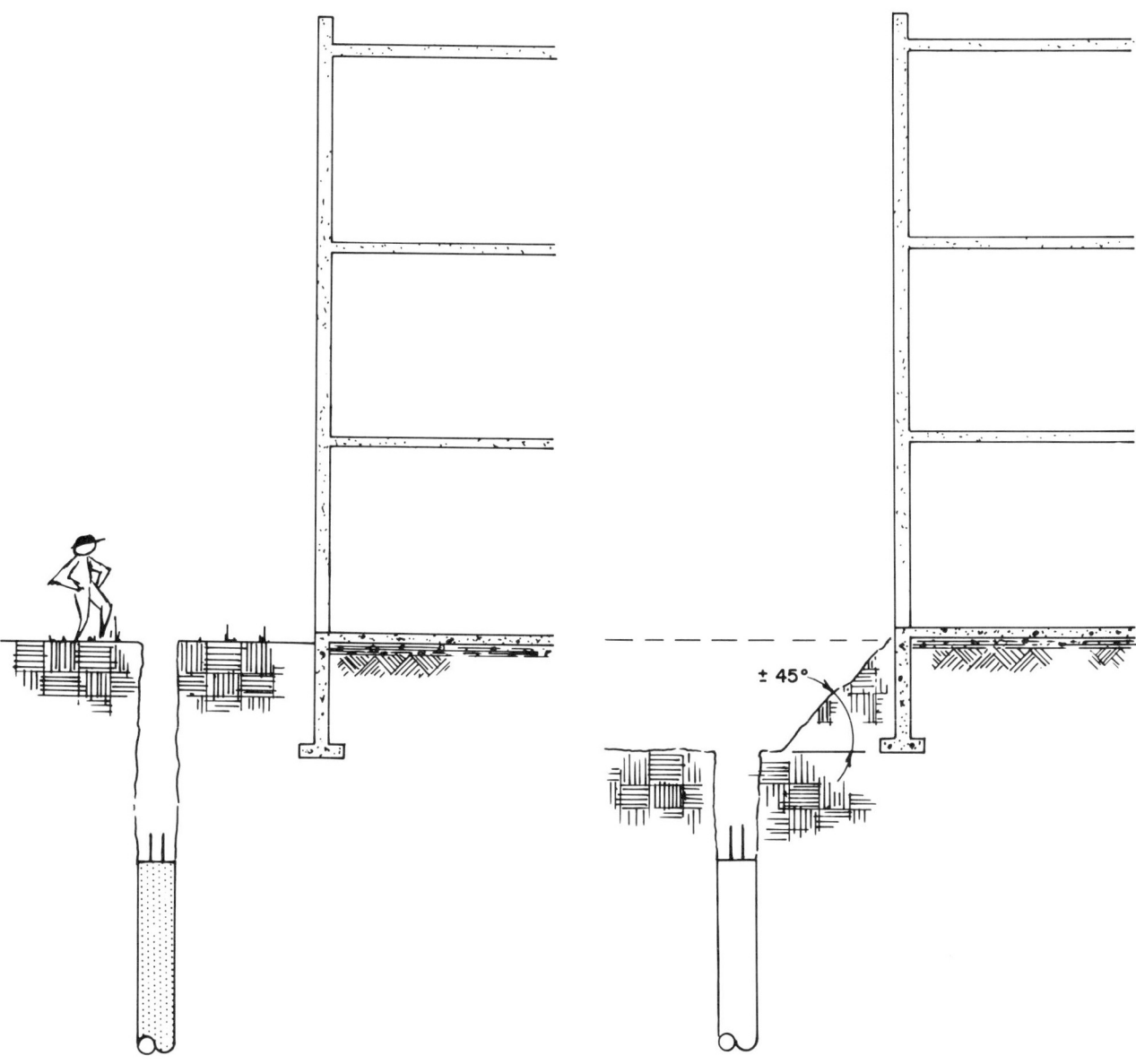

1.) Install Caissons

Figure 6.4.1 - Step 1 Install Caissons

2.) Bulk Excavate to Footing Level

Figure 6.4.2 - Step 2 Bulk Excavate

widely used for this general configuration.

One major restraint in determining shoring and underpinning details is the willingness of the adjacent property owner to grant permission for the installation of tiebacks on his property. If the new development is a fairly large scale project, the cost of earth retention and underpinning are minor in comparison to the overall project cost. Earth retention is required on urban redevelopment sites to stabilize adjacent streets and property. As mentioned in previous chapters, constant monitoring of the existing structure for settlement and deterioration due to vibrations from the new construction is mandatory.

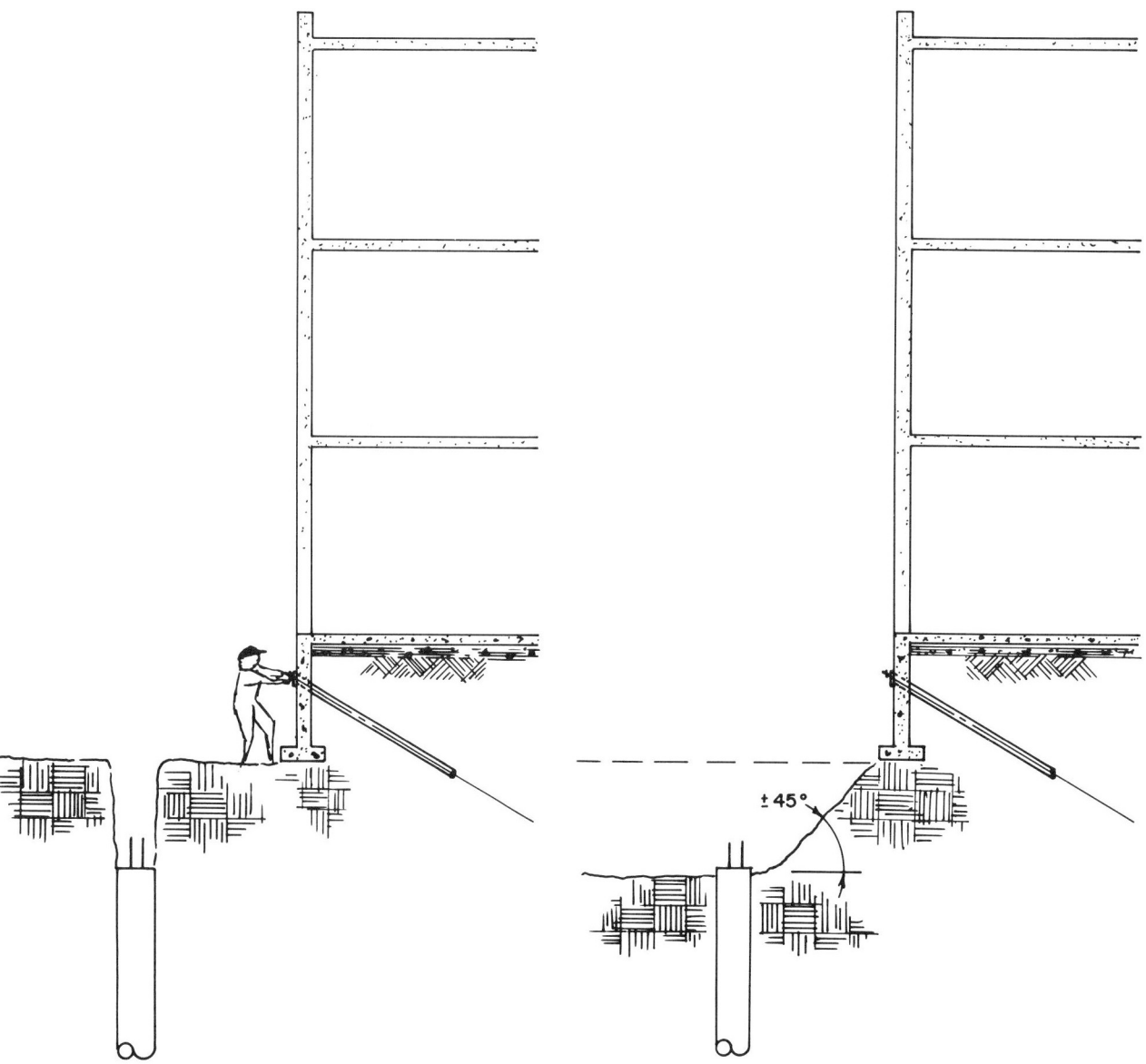

3.) Stabilize Existing Foundation

Figure 6.4.3 - Step 3 Stabilize Foundations

4.) Complete Bulk Excavation

Figure 6.4.4 - Step 4 Complete Excavation

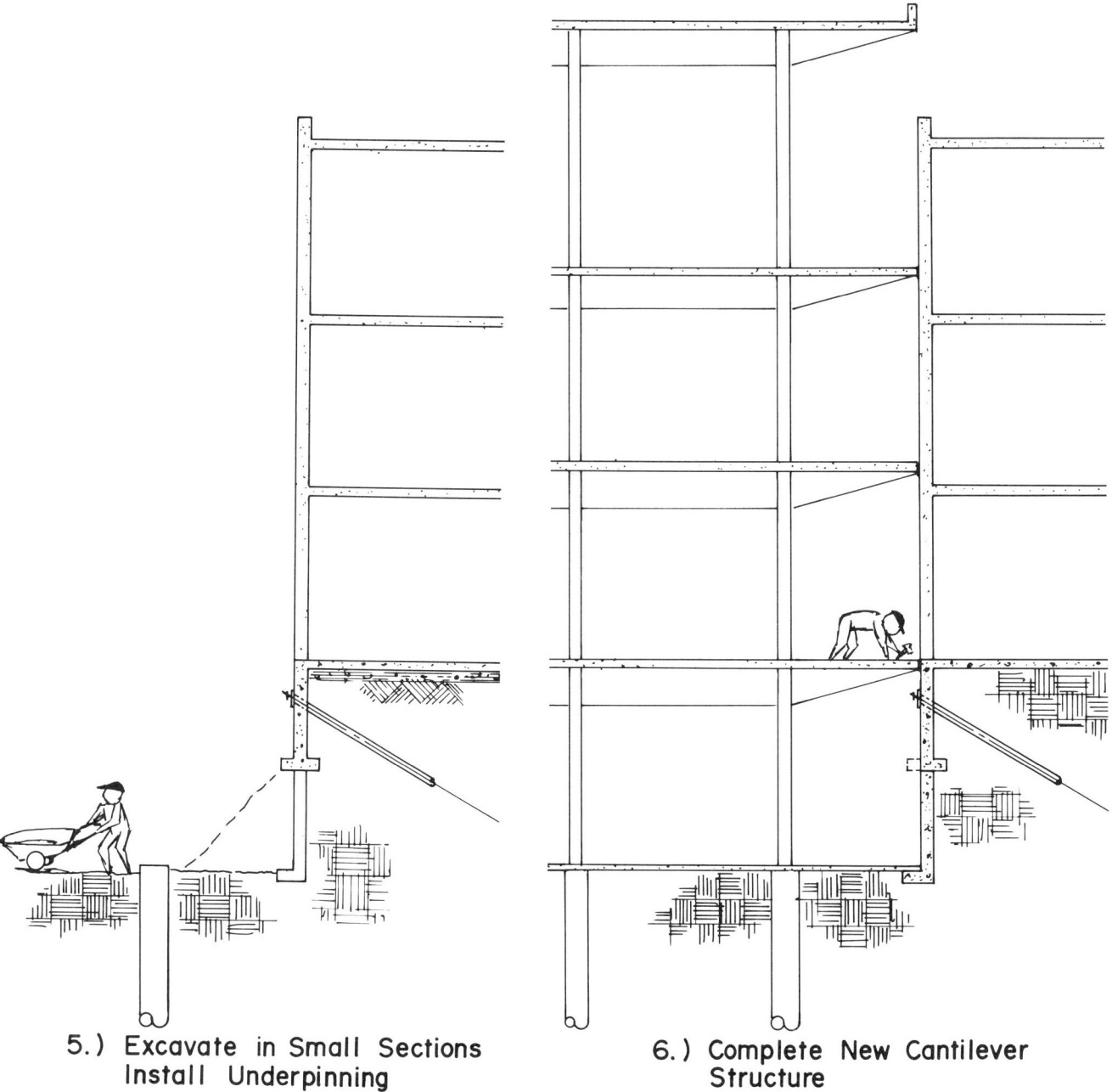

5.) Excavate in Small Sections Install Underpinning

Figure 6.4.5 - Step 5 Underpin

6.) Complete New Cantilever Structure

Figure 6.4.6 - Step 6 New Structure

5. Vertical Addition With Separate Structure

Project Study 6.2 dealt with the retention of part of a heritage structure where the redevelopment was considerably larger than the original building. This case study will illustrate a method of retaining a sound structure with a footprint approximately the same size as the new development. This approach has been used in "air rights" developments over heritage structures, and in the case of Grand Central Station, New York over a designated heritage space.

The original structure must be sound and of non-combustible construction generally meeting current fire codes. Any deficiency in the fire rating can be upgraded by the application of additional fireproofing material.

The reconstruction would involve threading a totally new vertical and wind-resisting structural system through the existing structure to support the new frame above. A transfer system is normally required immediately above the original building. This space is used as a plenum for transferring mechanical and electrical services. This approach is more feasible when the new construction has a totally different structural grid than that of the original. The new columns can then be threaded through the existing building. This process is a difficult and costly approach, normally reserved for major redevelopments over very significant heritage properties.

6. Vertical Addition Supported By Existing Structure

The vertical addition of new construction over an existing heritage structure can often be accomplished by reinforcing the existing structure. As a general rule the new construction should have less volume than the original building. This approach has been used most successfully when the original building was designed for warehouse loading. In an adaptive re-use project the new use is generally commercial, office, or residential. Floor loadings for these uses are significantly less than the original warehouse design loads. Considerable excess capacity is then available in foundations and columns, which in turn allows vertical additions equivalent to the original height. This does however, create problems in the wind-resisting elements of the original construction. The total wind load may have more than doubled with the addition.

The addition of new bracing or shear walls placed strategically in the existing building can efficiently overcome this difficulty.

Structure and foundations are two major costs and scheduling elements in any project. The proposed approach can lead to considerable savings in money and time when redeveloping a site while retaining an aesthetically pleasing heritage element. The techniques discussed were used effectively in Chapter 5, Project 17.

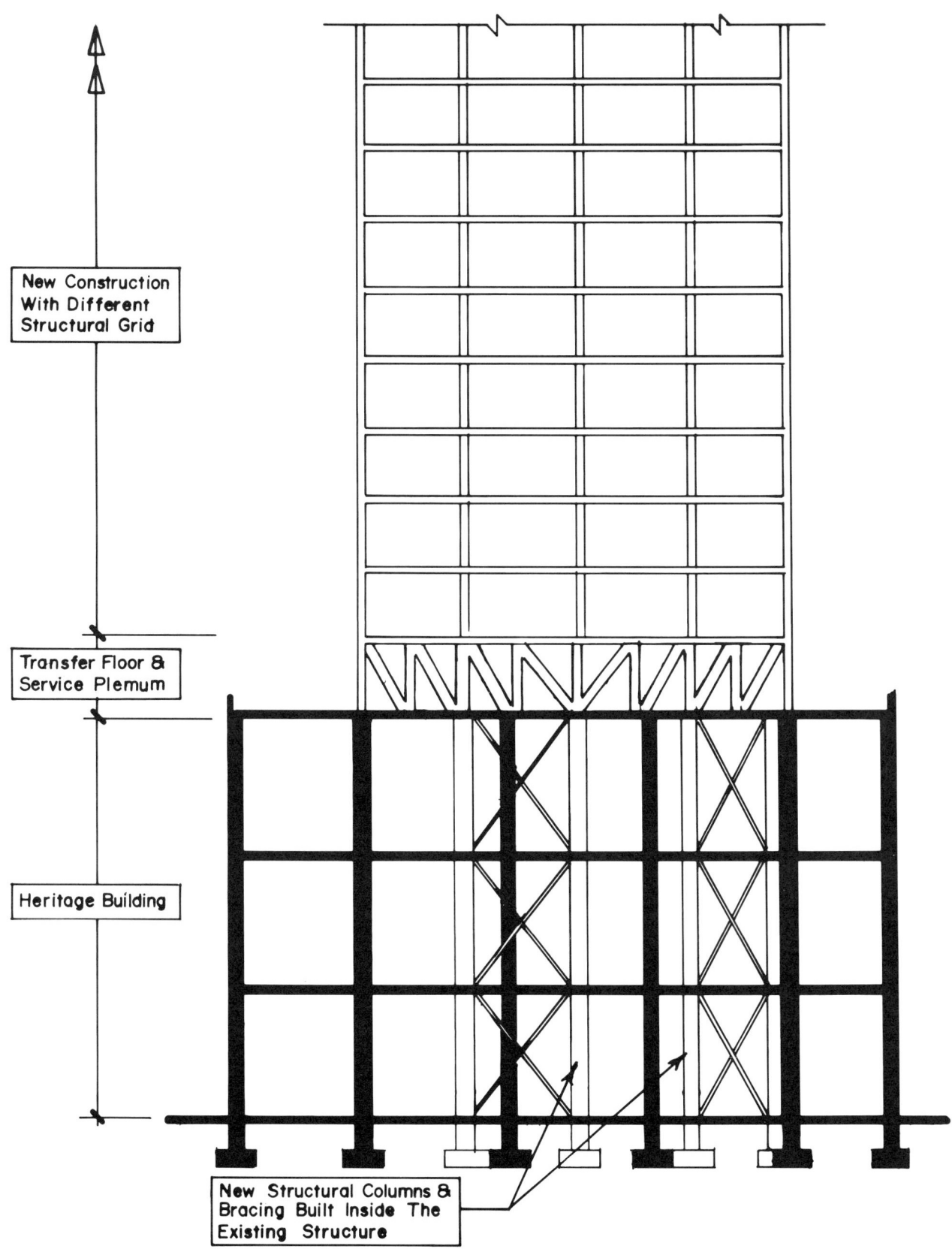

Figure 6.5.1 - Building Section - Separate Structure

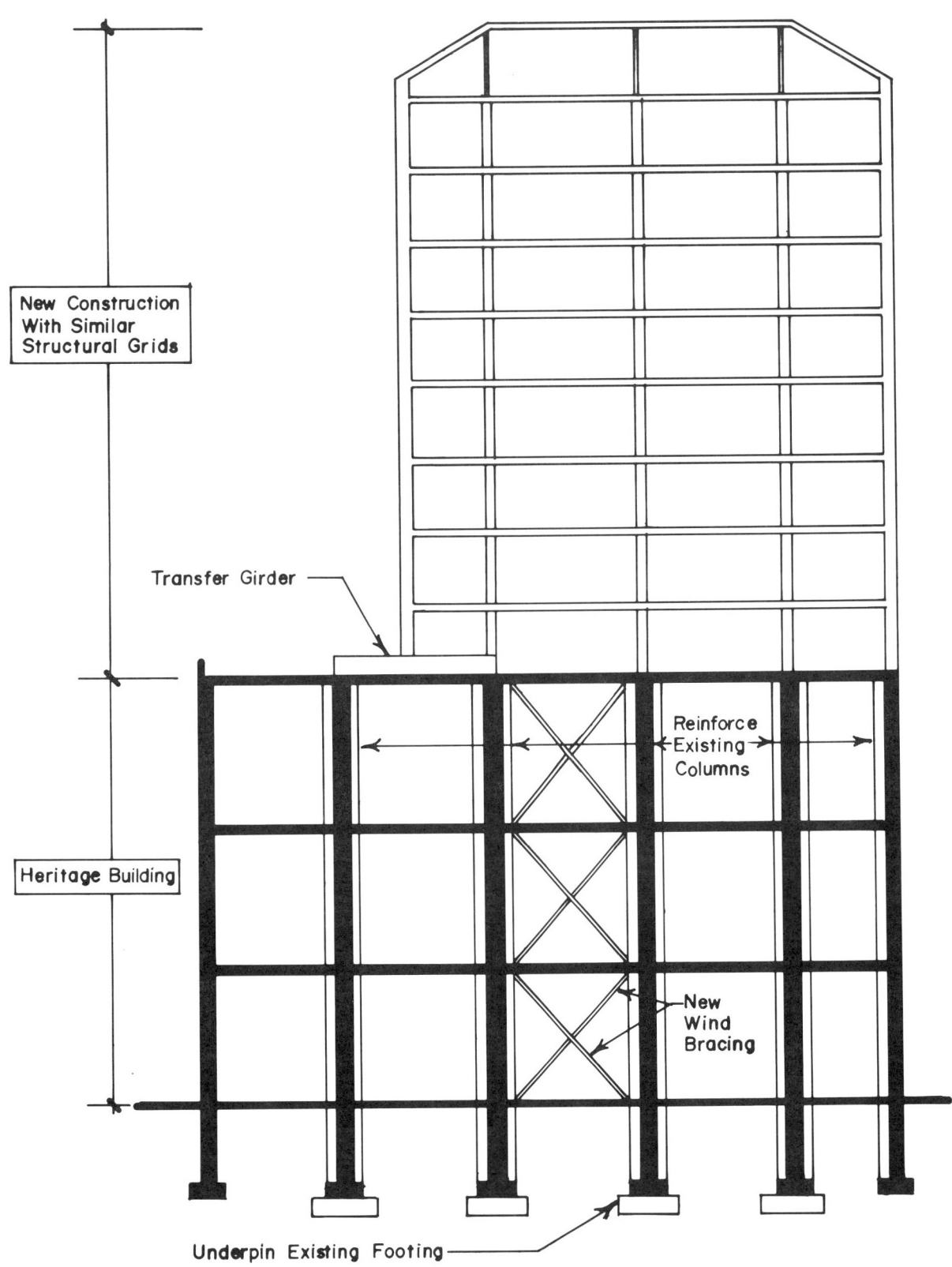

Figure 6.6.1 - Building Section - Same Structural Grid

ECONOMIC AND SCHEDULE EVALUATION

Heritage conservation is similar to most other human activities - both the costs and benefits must be considered. Unfortunately in the case of preservation of architectural heritage these costs and benefits are often intangibles and do not lend themselves to a quantitative analysis. What can be reasonably quantified is the capital cost to retain certain significant heritage elements of a building, while still creating a viable new project. The duration of the construction process and the influence of the heritage component on that schedule is the second area that is quantifiable.

Current experience indicates that the cost of renovating a basically sound structure will be very close to the cost of equivalent new construction. The real benefit from this type of redevelopment can be a shorter construction process. The planning and design duration can be compressed considerably because of the many givens, or restraints, in an existing structure. The two most time consuming elements in any new construction are the mounting of the structure and installation of the exterior cladding. Both of these elements are already in place in an adaptive re-use project.

FACADE RETENTION

Scale is the most important element in the economic feasibility of facade retention. The larger a project the more favourable the economics of saving an existing facade. The example of "53 State Street" (See Chapter 5) with the retention of a twelve-storey facade, involved a capital cost of less than one percent of the total project budget. Had this facade been removed, additional demolition costs would have been incurred. Replacing the existing wall at this location would have been more expensive.

Scheduling impact, again, is a question of scale. During large redevelopments the retention of the facade normally involves a small part of the site. At least two other sides of the site are normally available for construction access. Hence there is a negligible impact on the overall construction schedule.

Current costs for the panelization of facades using the shotcrete system are approximately $300 per square metre of wall surface. This cost compares favourably with the expense of duplicating an historically significant wall with new materials. There is also the intangible benefit of having retained the original construction.

UNDERPINNING

The excavation for any new structure adjacent to or under an existing building is costly and time consuming. Current costs of shoring a vertical excavation face run approximately $250 per square metre of wall surface. Underpinning of an existing structure can double or triple this basic cost. The retention of an existing facade during excavation is particularly complicated as illustrated in Project 1 of this chapter. As with most complicated construction projects it is important that experienced professionals be involved in evaluating the alternatives.

When excavation must take place on an historic site, there are several alternative methods. The historic elements can be retained or demolished and reproduced with new materials later in the construction process. Alternatively the elements can be panelized and temporarily stored to be reincorporated in the site later on. Because of the large number of variables a site-specific analysis must be carried out for each project. The tangible costs must be weighed against the intangible benefits from any of these options.

Chapter 7

INNOVATIVE SOLUTIONS

Every redevelopment of a heritage property presents a unique set of restraint and challenges for the design team. The mixture of new and old technology with existing building forms and new uses creates an infinitely variable set of circumstances. It is these circumstances that provide ample scope for a creative mind to find a new and better way to accomplish the desired result. The following sections describe a few outstanding examples of this process.

POST-TENSIONING OF EXISTING STRUCTURES

Post-tensioning consists of applying a high tensile load to steel strands to induce a compressive load in the member providing the resisting force. If the strands are draped, transverse loads can also be induced. This in effect pulls the structure up by its boot straps. A sixty-year-old parking garage in Cambridge, Mass. was restored in this manner. We were unable to find a similar application in Canada, but certainly the skills and technology exist in most parts of the country to use this technique. In the Cambridge example the one-way concrete joist frame was badly deteriorated. The load-carrying capacity of the joists was restored by threading steel cables through the existing structure as shown in Figure 7.1. The cables were then tensioned to provide an uplift at midspan of the joists.

Post-tensioning also formed part of the recent renovation of the Lions Gate Bridge in Vancouver, B.C. Movement along the suspension cables combined with foundation settlement reduced the load capacity of the north secondary tower. To prevent further settlement, a concrete collar was post-tensioned to the existing pier as shown in Figure 7.2. The collar transfers the tower loads to new pipe piles driven to stabilize the foundation.

To eliminate the eccentricity in the tower, a rocker bearing was installed in a hole drilled above the pile collar. The upper and lower portions of the pier were then separated by horizontal line drilling at the rocker level. The tower base is free to rotate on the rocker bearing as the top of the tower moves with changing bridge loads and temperatures.

A similar application of the post-tensioning technique would allow a footing to be enlarged for increased load capacity.

Shotcrete Panelization

The project study on Edmonton's Rothesay Apartments (see Chapter 5) describes the use of shotcrete to facilitate the dismantling of masonry walls. The basic principle involves applying a reinforced shotcrete back-up and sawing the wall into panels. This approach yields a product not unlike factory-made brick-veneer panels. The potential for damage, theft or loss of individual components is minimized when using this system. It is difficult to lose three-metre square, one tonne panels.

Photo 7.1: Rothesay Apartments, Edmonton

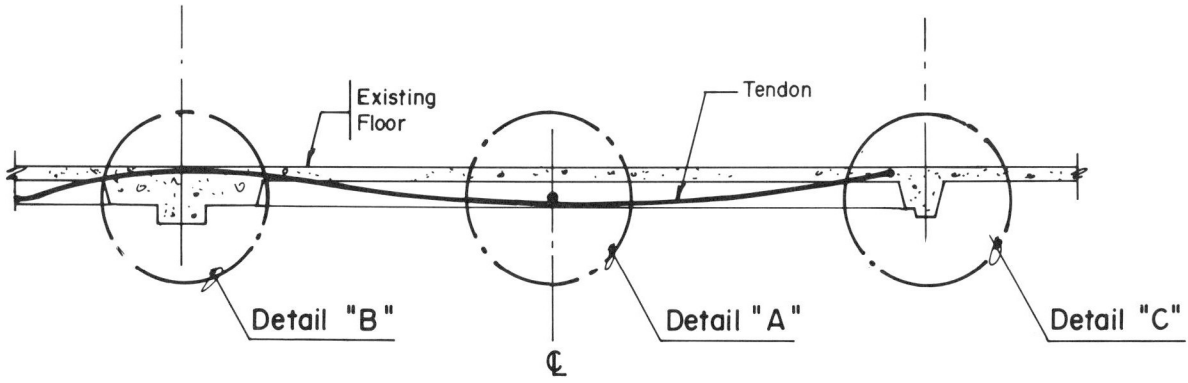

CROSS SECTION

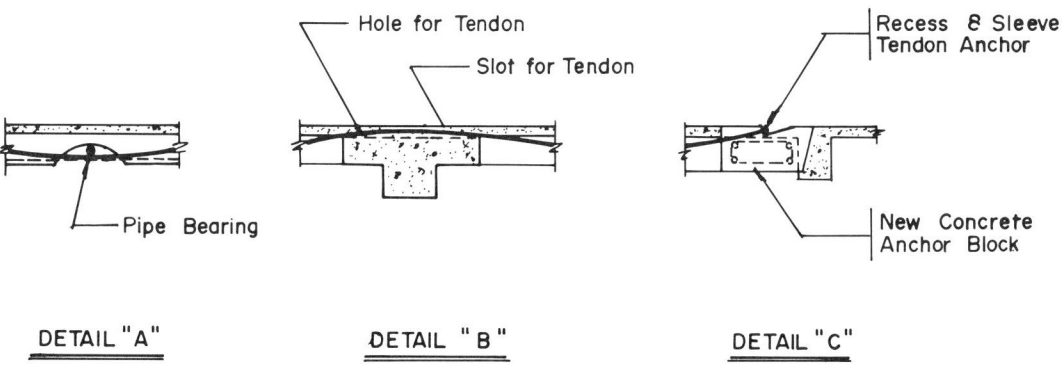

Figure 7.1 Post-tensioned Floor Repair.

To use this technique to its fullest advantage, the shotcrete must bond to each individual masonry unit. This will eliminate reliance on the existing mortar to hold the panel together. The panel must have sufficient stiffness to prevent flexural debonding of the masonry. When there are corner panels with large returns, the addition of steel bracing may be necessary. The required bond to the existing masonry can be provided by the shotcrete without bonding agents if the surface is sound and has been cleaned by sandblasting. The shotcrete must be left in its natural gun finish as trowelling the freshly applied material could break the bond. If the bond must be confirmed, samples can be cored from the wall and tested.

Severely deteriorated walls may fail to provide the required bond between the shotcrete and masonry. A solution for this is to drill small holes through the masonry joints. Tie rods can then be threaded through these holes and used to attach anchor plates or wood lagging.

If stored outdoors, the panels must be protected from the elements. The covering should be a loose tarpaulin that allows free circulation of air around the pieces. Airtight covers tend to initiate the growth of moulds and mildew which can result in staining.

Shotcrete panelization could possibly be extended to create insulated sandwich panels. Research has been carried out on the bond between shotcrete and sprayed urethane insulation. Further research will be required to determine the bond between older masonry and sprayed insulation, and to determine the effect of the impermeable insulation on the moisture content of various masonry materials.

Reinforced Masonry

Adaptive re-use projects often require the reinforcement of masonry walls. Walls often lack sufficient strength to withstand flexural stresses imposed by today's earthquake design requirements. Projects can also

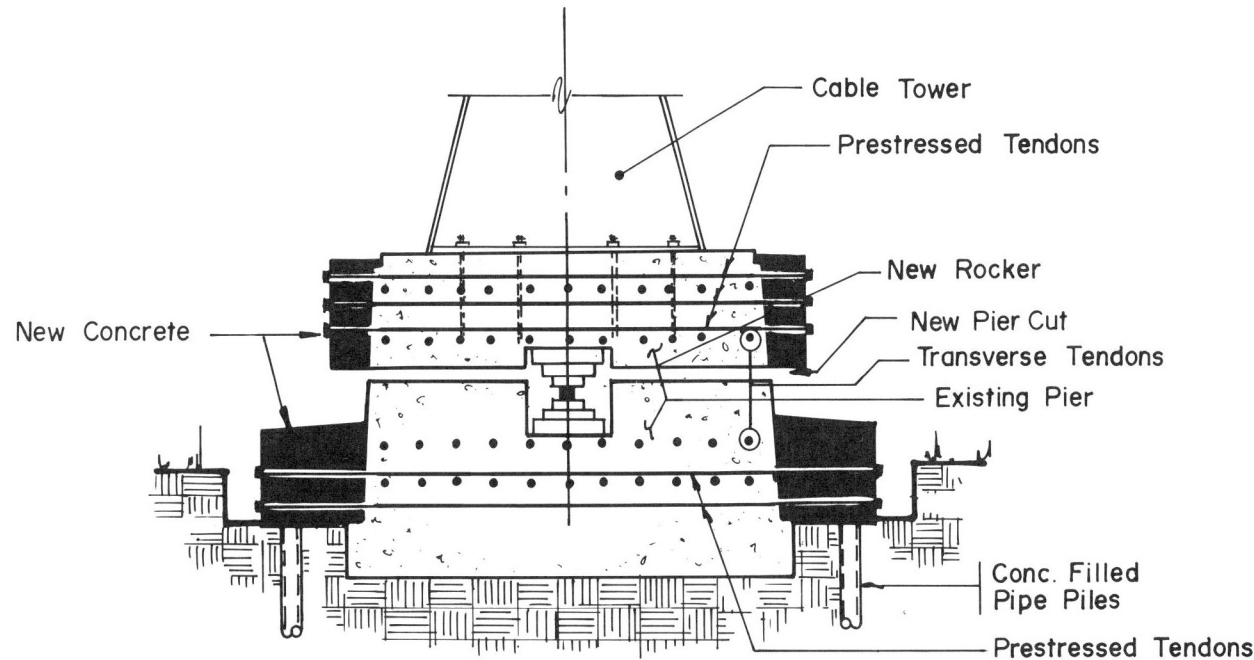

Figure 7.2 Lions Gate Bridge Repair

include the removal of floors, increasing the freestanding height of walls, while diminishing their strength.

In some cases, the wall can be strengthened by installing wire reinforcing in mortar joints. This method does not allow normal depth of cover for corrosion protection. Galvanized wires should be used, and in extreme cases, stainless steel.

The wires are covered with mortar when the joints are repointed. The system gains its strength not from the size of the reinforcement but rather from the quantity of wires. It is feasible to install a wire in each horizontal joint in a wall. This would give a spacing as close as 75 mm in a brick wall. There is even the potential to post-tension or prestress these wires under certain conditions.

Epoxy Reinforcement

Steel bar reinforcement can be epoxy glued to the face of a concrete wall to increase its flexural strength. A typical example is shown in Figure 7.3. In a similar manner, new reinforcement can be bonded to the surface of existing reinforced concrete, wood, or steel beams and slabs. Considerable research data is now available on the bond strength of epoxy joints for various materials. As discussed in previous chapters the only serious drawback to this method is the low heat tolerance of the current brands of epoxies.

Torch Straightened Steel

Many specialist tradesmen have developed unique skills. A few phone calls to people involved in conservation can lead to an individual with the skills required to solve a seemingly impossible problem. The business card of one such tradesman reads "Have Torch Will Travel." Mr. Stitt's only tool is a welder's torch. He has a keen eye for the colour of hot metal, to coax bent structural steel shapes back into line without shoring.

Summary

Consultants with experience in repair or rehabilitation can often recommend unique, feasible techniques to allow conservation of our built heritage. Specialists in any field have access to a network of people in their field. These networks can be formal, such as the Association of Preservation Technologists. Informal networks of personal contacts exist in all fields. These networks are an invaluable means of locating specialized skills and expertise. The increasing use of computer data-bases gives instant access to formal research material. Some of the on-line computer services allow "chatting" with people almost anywhere in the world. As these computer services become more selective and specialized, hopefully a conservation-technology network will come into existence.

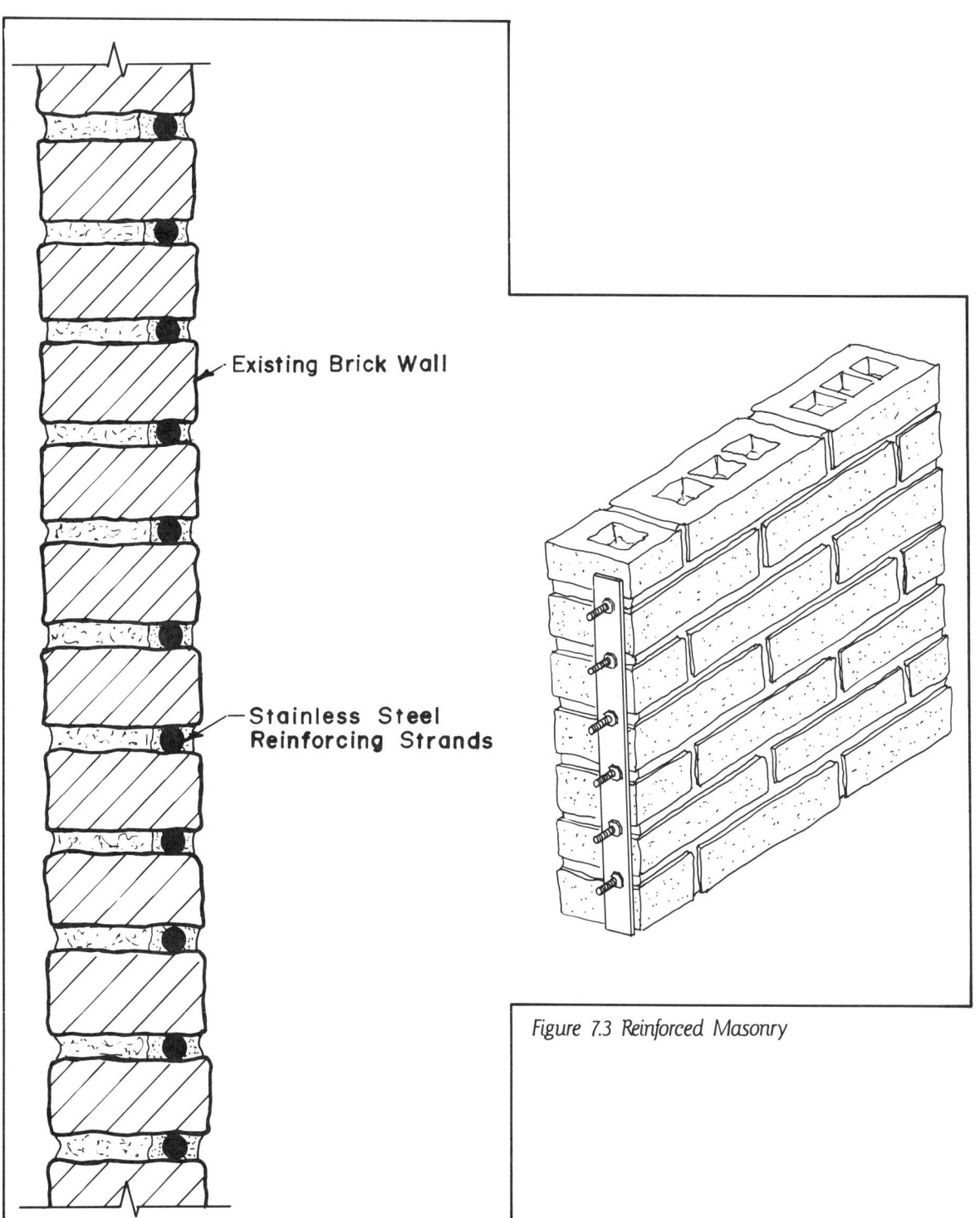

Figure 7.3 Reinforced Masonry

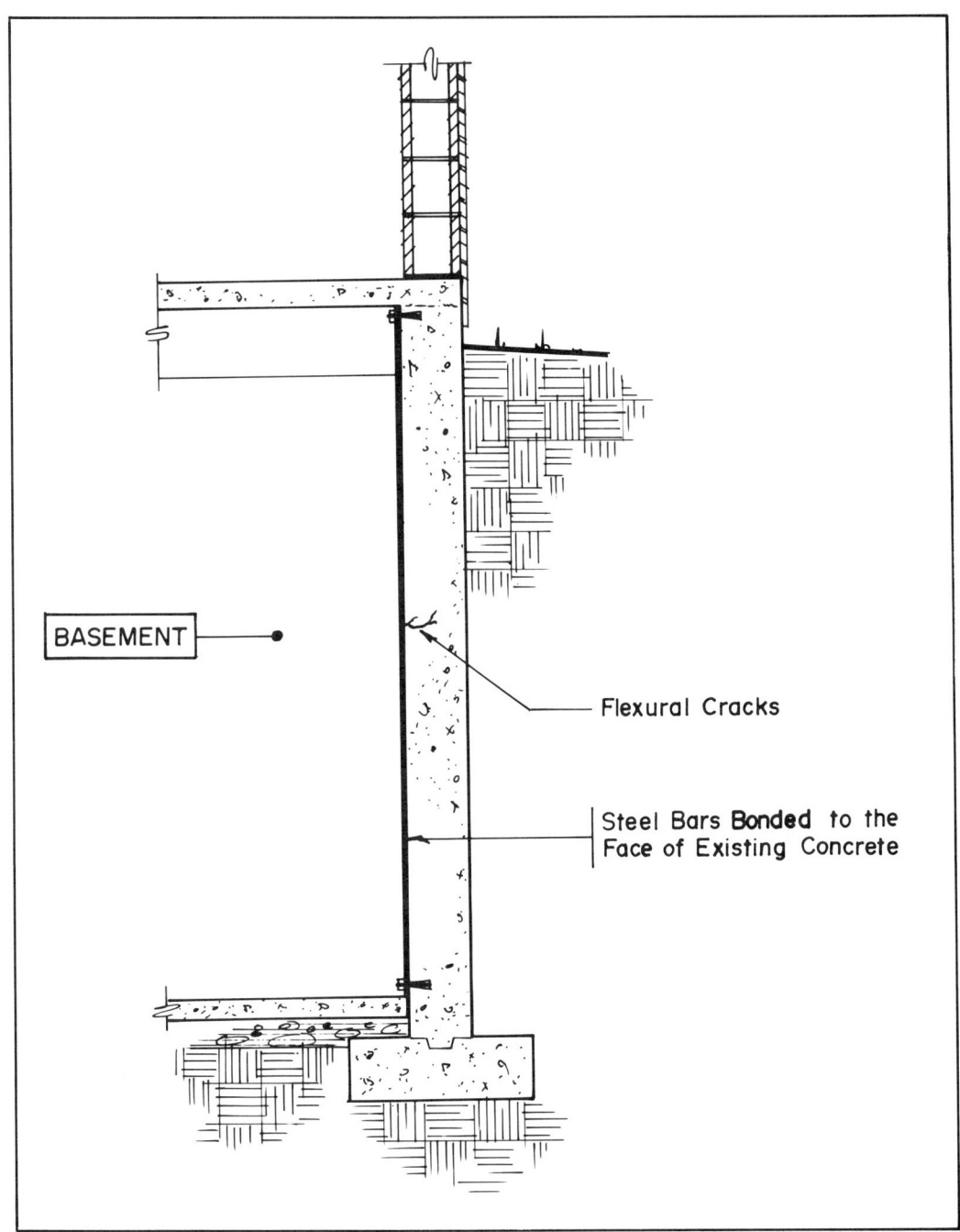

Figure 7.4 - Epoxy Bonded Reinforcement

Chapter 8

SUMMARY

PERSONAL IMPRESSIONS

The personal contact with people involved in heritage conservation was the greatest source of satisfaction during the compilation of this book. These people covered the entire range of involvement, including developers, historians, fellow design professionals and government conservationists.

The common sentiment displayed by these people was extreme pride in their particular project. Several of the developers explained in great detail the trials and tribulations of dealing with the local preservation activists and building inspectors. They then went on to tell about the completed project, and their other heritage projects with a zeal of the newly converted.

COMMON DENOMINATORS

The most common structural engineering challenges to be solved during heritage conservation projects were found to be:
- unauthorized structural renovations during the life of the project
- the lack of original construction drawings, and inaccuracies in any that were found
- the difficulty in obtaining concessions from building code authorities

In fairness to our building inspectors, it should be noted that project designers universally express dissatisfaction with the approval process for historic structures. In spite of this, they are still able to create a viable project within the imposed limitations.

FACTORS IN THE DECISION PROCESS

The decision to proceed with a conservation process is complex. Many of the factors are intangibles. They defy the application of rigorous economic and engineering analyses. Based on the experience gained in the research for this book, I would like to offer the following list of considerations to aid in the decision-making process. It is far from complete and the items are not necessarily ranked in order of importance.
- community involvement in the project
- magnitude of the undertaking in relation to the resources of the proponents
- the ability of the completed project to serve a useful function
- the future prospects of the surrounding area
- the imagination or vision of the design consultants at the feasibility stage
- realistic budgeting by the proponents and designers
- the degree of deterioration in the structure at the time conservation is contemplated

These items can also be a checklist for ensuring the success of a preservation project once the decision is made to proceed.

Among these factors, I feel that the ability to demonstrate a useful function for the preserved structure is of prime importance.

CURRENT AND FUTURE TRENDS

In the pure engineering sense, our biggest hope for new aids to conservation lies in the materials science field. The relatively small scale of the conservation industry does not allow extensive research into materials. However, developments in other areas will often spin-off new technologies to other related sciences. Advances in space technology and contemporary building science technology will undoubtedly benefit heritage conservation in the near future.

The most obvious area of concern at the present time is with polymers. Readily available epoxies have several major drawbacks. They are brittle, impermeable and have a low heat tolerance. Perhaps space research will produce the ideal sealant/adhesive. It should have superior compressive, tensile and bond strength. It should stick to any surface, regardless of temperature or moisture content. It must retain its strength and elasticity at very high and low temperatures. Provision should be made to adjust the elastic properties to match those of the materials joined. The perfect material would also have the ability to "breathe" while being waterproof at the same time. In view of the significant progress made with polymeric materials in the last few years, there is hope that most of these attributes will be available in one product during this decade.

In the political realm the co-operation between the private sector and local government is the most encouraging trend. The initiative displayed by both the private and public sectors in one Canadian city are outlined in Appendix A. Hopefully similar initiatives are occurring simultaneously in other Canadian cities.

One element lacking from the political side of conservation is co-operative planning between other interested groups. An attempt must be made by local historical boards and conservation groups to lobby owners of historic properties well in advance of any proposed redevelopment.

In conclusion, an encouraging note to those concerned with the disappearance of our architectural heritage. Canada has seen a resurgence of interest in all heritage related areas in the last few years. This interest has filtered into the conciousness of all the major property owners across the country. The mood and opportunities are there for co-operation between all groups concerned with the conservation process.

APPENDIX A
Development Incentives Applicable to Heritage Buildings, City of Edmonton

The preparation of a Register of Heritage Buildings in the City of Edmonton raised fears among the owners of these properties that mandatory conservation requirements might be imposed on designated buildings. A dialogue was started between the heritage building owners, the City Planning Department and other civic departments.

The end result of these deliberations was nine recommendations to City Council. These recommendations are:

1. That the City lease at least twenty per cent of its office space requirements in Heritage Buildings.
2. That the Municipal Tax Assessment Department establish a specific class of Business Tax for owner/occupants or tenants in Heritage Buildings.
3. That the Tax Assessment Department implement a five-year tax-relief system for owners of rehabilitated Heritage properties.
4. That the Provincial Government amend the Municipal Tax Act to allow the exemption of taxes imposed on Heritage properties.
5. That the Provincial Government provide funds to Heritage building owners in the form of low interest loans, grants or subsidies to assist in the upgrading, maintenance and repairs of these properties. These funds would also be available to allow government purchase of significant historical properties threatened with demolition.
6. That the Provincial Government establish legislation enabling mortgage guarantees to conventional lenders for heritage properties.
7. That the feasibility of transferring the excess development rights from heritage properties to former industrial land in the central area of the City be determined.
8. That the Land Use By-Law be amended to exempt heritage properties from certain requirements if they are to be rehabilitated. These exemptions would apply to: amenity areas, loading facilities, parking requirements and building envelope.
9. That the Building Inspection Branch appoint a person who will be a specialist in the processing of applications concerning heritage properties.

GLOSSARY

ADAPTIVE RE-USE: Implies the recycling of an older structure, often for a new function. Extensive restoration or rehabilitation of both the interior and exterior is usually involved.

ARCHITECTURAL CONSERVATION: Refers to the physical intervention in a building to counteract deterioration or to ensure its structural stability.

BENTONITE: A clay composed principally of minerals of the montmorillonite group, characterized by high absorption and very large volume change with wetting or drying.

CAISSON: A deep foundation unit formed by excavating inside a wood, concrete or steel casing.

DYNAMIC ANALYSIS: Stress analysis of structures subjected to varying loads.

EPOXY: Very strong glue; often comes in two parts which must be mixed before using.

EXCAVATION SHORING: Props or posts of timber or other material that provide temporary support to excavation walls.

FACADE RETENTION: The process of incorporating an historically significant building exterior in a new development. The facade is normally retained in its original location.

LAGGING: Heavy timber used in underground work to withstand earth pressure.

PHOTOGRAMMETRY: The science of measurement using photographs.

POLYMERS: Rubber or resin consisting of large moleclues formed by polymerization.

POST-TENSIONING: A method of pre-stressing reinforced concrete using high strength steel tendons which are stressed after the concrete has hardened.

PRESERVATION: The broad range of processes associated with the restoration and adaptive re-use of historic structures.

RAKER: A sloping brace used to support excavation shoring.

RECONSTRUCTION: Involves the re-creation of a non-existent building on its original site.

REDEVELOPMENT: Similar to Adaptive Re-Use but on a larger scale where a major addition is constructed on the site, while maintaining the most important heritage elements.

REHABILITATION: Is often used interchageably with renovation to describe the modification of an existing building. This process extends the structure's useful life through alterations and repairs while preserving its important architectural, historic and cultural attributes.

RENOVATION: A term used to describe various levels of intervention including remodelling, recycling, and rehabilitation.

RESTORATION: The process of returning a building or site to a condition that existed at a particular previous period of time.

RETROFITTING: Involves the upgrading of a building to meet code requirements (i.e. fire or emergency exits). This process often includes the installation of new insulation as a means of energy conservation.

SEISMOGRAPH: An instrument used to record the durations and amplitudes of earth shocks.

SELECTIVE DEMOLITION: The deliberate razing of certain parts of a building, while leaving other parts intact.

SHOTCRETE: Mortar or concrete projected at high velocity onto a surface. Also known as gunite.

SLURRY: A watery mixture of soil and water that will flow.

SPALLING: The development of small fragments or chips of concrete, brick or stone through deterioration.

STABILIZATION: Is a process of intervention which may be used as an interim measure on a severely deteriorated building.

STRAIN GAUGE: A sensitive instrument to measure small movements in structures from which the strains can be calculated.

TERRA COTTA: Cast and fired clay units, usually large and more intricately detailed than ordinary clay bricks.

UNDERPINNING: To provide new supports beneath an existing structure without removing the superstructure, in order to increase the load capacity.

BIBLIOGRAPHY

Alberta Labour. Building Standards Branch. *Alberta Building Code.* 1981.

American Association For Testing Materials. *Epoxy - Resin - Based Bonding Systems for Concrete.* ASTM C881-78.

American Concrete Institute. *Formwork For Concrete.* SP4, Fourth Edition, 1981.

American Concrete Institute. *Guide for Repair of Concrete Bridge Superstructures.* ACI Report 546.1R-80.

American Concrete Institute. *Recommended Practice for Concrete Formwork.* ACI 347-78.

American Concrete Institute. "Recommended Practice for Shotcreting". ACI 506.66, *ACI Manual of Concrete Practice.* 1982.

American Concrete Institute. "Specification for Materials, Proportioning and Application of Shotcrete". *ACI Manual of Concrete Practice.* 1982.

American Concrete Institute. *Standard Specification for Bonding Plastic Concrete to Hardened Concrete with a Multi-Component Epoxy Adhesive.* ACI 503.2-79.

American Concrete Institute. *Standard Specification for Repairing Concrete with Epoxy Mortars.* ACI 503.4-79.

American Society of Civil Engineers. *Evaluation, Maintenance and Upgrading of Wood Structures, Subcommittee on Evaluation, Maintenance and Upgrading of Timber Structures.* 1982.

American Society of Civil Engineers. *Evaluation, Maintenance and Upgrading of Wood Structures.* New York

Body, Trevor "Prairie Architecture: Prairie Forum Special Issue". *Journal of the Canadian Plans Research Council,* Fall, 1980

Brochers, Perry E. "Architectural Photogammetry in Restoration". O.M. Bullock, reprinted in *The Restoration Manual,* 1966.

Buckland, Peter G. "The Lions Gate Bridge - Renovation". *Canadian Journal of Civil Engineering.* August, 1981.

CSA Standard. *Access Scaffolding For Construction Purposes.* S269.2-M1980.

CSA Standard. *Code of Practice for Safety in Demolition of Structures.* S350-M1980.

CSA Standard. *Falsework for Construction Purposes.* S269.1-1975.

Chae, Y.S. *"Design of Excavation Blasts to Prevent Damage".* ASCE, Civil Engineering, April, 1978.

Concrete. "UK Debut for German Repair Technique". August, 1983

Concrete Construction. *"Slabjacking Art and Science".* February, 1969.

Concrete Construction. "Shotcrete for Building Repairs". May, 1981.

Concrete International. "State-Of-The-Art Report on Fiber Reinforced Concrete". May, 1982.

Feildon, Bernard M. *Conservation of Historic Building.* Butterworth, 1982.

Fuller, J.D. and Kriegh, J.D. Maintenance and Repair of Concrete and Masonry Structures: Epoxy Pressure Grouting, Construction Engineering Research Laboratory. Champaign, Illinois, July, 1971.

Gifford, E.W.H. and Taylor, P. "The Restoration of Ancient Buildings." *The Structural Engineer,* October, 1964.

I.C.O.S. Company. *The I.C.O.S. Company in the Underground Works.* Milano, Italy, September, 1969.

Kalman, Bailey, Wagland. *Recycling Public Buildings for the Arts.* Encore, Corpus, 1980.

Kubler, Hans. *Wood as Building and Hobby Material.* John Wiley & Sons, 1980.

Lardner & Sandori. "Foundations: Driven Piles". The Canadian Architect. February, 1983.

Lardner & Sandori. "Foundations: Shoring". *The Canadian Architect.* July, 1982.

Lardner & Sandori, Foundations: Underpinning. "*The Canadian Architect.* May, 1982.

Northwood, T.D. and Crawford, R. "Blasting and Building Damage". *Canadian Building Digest.* #63.

Portland Cement Associates. *Slabjacking Concrete Pavement.* ISO6OP.

Prentis and White. *Underpinning.* Columbia University Press, 2nd Edition, 1950.

Prudon, Theodore H.M. "Wooden Structural Members: Some Recent European Preservation Methods. "*Association for Preservation Technology Bulletin.* Vol. VIII, No. 3, 1975.

Rainer, J.H. "Effect of Vibrations on Historic Buildings: An Overview". *Association for Preservaion Technology.* Vol. XIV No. 1, 1982

Ringe. Historic Preservation of Engineering Works. *Proceedings of Engineering Foundation Conference.* New Hampshire, June 25 - 30, 1978

Stumes, Paul "Testing The Efficiency of Wood Epoxy Reinforcement Systems". *Association for Preservation Technology Bulletin.* Vol. VIII, No. 3, 1975.

Stumes, Paul "The Application of Epoxy Resins for the Restoration of Historic Structures". *Association for Preservation Technology Bulletin.* Vol. III, No. 1, 1971.

Stumes, Paul "The W.E.R. System Manual". *Association for Preservation Technology.*

Szado, T. "Plywood Reinforcement For Structural Wood Members with Internal Defects". *Association For Preservation Technology Bulletin.* Vol. IX, No. 1, 1977.

Toplis, Colin *Demolition, Construction Press.* 1982.

U.S. Department of Commerce. *Selected Methods for Condition Assessment of Structural, HVAC, Plumbing and Electrical Systems in Existing Building.* National Bureau of Standards. NBSIR 80-2171.

Index

accelerograph 21
adaptive re-use 73, 82, 105, 106, 107, 122
additions 20, 84, 122, 143
Alberta Building Code 17
Alberta Association of Architects 72
ALCAN 114-117
American Concrete Institute 40
ARCOP 84, 117
Assiniboia Hall 106
Association of Preservation Technologists 149
Athabasca Hall 105
authenticity 12
bacteria 56
band aid repairs........................... 99
Barrington Place 92
Bay Street, 330 89
bentonite 26
Bittorf Holland Christianson........ 104, 105, 107
Boston 120
brown rot 57
Bureau de Postes 88
Calgary 20, 84
Canada Permanent Building 50
Canadian Imperial Bank of Commerce ... 40, 110
Canadian Standards Association............ 15
Capuchines Shrine 36
Carlson Construction 105
Carnegie Library 37, 82
carpenter ants 58
chemical grouting 49
chemical slurry........................... 27
Chicago 31
Chicago well 30
coal 51
cold 51
computer data-bases 149
concrete 16
construction delivery 10
controlled blasting 21, 117

creep 59
dead shores 43
Demec strain gauge 15
deterioration, wood frame 56
dewatering 29
dismantling................. 37, 80, 84, 90, 93
do-it-yourself 11
drawings, as-built 14
Duggan House......................... 64, 70
Edmonton 7, 38, 42, 50, 70, 102, 110, 147
electromagnetic detector 21
epoxy.................... 38, 50, 62, 149
evaluations 14, 15
excavation shoring 23-29
facade retention 87, 100, 106-108,
                                  121, 126, 146
First Presbyterian Church 50
flatjack 47, 49
flying shores.............................. 47
foundations, residential 51
fungi 56
Grand Central Station 143
Grandin House 35
ground freezing 27
Halifax 92
High Level Bridge 7
Holland A.M. 80
Holland Cummins Partnership 72
Holinsworth Building 20, 84
hydrojet 19
Imbrook Properties 89
insects 57
intuition 16
intumescence 50
Laing Stress Building 37
latex 38
Lions Gate Bridge 148
log house............................. 67-69
Maison ALCAN 114-118

Manhattan	37
Manitoba Teachers College	97
masonry	16, 39, 72, 75, 82, 148
Mexico City	36
microwaves	19
minor additions	20
Montreal	108, 114
mudjacking	49
National Building Code	19, 23
National Capital Commission	86
New York	143
Noranda Builders	80
Norway	49
Olympia & York	120, 124
Ottawa	17, 53, 75, 86
Ottawa River	17
P&M Construction	107
pacometer	16
Page & Steele	93
panel underpinning	31
panelization	80, 136, 147
Parks Canada	88
PCL Construction	84, 93, 106
peak particle velocity	21
Pembina Hall	103
petrographic examination	16
photogrammetry	15, 28, 49, 97
pioneer structures	66-68
polymers	38-40, 152
post-tensioning	62, 110, 147
Prairie Partnership	100
Quebec City	88
Queens Quay Terminal	9, 40, 122-125
Quinn Dressel Associates	90, 117, 120
Quinn Dressel Jokinen	80
radar	20
rakers	26, 33
raking shores	47
rebound hammer	16
Regina	96
relocation	49
Rideau Canal	7
rock excavation	21
rock saw	23
root piles	27, 33-34
Rothesay Apartments	38, 80, 147
sand jack	49
Saskatchewan Legislature Building	36, 50, 96
scaffolding	43
segmented piles	36, 96
seismic upgrading	82, 108
selective demolition	19, 80, 84, 87, 93, 106-108, 117, 121, 133

seismograph	21
sheet piling	26
shotcrete	26, 36, 80, 82, 137, 147
shrinkage	58
silent explosives	19
slabjacking	49
slurry trench	25
sprinklers	18
St. Albert	36
St. Brigid Church	74
State Street, 53	120, 143
Stitts	149
structural steel	16, 149
subliming materials	50
sulphates	52, 54
Sussex Drive, 527	86
sweat equity	11-12
swelling clay	54
tangent piles	25
tannic acid	17
temporary supports	43
termites	57
terra cotta	12, 84
thermic lance	19
tie back anchors	26
timber	15, 79
Toronto	79, 89, 122
Toronto Free Theatre	21
transfer systems	40, 122
Trizec Corp.	84
Ukrainian Heritage Village	9
ultrasonics	16
underpinning	29-35, 84, 87, 97, 108, 110, 117, 121, 146
University of Alberta	102-107
University of Quebec	108
Upper Canada Village	9, 12
Vancouver	37, 82, 147
W&R Foundations	97
water	53
wave propagation test	15
well cribbing	30
WER system	40
white rot	57
windsor probe	16
Winnipeg	98
Winnipeg Housing Rehabilitation Corp	100
wrecking ball	19
WZMH	89, 121
x-ray	16
Zeidler Roberts Partnership	122